Unwording the World

Unwording the World

Samuel Beckett's Prose Works After the Nobel Prize

Carla Locatelli

University of Pennsylvania Press
Philadelphia

Library of Congress Cataloging-in-Publication Data
Locatelli, Carla.
    Unwording the world : Samuel Beckett's prose works after the Nobel prize /
Carla Locatelli.
        p.   cm.
    ISBN 0-8122-8232-9
    1. Beckett, Samuel, 1906–   —Prose. I. Title.
PR6003.E282Z7715 1990
848'.91409—dc20   89-28854
                                                                   CIP

Jacket illustration. *Light Inscriptions*. Photograph by Ann Matter.

Per Maria e Gianni, *sine qua non*

Contents

Preface

Unwording the World: Samuel Beckett's Prose Works After the Nobel Prize investigates the successful realization of the Beckettian project to produce a "literature of the unword," and examines the hermeneutical and epistemological implications of such an innovative attempt. It also illustrates how Beckett's structural and semiotic subtractions contribute to an unprecedented and unforeseeable development of postmodernist writing.

Beckett's "literature of the unword" has shown, by means of successive and daring reductions, that experience is always already a hermeneutics of experience, and that what is often mistaken for reality is only the result of conceptual unification. Through the analysis of some of his later texts, read in the context of his previous works, and particularly through a systematic reading of *Company* (1980), *ill seen ill said* (1982), and *Worstward Ho* (1983), it becomes clear that earlier negations were transformed by Beckett into powerful cognitive subtractions, as a hermeneutics of suspicion was being challenged by an imperative which activated the condition of ignorance as an instrument of knowledge.

Although Beckett had described his desire to dissolve the "terrible materiality of the word surface" as early as the 1930s, it is not until the completion of the so called "Second Trilogy" in the 1980s that the value and scope of his "poetics of indigence" could be understood not only in aesthetic and philosophical, but also in cognitive and theoretical terms. In fact, this is the aim of the present study, which does not contemplate a detailed reading of every prose piece produced after 1969, but which elucidates Beckett's enterprise by relating it to some of the major cultural issues raised by the intellectual communities in which he has moved.

The role of representation and the structure of communication, which are very important in all of Beckett's works, become absolutely central in his later prose, because the critical self-reflexivity of these texts shows both the ineliminability of representation in the human structuring of experience, and the quality of communication as an event, a quality best underscored by Beckett's subtractive communicative strategies. His way to the "literature of the unword" is in fact an active and lucid "un-wording," the practice of an actual communicative process which moves against naive referential fallacies and logocentric closure.

Far from being confined to the production of aesthetic self-reflections and metanarrative conceptualizations, Beckett's unwording probes into issues of the cultural encoding of meaning, not only to denounce the conventions of literary discourse, but to reveal the epistemological function of linguistic representation, and the intrinsic hermeneutical quality of our being. His linguistic subtractions do not just mirror the world of literary artifacts, but they unword the world as it comes to us, because they deconstruct concepts and figures as they constitute the world we perceive. In other words, Beckett exerts his subtractive practice at the very core of saying, so as to reveal the human impossibility of avoiding representation, as well as to show that saying determines the visibility of all mental and physical realities. Furthermore, the aesthetic doubling of linguistic representations in Beckett's later works produces the revelation of the "event-quality" of communication, independent of the degree of referential assumptions, and shows that any subject can be constituted only as the perceiver-perceived of an interpreted world.

It is obvious that the subtractive practice typical of Beckett's later works ignites a powerful deconstructive process, and that his "literature of the unword" should never be mistaken for a thematics of silence. His unwording is the function of an active communication which regards the structure of reality, and not the object of such communication. Thus, the "literature of the unword" should be understood as a process, not as a negation nor, even less, as the object of a negation. Beckett's "Second Trilogy" shows that only the strategic practice of unwording produces a designative suspension, rather than a refusal of naming, so that (the visibility of) the world can be shown as the result of our unavoidable interpretive representations.

The completion of this book would not have been possible without the help of a vast number of friends and the support of institutions whom I wish to thank here.

I am particularly grateful to Paul Korshin, whose support, encouragement, and advice were constant throughout the compilation of the manuscript, and to Ann Matter and Angela Locatelli, who made the process of writing a challenging and rewarding intellectual experience. Without them this book would simply not have been the same, even if it is obvious that its shortfalls are entirely my own. Furthermore, I would like to thank friends and colleagues on both sides of the Atlantic whose conversations and encouragement have nurtured this project in ways that may even be unknown to them. Among them: Bob Lucid, Wendy Steiner, Elaine Scarry, Gerald Prince, Stuart Curran, Barbara Johnson, J. Hillis Miller, Terence Hawkes, Giovanna Jung, Marcello Pagnini, Cesare Segre, and Sandro Serpieri.

Most of the research for this book was carried out at the University of Pennsylvania, and the courtesy of the staff at the Van Pelt Library deserves my acknowledgment, together with the Librarians at the University of Texas, Austin and at the British Library in London. I would also like to thank the United States Information Agency who welcomed me in their International Visitors Program which allowed me to meet with colleagues throughout the United States in the Spring of 1983, and the British Council for their invitation to take part in the Summer Seminar at Trinity College, Cambridge in 1986.

Special thanks go to the Italian Ministry of Education, and particularly to the Istituto Universitario di Lingue Moderne of Milan for their generous financial contribution towards the publication of this book.

I am grateful to the University of Pennsylvania Press, and especially to Alison Anderson, for the care and dedication with which this book was brought to publication.

News of Samuel Beckett's death on December 22, 1989 reached me as the final copy of this book was being prepared.

The implications of this loss cannot yet be fully assessed, even if Beckett's presence will never be obliterated from Western culture.

Introduction

"Hieroglyphics Traced by Inspired Perception"

Samuel Beckett's literary production since the early 1970s has provided indisputable evidence of the openness of his corpus of writings and of the evolution intrinsic to his work. In fact, he has devised unexpected expressive possibilities, and has found new linguistic solutions to what has been the central problem of his poetics: the establishment of "more authentic, more ample, less exclusive relations between representer and representee."[1]

In 1983, the publication of *Disjecta,* "Miscellaneous Writings and a Dramatic Fragment," made easily available a collection of important critical pieces that confirm Beckett's central aesthetic concerns, as well as the flexibility and mobility of his responses to the variety of problems he has successively perceived. This useful book makes it possible to trace an evolving aesthetic theory—by no means a closed system—and to see how Beckett's observations imply radical gnoseological issues and produce an unmistakably Beckettian hermeneutics of experience. It is true that Beckett's plays, novels, and poems are enough to map out such an achievement and to indicate such an interpretation, but the readiness of some critics to see "symbols" rather than produce elucidations has made those encoded messages even more latent, even more elusive. It is no wonder that already in 1936 Beckett was ironically denouncing "allegory, that glorious double-entry, with every credit in the said account a debit in the meant, and inversely," and was instead praising an art structured as a "single series of imaginative transactions."[2]

In retrospect, it is easy to see that in those years Beckett was indicating what type of novel he would *not* want to write; but not too many years later he had produced a personal idiolect and absolutely innovative works. The witty irony of his production in the 1930s (including *Whoroscope,* 1930; *Echo's Bones and Other Precipitates,* 1935; "Dream of Fair to Middling Women," 1932; *More Pricks than Kicks,* 1934; and *Murphy,* 1938), and the critically amused remarks in his essays ("Dante . . . Bruno. Vico. . Joyce," 1929; "Le Concentrisme," ca. 1930; and *Proust,* 1931), point to the *pars destruens* of his project, to a critical attitude which was to culminate, however, in the highly creative innovations of his later works. The *pars construens* of Beckett's poetics can clearly be seen in the 1950s, when *The Trilogy* and *Texts for Nothing* (1955), *Waiting for Godot* (1952), and *Endgame* (1958) provide the full appropriation of a precise voice, the delineation of a universe, and the recurrence of a number of unmistakably idiosyncratic motives.[3]

The continuity of his production is attested, up to his most recent works in the 1980s, when that voice, that world, and those motives demonstrate, in Beckett's own words, that "there are many ways in which the thing I am trying in vain to say may be tried in vain to be said."[4] He kept finding new and "many ways," even when the lucid virtuosity of his previous achievements had seemed to deny any further possibility of expanding his expressivity. For example, after *The Unnamable* (1953) many critics have voiced a profound surprise when confronted with *Texts for Nothing* (1955), because it was generally thought that Beckett "would not be able to push further his quest."[5] Beckett himself confessed: "*Malone* grew out of *Molloy, The Unnamable* out of *Malone,* but afterwards—and for a long time—I wasn't at all sure what I had left to say."[6]

The present study will focus primarily on Beckett's late production, and particularly on major prose works written after receiving the Nobel Prize on October 23, 1969. *Company* (1980), *ill seen ill said* (1981), and *Worstward Ho* (1983) will be analyzed in detail, foregrounding some specific aspects of the texts and relating them to precise epistemological and aesthetic issues. I believe that the development of Beckett's "poetics of indigence" brought him to an unforeseeable, radical change in the 1970s, transforming his gnoseological quest into a modern epistemological analysis, based on a critical, self-reflective use of language. By means of progressive subtractions, the early questions regarding space, subjectivity, and basic realities were transformed into epistemological issues, implying a sense of reality as interpretation, and focusing on language in relation to the crucial problem of the "thing-structure" and "proposition structure" of reality.[7] Beckett does not provide any answers as to the priority of one over the other, nor does he seem interested in finding such answers, but he keeps telling us how implicated we are with both language and "things." His way of showing the depth of our involvement proceeds through subtractions, almost as if by means of a reduction it were possible to indicate those borders from which cognition and truth have an elementary, minimal origin. Methodologically, Beckett could thus be compared to Husserl, whose "reductions" constitute a process, a dynamic, investigative device, well known to the analyses of descriptive phenomenology. Obviously, Beckett's investigation develops on and through literature, and in a non-transcendental direction. Unlike Husserl, he is not looking for an irrefutable foundation of knowledge, but his "unwording"[8] reveals to him the pervasiveness of language, a discovery which in itself is charged with an important cognitive significance.

Thus, new epistemological meanings regarding the relationship between human consciousness and a spatio-temporal world are produced in his late works, when language and reality are no longer conceived as being susceptible of separation. If in his earlier literary production Beckett had used language to scan reality, and reality to denounce the "falsifications" of language and literature, he has since then used language as inseparable from reality, no longer maintaining the possibility of their opposition. I would say that an earlier "hermeneutic of suspicion," animated by a demystifying desire, is transformed into a later "hermeneutic of experience" that does not contemplate the possibility of any final denouement, not even the demystifying urge of his earlier production. Beckett's works remain "hieroglyphics,"[9] not only because time proves that many new possibilities of reading develop around and because of them, but also because the resistance to a final semantic appropriation of their meaning compels interpretations to multiply, ever to be engulfed by "an art that is perfectly intelligible and perfectly inexplicable."[10]

Evolving Epistemic Coordinates

It is easy to see a different use and conception of language if we compare some early works with later ones. To this end I will consider different sets of examples, dealing in turn with the epistemic coordinates of 1) subject, 2) time, and 3) space. As a matter of fact, they map out Beckett's fictional world, inasmuch as they are the only recurrent thematic and structural elements of his entire production.

In *Murphy* (1938), for example, Beckett was clearly denouncing literature as an artifact when he structured a character like Celia, introduced at the very beginning of the "Second Chapter" as follows:

Age.	Unimportant
Head.	Small and round
Eyes.	Green

Complexion.	White
Hair.	Yellow
Features.	Mobile
Neck.	13¾″
Upper arm.	11″
Forearm.	9½″
Wrist.	6″
Bust.	34″
Waist.	27″
Hips, etc.	35″
Thigh.	21¾″
Knee.	13¾″
Calf.	13″
Ankle.	8¼″
Instep.	Unimportant
Height.	5′ 4″
Weight.	123 lbs [11]

The use of hyper-detailed elements of description, arranged in an ironic sequence, lays bare the technique through which characters are defined and created in conventional mimesis. A totally different typology of characters is present, over forty years later, in *Company* (1980), where the protagonist is "enacted" rather than narrated, and the conventions of literary portraiture are challenged but not denounced, because a truly critical mimesis replaces a didactically demystifying one. The "novel" opens with these words: "A voice comes to one in the dark. Imagine." In "Fragment 8," a few pages later, we find this "description," aiming at the identification of such a character:

> If the voice is not speaking to him it must be speaking to another. So with what reason remains he reasons. To another of that other. Or of him. Or of another still. To another of that other or of him or of another still. To one on his back in the dark in any case. Of one on his back in the dark whether the same or another. So with what reason remains he reasons and reasons ill. For were the voice speaking not to him but to another then it must be of that other it is speaking and not of him or of another still. Since it speaks in the second person. Were it not of him to whom it is speaking speaking but of another it would not speak in the second person but in the third.[12]

Here the reconstruction of a character can only occur a posteriori through a series of hermeneutical hypotheses concerning identity, hypotheses which "take time" and require referents, as in real life. The transformation of a transgressive portraiture into a visible process of narration, mirroring the actuality of the process of identification, constitutes a radical and constructive critique of both the traditional positing of identity and of traditional mimesis. It seems to me that Beckett has fully achieved in *Company* the results he had praised in *Proust:*

> the identification with Albertine is retrospective [. . .] and proceeds to her acquaintance by a series of subtractions. [. . .] Thus is established the *pictorial* multiplicity of Albertine that will duly evolve into a *plastic* and moral multiplicity, no longer a mere shifting superficies and an effect of the observer's angle of approach rather than the expression of an inward and active variety, but a multiplicity in depth, a turmoil of objective and immanent contradictions over which the subject has no control.[13]

> Proust is too much of an affectivist to be satisfied by the intellectual symbolism of a Baudelaire, abstract and discursive. The Baudelarian unity is a unity 'post rem,' a unity abstracted from plurality.[14]

Beckett's rejection of philosophy, as we shall see, is actually motivated by a similar distrust for "*post rem*" concepts and abstractions as means of cognition. It is not surprising, however, to discover, a posteriori, that it is precisely the desire to be "faithful" to reality that leads him to produce the epistemological meanings of his late works. He sees art as an "evocative experiment" of "penetration of reality" through "inspired perception," whereas philosophy appears to him flawed, because of its teleology, always tending towards intelligibility.

> The most successful evocative experiment can only project the echo of a past sensation, because, being an act of intellection, it is conditioned by the prejudices of the intelligence which abstracts from any given sensation, as being illogical and insignificant, a discordant and frivolous intruder, whatever word or gesture, sound or perfume, cannot be fitted into the puzzle of a concept. But the essence of any new experience is contained precisely in this mysterious element that the vigilant will rejects as an anachronism.[15]

Comparing *From an Abandoned Work* (1958) and *That Time* (1976), on the issue of temporality provides another instance of the great changes which have occurred in the use and conception of language between early and later works.

There is a great variation in rendering the semantics of "ending," a variation that presupposes a great change in the perception of time:

> Over, over, there is a soft place in my heart for all that is over, no, for the being over, I love the word, words have been my only loves, not many.[16]

> was that it something like that come and gone come and gone no one come and gone in no time gone in no time[17]

The first example, from the earlier work, suspends the designation of an end, even after having invoked it so many times, when this end ("over, over") tends to become the vision of an existential ending ("the being over"). A relieving irony shifts the semantic axis of discourse, from death to words ("the being over, I love the word"), so that the idea of death is really submerged by the paradoxically declared "love for words." On the other hand, the second example actually expresses the ending, not only because those are the words spoken at the literal end of the play, but because the pun is no longer functional to the creation of a nonsensical humor. The "love for words" exhibited in the concatenation of the second fragment does not keep the evidence of ending at bay, but shows that words cannot control death ("gone / in no time / gone in no time"). It is no longer possible to avoid seeing the speaker engulfed by time, as he is necessarily wrestling with it, even while playing with language ("in no time gone / in no time"). The power of rhetoric is silenced, as words literally fade, one after another. Furthermore, the absence of diacritical marks in the passage produces a semantic freedom in the reconstruction of experience that foregrounds the interpretive role of memory, which actually changes past events. Besides, the conventional nature of the rhetoric of temporality is very clearly displayed. As time passes questions multiply, and from the need of a precise chronology (a "wrong" question), grows the positive awareness of an inescapable, irreversible duration:

> or was that another time all that another time was there ever any other time but that time[18]

Clearly, the protagonist is trying to remember an exact chronology, but he comes to realize the meaninglessness of such a question. The continuity of the remembering subject with the content of his remembering reveals to him that there is no other time "but that time," which is actually also the same as "this" time. Temporal indexes are shown as purely conventional indications, devoid of "real" meaning, and producing only the illusion of an ontological difference.

In *From an Abandoned Work* Beckett had didactically stressed a similar, yet opposite illusion: one about "sameness," rather than "difference," but again the result of logocentric abstraction:

> So in some way even olden things each time are first things, no two breaths the same, all going over and over and all once and never more.[19]

The expression of an irreversible and ineliminable temporality has been central to Beckett's artistic concerns since the very beginning of his literary career. He started like Proust, "from the negation of death to its affirmation," even though he ends by implying the non-oppositional continuity of the present. His presentation of Proust's work shows the potential development of his own:

> From the victory over Time he passes to the victory of Time, from the negation of death to its affirmation. Thus, at the end as in the body of his work, Proust respects the dual significance of every condition and circumstance of life. The most ideal tautology presupposes a relation and the affirmation of equality involves only an approximate identification, and by asserting unity denies unity.[20]

"The dual significance of every condition and circumstance of life," that irreducible ambiguity which "asserting unity denies unity" constitutes the starting point of Beckett's gnoseological explorations and aesthetic representations. After all, however critical they may seem, these assertions in *Proust* produce another perfectly closed conceptual discourse. Dissatisfied with it, Beckett began trying to produce a radically different type of assertion, in a form of discourse really open to duration. When art began to appear to him as an evocative tautology that repressed its temporal difference, he started pursuing the "Beneficient Fecundity of the Imperfect,"[21] both linguistically and existentially. Imperfection alone could suspend the closure of discourse, and even the absoluteness of the idea that being born is the greatest sin, an idea dogmatically announced in *Proust:* "el delito mayor/ del hombre es haber nacido."[22] In the light of impotence, and thus through impotence, Beckett devoted his life to the investigation of time and being, but without suspending them in the course of his "abstractions." Thus, his works oscillate continuously, covering the span between the conceptual extremes of life and death, of sameness and difference, of language and things, until they manage to express time as pure duration, having no real beginning and no real end, even when beginning and end are denoted by language.

His latest works "fail as no other dare fail,"[23] because they refuse all the guarantees of the *logos,* the law and order of a compact discourse. They constitute an unprecedented art of the "penultimates," reproducing life as quintessentially penultimate, not in relation to a conceptual end, but because of the process of phenomena, determinable and terminable only a posteriori. In Beckett's latest works life ends when the "traces" of identity can be composed in a perfected unity: when they become "signs" of a subject. Such a unity does not pertain to phenomena, which are temporal and irreducibly dispersed, problematic and "plural," but it belongs to a subject when he is determined, "finished," no longer there. A Beckett, that is, who in the 1930s praised Proust for having written: "A being scattered in space and time is no longer a woman but a series of events on which we can throw no light, a series of problems that cannot be solved,"[24] can today express in *That Time* the paradox of our vanishing constitution:

come and gone no one come and gone.[25]

Beckett produces a transcription of identity as presence-absence: "come and gone *no / one* come and gone." Furthermore, by leaving open the choice of a prosodic pause he engenders two opposite meanings: "one come and gone" vs. "no one come and gone." The fact that the time of reading, rather than the sentence structure, determines meaning (as a hermeneutical hypothesis), creates "a dual significance" rather than a conceptual contradiction. Identity is thus expressed as a temporal process, a continuity from "no one" to "one." We must notice, however, that the full definition of the subject can be achieved only a posteriori, when he/she is absent: "*one* come and *gone.*" As we can see from these examples, the epistemic coordinates of Beckett's universe have undergone a remarkable metamorphosis in the course of the years, even if the basic semantic coordinates of his vision are still focused on perceiver-perceived and those of his art on representer-representee.

With regard to the treatment of space in his narratives, Beckett has moved from meticulous and obsessive descriptions of space (often aiming at ridiculing the "objectivity" of scientific precision), to the choice of paradoxical places (with a special preference for cemeteries, benches, and nettle fields), to a systematic mixing of landscapes and "skullscapes." In his late works, a pervading syncretism combines physical and mental traits, and space acquires a new mobility, expanding the previously complex structure of point of view. Thus the reader is made aware of the fact that there is no such thing as *one* point of view expressing one subject's perception of space.

In fact, the subject is always "plural," since even in "one" subject there are successive points of view. Besides, the temporal component of space enters representation because the extension of space is shown to be both spatial and temporal, from the very minute in which space is posited. In this sense we can see again a Beckettian hermeneutics of experience and a portraiture of the world as interpreted world. This late Beckettian "cosmogony" is reminiscent of Heidegger:

> World is never an object that stands before us and can be seen. World is the ever non-objective to which we are subject as long as the paths of birth and death, blessing and curse keep us transported into Being.[26]

Beckett's late designations of the world are not purely mental: the world is given as interpretation, but it is not the result of an abstraction. The real movement of "birth and death, blessing and curse" is shown as keeping us intimately participative in it. At the same time, Beckett manages to indicate the ineliminable role of language in the constitution of that world, which can thus be portrayed as participated-interpreted, as a "dual reality."

Moreover, through incongruous references and critically self-reflected designations Beckett manages to indicate also the spatialization intrinsic to language. The showing of an essential space category working in it pushes the idea of the interpretive structure of the world even further. Thus, in Beckett's late works space is always a "place of remains," the residuum of existential movement and of interpretations:

> Place of remains where once used to gleam in the dark on and off used to glimmer a remain. Remains of the days of the light of day never light so faint as theirs so pale. Thus then the skull makes to glimmer again in lieu of going out.[27]

Still (1974) and *For to end yet again* (1975) inaugurate the late phase of the search, and constitute the first achievements in a spatial representation where the thing is "suspended" in order to reflect (on) the nature of space and vision. In *First Love,* written in the 1940s, Beckett had already expressed the need to produce a better representation of space, and had found in a metalinguistic self-reflection of discourse an original means of designating the intrinsic mobility of the world:

> I returned to the bench, for the fourth or fifth time since I had abandoned it, at roughly the same hour, I mean roughly the same sky, no, I don't mean that either, for it's always the same sky and never the same sky, what words are there for that, none I know, period.[28]

Although "there are no words for that," Beckett transformed the atemporality of description into the dynamics of narration in *Still*, where space can be described as being and not being the same, because of time:

> So quite still again then all quite quiet apparently eyes closed which to anticipate when they open again if they do in time then dark or some degree of starlight or moonlight or both. Normally watch night fall however long from this narrow chair or standing by western window quite still either case. Quite still namely staring at some one thing alone such as tree or bush a detail alone if near if far the whole if far enough till it goes. Or by eastern window certain moods staring at some point on the hillside such as that beech in whose shade once quite still till it goes.[29]

Space is one of the most profoundly investigated and metamorphosized elements in Beckett's works. Undoubtedly this is because of the many aspects and components of the determination, and subsequent representation, of space. In earlier works Beckett was trying to liberate space from subjectivity, but he soon abandoned this objective concern together with an epistemology typical of the *nouveau roman*. In *Proust* he expressed a profound admiration for the narrator because:

> The notion of what he should see has not had time to interfere its prism between the eye and its object.[30]

Beckett's preoccupation with "interfering prisms" can be found also in his later works, but it is focused on affective rather than cognitive attitudes. In recent times, a purely objective space or a purely mental one is transformed into the vision of a relational, functional space, no longer objective or totally abstract. On the way to the representation of a cogently interpreted space, the world successively becomes: the "non-self" and the "as said," always oscillating between objectivity and subjectivity. In *First Love* the world is "that residue of execrable frippery known as non-self";[31] in *Imagination Dead Imagine* it is "as said" by someone who is portrayed "as seen" by an external observer:

> No trace anywhere of life, *you say* [. . .] Islands, waters, azure, verdure, one glimpse and vanished, *omit*.[32]

Beckett's vision evolved gradually: he worked with changing light, (a true protagonist of his epistemic spatial tales), with complementarity of colors and positions, with oppositions between figures and grounds, as well as with different emphasis on the psychological elements of perception. Gestalt and desire, memory and imagination, impersonality and affectivity play complex roles in each of his recent representations of space. *Ill seen ill said* (1981) is, in this respect, a masterpiece: it proves how far his expressive search did go, and constitutes the climax of this original and very modern representation of space as articulated, existential, and interpreted. "Fragment 6" is an example of the complexity of Beckett's achievement:

> To the imaginary stranger the dwelling appears deserted. Under constant watch it betrays no sign of life. The eye glued to one or the other window has nothing but black drapes for its pains. Motionless against the door he listens long. No sound. Knocks. No answer. Watches all night in vain for the last glimmer. Returns at last to his own and avows, No one. She shows herself only to her own. But she has no own. Yes she has one. And who has her.[33]

The protagonists of this vision are many: an "imaginary stranger," a "she," and different eyes: open or closed, physical or mental ("his own," "her own" consciousness). The old Beckettian desire to represent one's own perceiving consciousness together with the representation of self as the content of that consciousness is reformulated as an open-ended question, as an oscillation whereby self is portrayed as differing from self ("But she has no own. Yes she has one. And who has her."). This subject/subject split combined with a subject-subject confrontation conveys the idea of a polymorphic space, a space no longer reducible to the objective/subjective polarity. Furthermore, the presence of the observer of an observer (an invariant element of Beckett's recent "novels") constitutes a multiplication of viewpoints which expresses the irreducibly interpretive nature of reality, a reality knowable only as a series of successive, personal objectifications. Besides, the non-hierarchical organization of instruments of observation and of observers, shows a mistrust in the possibility of multiplying cognitive power through the excellency of a single, closed procedure. The analytical ideology from which the text proceeds engenders a hermeneutics of reality, as the hope of cognitive objectivity fades away. The description of a place becomes a "polylogue," a discourse of interactions, the representation of open, plural, and evolving determinations. In a crucially significant essay on painting, written shortly after the end of World War Two, Beckett expressed his radical critique of representational arts, and blamed the myth of objectivity for the unfortunate atemporality of realistic representations.

He praised the painter Abraham van Velde for being able to show "la chose en suspens," "the thing fixed by the need to see it, and by the need to see." "The skull," Beckett added, "has the monopoly of this article."[34] More recently, in 1966, Beckett wrote a critical presentation of his friend Avigdor Arikha's drawings which reveals his evolved phenomenology of space, and which illuminates Beckett's own works:

> Siege laid again to the impregnable without. Eye and hand fevering after the unself. By the hand it unceasingly changes the eye unceasingly changed. Back and forth the gaze beating against unseeable and unmakable. Truce for a space and the marks of what it is to be and be in face of. Those deep marks to show.[35]

The dynamism of this description cannot go unnoticed: space has become intrinsically mobile and metamorphic. "The unseeable and unmakable" are the terms *a quo* and *ad quem* the "unself" moves. Gaze, eye, hand perform the endless subtractions that prove how impregnable a non-denotable space can be. It is unfortunate that "the impregnable without," which is a synthetic formula for a "true to life" world, has led critics to overlook, or even ignore, the referential quality of Beckett's discourse on space. It is unfortunate that his refusal of simplification and the dynamism of his representations make the critics talk of mental realities or of metanarratives. Probably these reductive readings are due to the fact that Beckett's ideas of space, time, and subjectivity were (and perhaps still are) so avant-garde that conceptual frames of reference and descriptive instruments for his discourse have yet to be devised. The recent convergence of different trends of thought and disciplines into modern hermeneutics, however, helps us to understand Beckett conceptually, even when it is clear that the work of art tells us something in such a way that its message can never be circumscribed in a concept.[36]

Artistic "Coefficients of Penetration" Versus Philosophical Intelligibility

The fact that Beckett has continually emphasized his difference from philosophers does not mean that he should not be seen as a truly modern thinker. In fact, I will argue that, by defending the specificity of his discourse even against traditional philosophers, and by pursuing in all directions his subtractive analysis of experience, Beckett has provided the presuppositions for considering his work as intrinsically philosophical and exquisitely hermeneutical. I think that *systematic* philosophy and *conceptual* intelligibility are the "distortions" that engaged him in a war against traditional philosophy. When he compares the high "coefficients of penetration" experienced by the artist to the flatness of philosophical intelligibility, he is defending an anti-intellectual attitude and the value of "the verbal oblique."[37] Systems and concepts are extraneous to his work, but the recent conception of philosophy as interpretation, the modern idea of philosophy as hermeneutics, leads me to recognize Beckett as one of the major contributors to this field of study.[38] Precisely by maintaining and preserving his difference from traditional philosophers, Beckett appears, in retrospect, to have been throughout his entire career a truly modern one, even an anticipator of modern hermeneutics. He has repeatedly stated his dissimilarity from traditional philosophers. But it seems to me that, before interpreting his words as the expression of an absolute refusal of philosophy *tout court*, we must place them against the background of the definitions and trends of philosophy historically available to him. Beckett rejected philosophical discourse because of its incapacity to deal with chaos, and because of its non-contradictory, abstract language. We must remember, however, that this type of discourse has recently been criticized by philosophers themselves, and charged with being logocentric and metaphysical.[39] Therefore, the question of Beckett's refusal of philosophy should be re-addressed, particularly as it becomes clear that Beckett's unwillingness to be compared to a philosopher is functional to the recognition of the radically new type of discourse he was developing. If Beckett's discourse were firmly classified as "purely" literary, such classification could not stand today, after the historical changes that have brought about new and flexible typologies of discourse. The recognition of Beckett's originality implies a reconsideration of previous definitions of genres and boundaries of discourse, in the light of their constant modifications. His work is so dynamic that it defies traditional genre definition and discourse typology, just like Lucretius' and Dante's. In the terminology of Thomas S. Kuhn, it has certainly disturbed the dominant paradigm of "normal science" and has established the evidence of a modern scientific revolution.[40]

In an interview with Gabriel D'Aubarède in 1961, Beckett decreed the untranslatability of literature into philosophy, and emphasized the specificity of aesthetic discourse:

Interviewer: Have contemporary philosophers had any influence on your thought?
B: I never read philosophers.
I: Why not?
B: I never understand anything they write.
I: All the same, people have wondered if the existentialists' problem of being may afford a key to your works.
B: There's no key or problem. I wouldn't have had any reason to write my novels if I could have expressed their subject in philosophic terms.[41]

The impossibility of translating into a different type of discourse what his novels say is at the root of Beckett's refusal of philosophy. It was impossible for him to waive the empowering privilege of artistic discourse, its unique capacity of suspending answers while articulating a problematic discourse. If an answer had to be, it had to stem directly from the structure of the discourse articulating the problem. As in Proust,

the germ of the Proustian solution is contained in the statement of the problem itself.[42]

and

his explanations are experimental and not demonstrative. He explains them in order that they may appear as they are—inexplicable. He explains them away.[43]

In the same year, talking to Tom Driver, Beckett defined the specificity of the literary discourse, as the capacity of expressing "the mess." He described literature as a type of discourse which, unlike philosophy, is not subjugated to the laws of non-contradiction and of rational evidence:

The only chance of renovation is to open our eyes and see the mess. It is not a mess you can make sense of.[. . .] One cannot speak anymore of being, one must speak only of the mess. When Heidegger and Sartre speak of a contrast between being and existence they may be right, I don't know, but their language is too philosophical for me. I am not a philosopher. One can only speak of what is in front of him, and that now is simply the mess. [. . .] what I am saying does not mean that there will henceforth be no form in art. It only means that there will be new form, and that this form will be of such a type that it admits the chaos and does not try to say that the chaos is really something else. [. . .] To find a form that accommodates the mess, that is the task of the artist now. [. . .] There is the unexplainable, and there art raises questions that it does not attempt to answer.[44]

It is interesting to note that Heidegger was constructing a definition of thinking which comes very close to Beckett's desire not to provide answers, but "to persist in questioning." In *On Time and Being* Heidegger meditates on the end of philosophy:

Is not then the end of philosophy after all a cessation of its way of thinking? [. . .] The mere thought of such a task of thinking must sound strange to us. A thinking which can be neither metaphysics nor science?

   A task which has concealed itself from philosophy since its very beginning, even in virtue of that beginning [. . .]?

[. . .] If the answer could be given, the answer would consist in a transformation of thinking, not in a propositional statement about a matter at stake.[45]

The dissolution of philosophy is, according to Heidegger, a preparatory task, "content with awakening a readiness in man for a possibility whose contour remains obscure, whose coming remains uncertain."[46] Similarly, Beckett "continues to struggle with a perseverance that does not even signify a form of power, merely the curse of not being able to stop talking."[47] The devaluation of propositional statements about a matter at stake is essential to Beckett's idea of his art. Like Coleridge, he denies the possibility of adequate translation of literature into philosophy, because, like Proust, "he is less interested in what is said than in the way in which it is said."[48] Furthermore, Beckett seems to invoke a "transformation of thinking" in the light of the fact that "imagination, applied a priori to what is absent, is exercised in vacuo and cannot tolerate the limits of the real."[49] His longing for an experience "at once imaginative and empirical"[50] makes him contemptuous of "the vulgarity of a plausible concatenation"[51] (a "vulgarity" to which philosophy succumbs), and of "the penny-a-line vulgarity of a literature of notations,"[52] a vulgarity to which realistic art is bound to succumb as well. Implicitly we find in *Proust* a definition of Beckett's discourse; his works are neither novels, in the traditional, bourgeois sense of the term, nor philosophical essays, devoid as they are of the argumentative conceptualization and teleology that characterizes philosophical discourse.

The Creative Process: "A Turmoil of Objective and Immanent Contradictions"

It is impossible to describe Beckett's creative process if we ignore the profound gnoseological implications that the recurring, ever-changing presence of perceiver and perceived convey in his works.[53] If the pursuit of knowledge against consoling certainties made him at first acutely aware of the fact that "The observer infects the observed with its own mobility,"[54] the same pursuit disclosed to him the ineliminable role of language and the subsequent interpretive nature of our knowledge. Focusing on narratives, from *L'innommable* (1953) to the *Foirades* (written in the 1950s and 1960s), from *Textes pour rien* (1953) to *Comment c'est* (1961), from *Imagination morte imaginez* (1965) to *Le dépeupleur* (1967–70), Beckett explores the structure and the limits of the world and the structure and limits of experience. Narration does not eliminate the investigation of space and language, nor does it postulate, particularly in his later works, the possibility of a "true" opposition between subject and object. Often narration struggles with language as the tyrannical falsifier, as the pervasive forger of reality; the struggle is, at different times, ironic, lucid, and even sublime. In the 1950s and 1960s Beckett posited silence as the void that heals, the liberating hole in the net of language, the resistance of an absence that, fortunately, cannot be filled. Yet language is still the place of the struggle between betraying and naming, between unavoidable falsifying and unavoided bringing forth. Beckett's works grow between a necessary saying and the liberating unsaying of what has necessarily been said. In recent times it is possible to see the relevance of this deconstructive practice, which compels a radical transformation of reading. In the words of Barbara Johnson:

> Reading, [. . .] proceeds by identifying and dismantling differences by means of other differences that cannot be fully identified or dismantled. [. . .] The differences *between* entities [. . .] are shown to be based on a repression of differences *within* entities, ways in which an entity differs from itself. But the way in which a text thus differs from itself is never simple: it has a certain rigorous, contradictory logic whose effects can, up to a certain point be read.[55]

The transformation of reading into a practice of interpretive hypotheses in the light of difference has been theorized by Gadamer and Derrida, among others,[56] but the resistance that Beckett's texts have offered has haunted readers for years, long before modern hermeneutical theory could account for them. Their resistance to elucidation has multiplied approaches, in ways which foreground the major critical trends of our century. The dialectics of text-explanation have shown successive "failures" of both art and criticism, and produced the need for many returns to the "abandoned work," because of the modifications of the previously set limit of reading. Indeed, Beckett's texts show how the effects of a contradictory but rigorous logic can, up to a certain point, be read, and how this "certain point" keeps changing in time because of the "advancement of learning." Re-reading his texts is in a sense the opposite of déjà vu, because it produces the vision of something previously unseen, or maybe "ill-seen."

The "Beneficient Fecundity" of Obscurity and the Critical Struggle

The elusiveness and polyvalence of Beckett's works produce a fecund resistance, which can enrich theory and the critical practice. The evolution of modern hermeneutical theory can in fact often elucidate such a resistance and account for it. As John Pilling has observed:

> It would be difficult to find more dramatic illustration of the abiding fascination of Beckett's writing than the variety of approaches adopted by critics in response to it.[57]

"The multiplicity of ways in which commentators seek to elucidate ostensibly difficult and elusive texts"[58] has marked the history of Beckett criticism. It is interesting to notice that, as soon as his texts become reasonably "explainable" thanks to some theoretical frame or perspective, Beckett formulates a different discourse, charged with a new obscurity, which again and again compels the taking of new steps in the hermeneutical quest. Beckett's works are intertwined with the epistemological revolutions of the twentieth century, and Beckett criticism has to count on interdisciplinary perceptions in order to keep pace with the ever-changing evolution of the texts and the novelty of Beckett's discourse.

In the course of the last thirty years critics have emphasized the thematic and structural novelties of Beckett's works, and in so doing they have faced and dealt with several aesthetic and cognitive problems. It is interesting to note that elucidation has been a recurrent feature of their readings, even when the presuppositions of such readings were different and kept changing in time. My discussion will deal with most of the relevant critical contributions to the study of Beckett's works, and arrange them in a thematic-chronological sequence. Inevitable gaps and discontinuities in the realization of this plan will derive from thematic or methodological similarities which brought me to group together several works, or to establish immediate links among critical works separated in time. I will begin with a French critic who is not among the first to write about Beckett, but whose contribution constitutes a complex synthesis of several aspects of his works. Her book provides a comprehensive frame of reference for my "categorization" of different critical contributions.

In her study of Beckett's language and prose, Olga Bernal has powerfully emphasized how the namable is "dust" for him, and how this belief runs parallel to his critique of traditional representation. According to Bernal, Beckett reproduces a reality "that cannot be reduced to the aesthetics of modelization and elucidation which is typical of traditional aesthetics."[59] Indeed, anticipating the Heideggerian and Derridean critique of logocentrism, Beckett "represents a narrator deprived of the category of being entailed by language,"[60] and "manages to dissolve the three essential functions of language: the descriptive, enunciative, and predicative."[61] As a result of these erosions, in Beckett's novels "to think means to obstruct the conception and determination of a being in a pronoun and in a verb."[62]

The namable is the dust not only because "permanent reality, if any, can only be apprehended as a retrospective hypothesis,"[63] but also because naming implies an order which betrays the polymorphic continuum of phenomena. From the beginning of his career Beckett has been aware, and critical, of the ambivalence of naming:

> The old ego dies hard. Such as it was, a minister of dullness, it was also an agent of security. When it ceases to perform that second function, when it is opposed by a phenomenon that it cannot reduce to the condition of a comfortable and familiar concept [. . .] it disappears.[64]

Similarly, when the writer renounces his or her "old ego" he or she no longer aims at revealing unity and coherence, but "leaves behind all the forms of a knowledge that lead to the certainties which can yield order."[65] The refusal of criteria capable of producing reference and "notations," rather than discovery, is typical of Beckett's writing strategy. After all, he had lucidly announced his program to Axel Kaun in 1937:

> At first it can only be a matter of somehow finding a method by which we can represent this mocking attitude towards the word, through words [. . .] But it is not enough for the game to lose some of its sacred seriousness. It should stop. Let us therefore act like that mad (?) mathematician who used a different principle of measurement at each step of his calculation. An assault against words in the name of beauty.[66]

Critics have responded in different ways to these implications of Beckett's work: first, marveling at the novelty of this strange discourse and trying to relate it to a literary or philosophical tradition; then, focusing on it as "a comic complex and a complex comic,"[67] or investigating its language and structure (which was producing an altogether new idea of writing); and finally, recognizing how "there seems to be no limit in the number of inscriptions to be detected beneath the palimpsest."[68]

It is very difficult to sketch a synthetic but adequate map of Beckett criticism, even if mostly only around his prose works, because of the variety of contributions proliferating after his Nobel prize. I will not even attempt to be exhaustive here; what I will try instead is to indicate how differently the hermeneutical dialogue has involved readers, and how criticism about Beckett's prose works could be taken as a showcase of the major theories and techniques that have shaped criticism since the 1950s, and even earlier.

Georges Bataille and Maurice Blanchot's celebrated comments on *Molloy* (in 1951) and on *The Unnamable* (in 1953) illustrate the positive "misreadings" theorized by Harold Bloom, because they exhibit the working of writers' imaginations when struggling with eminent "strong texts."[69] Furthermore, they have had considerable influence on subsequent readings deriving from the hermeneutical areas of poststructuralism and deconstruction. Bataille's reading clearly indicates epistemological interests and his considerations are extremely modern. Not only does he perceive Beckett's "excess" in relation to the hermeneutics of suspicion as later theorized by Gadamer, he also shows how the problem of knowledge in Beckett does not end, but actually starts, with the perception of language as both inescapable and fallacious:

> An author writing while consumed with indifference to what he writes might seem to be acting out a charade; yet is not the mind that discovers this pretence also engaged in pretences—every bit as fallacious, but with the naïveté of unawareness? The truth, stripped of pretenses, is not to be so easily attained, for before we can attain it we must not only renounce our own pretenses, but forget everything, no longer know anything, be Molloy: an impotent idiot, "not knowing what [he] was going to do until it was done."[70]

Bataille stresses the seriousness of a struggle (not a charade), that wants "to make language into a façade" but must perforce use language as a weapon. Indeed, as he says of Beckett, his critics do not know what he is going to do until it is done, but when they do see his most effective impotence, his literature and language display "the authority of ruins."[71]

> [His] literature necessarily gnaws away at the existence and the world, reducing to *nothing* (but this *nothing* is horror) these steps by which we go along confidently from one result to another, from one success to another. This does not exhaust the possibilities available in literature.[72]

I find in Bataille's words the most convincing argument against the inclusion of Beckett's works among those of the "literature of exhaustion."[73] In fact, Beckett not only avoids the so-called postmodernist use of citation, metanarrative, and word-play, but uses literature as an antidote to logocentric closure, thus subverting the very sense of exhaustion. Blanchot masterfully described this radical openness, "producing an utterance without proper beginning or end,"[74] and developing "under the threat of the impersonal":[75]

> Perhaps we are not dealing with a book at all, but with something more than a book; perhaps we are approaching that movement from which all books derive, that point of origin where, doubtless, the work is lost, the point which always ruins the work, the point of perpetual unworkableness with which the work must maintain an increasingly *initial* relation or risk becoming nothing at all. One might say that the Unnamable is condemned to exhausting the infinite.[76]

Blanchot was among the first to link the death of the author to the interminableness of literature, that is, to a language that will never stop right where there is nothing to express and no power to do so.

Among the earliest Beckett critics it is worth recalling Edwin Muir, who related Beckett's *More Pricks than Kicks* (1934) to Sterne's and Joyce's works, on the ground of their "freedom of movement." Personally and acutely aware of a writer's practice, Muir could foresee the combinatory openness which was to become central to Beckett's style:

> he does give us the feeling that his dialogue could go on forever, and thus calls up a prospect of endless diversion.[77]

Implicit in the comparison with Sterne and Joyce is the recognition of an Anglo-Irish wit to which many critics have returned. Ruby Cohn, whose remarkable work has enriched Beckett criticism with multi-faceted observations, was among the first to study Beckett's humor. In *Samuel Beckett: The Comic Gamut* she addressed a number of issues that have become central to subsequent investigations. Her attention for the subtleties of Beckett's language games brought forth philosophical, psychological, linguistic, and interpretive issues that are still being investigated today. As early as 1962, Cohn was underscoring the fact that in Beckett's works "apparent opposites are only temporary aspects of a basic human substance," and that the meaning of Beckett's linguistic games exceeds an ephemeral comicality, because they are not mere *divertissement,* however playfully realized:

> The generalization of the human predicament is accomplished by an old Beckett comic device—merciless permutation, combination, and statistics.[78]

Furthermore, Cohn was among the first to foreground the "deliberate ambiguity" of Beckett's objects, of his protagonists, metaphors, and images, thus opening the way to further questioning in the direction of thematic and linguistic criticism. In her *Back to Beckett* (1973) she synthesized her own critical effort, stressing the inseparable double nature of Beckett's writing: its formal innovation and humanistic implications.

> I have tried to show that each of Beckett's genres examines the anatomy of that genre, but he does not write mere metagenre; he reveals how each genre delineates the human situation.[79]

In the case of Beckett criticism the separation of the two levels of investigation (formal/thematic) has not been so pronounced as for other writers, and I think that the twofold, "combined" nature of criticism is due to the innovative quality of Beckett's discourse. By saying this, I do not mean to ignore, on one side, the ever-recurring tendency to produce ideological readings, mostly oriented towards existentialist or religious issues, nor, on the other, the most recent postmodernist attempts to decode Beckett's structural and stylistic innovations in purely formal terms. I tend to regard both of these readings as either "symbolic" (and external to the textual production of meaning), or as excessively reductive (and focused on only one aspect of the text, however significant).

Overtly ideological and thematic readings have flourished particularly in France in the 1960s, and can be explained by historical attitudes in a country where "existentialisme" and "chrétienté" were fairly strong components of culture.[80] In the English-speaking world critics have adopted a different perspective from the very beginning, because their thematic readings were never divorced from the appreciation of the language and structure of texts. Philosophical allusions simply provided a background against which

Beckett's works could be discussed, so that their novelty could be fore-grounded in relation to pre-existing cultural roots. Besides Cohn, Hugh Kenner, Richard Coe, and John Fletcher, to name a few, set firm bases for subsequent investigations of the philosophic implications of the Beckett canon.[81] In more recent years, a number of critics have related Beckett's narrators, voice, language, or perspectives, to philosophic, cultural, and religious issues.[82] It is interesting to note how existentialism, Hegel, Schopenhauer, Heidegger, Husserl, and Christian mystics, have provided successive frames for readings, or at least, different suggestions for the appreciation of different aspects of Beckett's texts.

It is no wonder that the evolution of heuristic grids has interested one of the masters of the *Rezeptionstheorie* school of criticism.[83] In fact, Wolfgang Iser's *The Implied Reader* refers to Beckett's novels as perfect examples of how

> in the twentieth-century novel [. . .] the discovery concerns the functioning of our own faculties of perception. The reader is meant to become aware of the nature of these faculties, of his own tendency to link things together in consistent patterns, and indeed of the whole process that constitutes his relations with the world outside himself. [. . .] the reader realizes how far short of the mark are his attempts at consistency-building, since he has had to ignore so much of the potential content of the text in order to formulate his restricted interpretation. In this way, the reader is forced to discover the hitherto unconscious expectations that underlie all his perceptions, and also the whole process of consistency-building as a prerequisite for understanding.[84]

Even though I would hesitate to share Iser's specific notion of the indeterminacy of the text, I agree that a definite change in "horizons of expectations" can be detected in Beckett's readers during the last fifty years. Beckett produces texts that demand a constant evolution of "literary competence"[85] because they imply an understanding of art and reality as change. His representations are structured according to an evolving conception of experience, inclusive of an open epistemology that challenges atemporal consistency-building. In this sense, recent thorough studies, which have explored the entire Beckett canon, have provided empirical evidence for an evolving textuality produced by successive works, even though the definition of its meaning cannot be bound to the literality of texts. Furthermore, the very Beckettian idea of a "literature of the unword" would hardly be tenable if the text totally disappeared into reading.

Several critical investigations, starting with those of Lawrence Harvey, for example, point to the inner evolution of Beckett's structural motives.[86] Recently, S. E. Gontarski's analysis of Beckett's drafts has pointed out that

> revision is often toward a patterned disconnection as motives are organized not by causality but by some application of near symmetry.[87]

Indeed, it is possible to perceive a form of calculated intertextuality presiding over the evolution of the Beckett canon. James Knowlson and John Pilling, in *Frescoes of the Skull* (1982), base their learned exegesis of Beckett's later prose and drama on a subtle comparison of early and later works, taking into account Beckett's own criticism. Thus, the continuity of a creative process can be attested precisely at the points where the configuration of specific works keeps evolving in time. The accuracy of the authors' textual links greatly enriches the analytical discussion of recent works, and seems to point (pragmatically, if not theoretically), to a textual residuum that cannot be totally assimilated to the role of the reader. Rather, Pilling's comments about *For to End Yet Again* (published 1976) suggest the openness of an interminable dialectic between reader and text:

> Here is infinite riches in a little room for anyone prepared to puzzle their way through to a conclusion. One is gratified that the text reminds its readers that they need not, in doing so, think they have come to an end.[88]

However interminable, the text is not only a function of its readers, and however literal, it cannot have an inherent message, because it keeps undermining its stability of meaning. The movement of the signifier maps "the absence of everything in which presence is announced," be it the literality of the text or the exclusive role of the reader. As Derrida suggests:

> Only *pure absence*—not the absence of this or that, but the absence of everything in which presence is announced—can *inspire*, in other words, can *work*, and then make one work. [. . .] This emptiness as the situation of literature must be acknowledged by the critic as that which constitutes the specificity of his object, as that *around which* he always speaks. Or rather, his proper object—since nothing is not an object—is the way in which this nothing *itself* is determined by disappearing.[89]

The determination produced by disappearance is essential for the understanding of Beckett's dynamic reproductions, particularly in his later works. In fact, only the work*ing* of the text can configure his silence as a non-absolute, and as indeterminable in itself. Against a metaphysical silence Beckett produces a dynamic silence: he shows the other side of saying, not its opposite. In the words of Michel Foucault:

> There is no binary division to be made between what one says and what one does not say; we must try to determine the different ways of not saying such things. [. . .] There are not one but many silences, and they are an integral part of the strategies that underlie and permeate discourses.[90]

The definitions of Beckett's "many silences" lie at the core of a vast number of exegetical efforts, and the problematic, ambiguous nature of silence is indeed well foregrounded by the exegetical results. They have shown the evolving meaning and different functions of what superficially could appear as a monolithic, invariable element of Beckett's art. Blanchot's awareness of the problematic definition of silence in the early 1950s is striking, inasmuch as it pointed to what can now be seen as the un-iconic quality of silence, and its differential nature, a difference which actually permits the working of language:

> when the talking stops, there is still talking; when the language pauses, it perseveres; there is no silence, for within that voice the silence eternally speaks. [. . .] What is this void that becomes the voice of the man disappearing into it?[91]

In the 1960s, Northrop Frye remarked how "in a world given over to obsessive utterance [. . .] to restore silence is the role of serious writing,"[92] and David Lodge ended his penetrating analysis of *Ping* with an observation on the quality of Beckett's language which implies the cognitive value of his silence: "Its language is not void; its words do not merely demonstrate their emptiness. It is, like any literary artifact, a marriage of form and meaning."[93] In the 1970s, E. M. Cioran confessed his regret at not having counted the many instances in which Beckett

> refers to words, where he reflects upon words—"drops of silence in silence," as they are described in *The Unnamable*. Symbols of fragility transformed into indestructible foundations.[94]

Recently, Floyd Merrell has seen Beckett's narratives as a perfect answer to Derrida's need of "a speech which maintains silence." He explains how "Silence erases the continuity of 'syntax.' It exists, appropriately, on the 'semantic' plane—or better, it is the equivalent of zero, the void."[95] Although the metaphorical use of such terms as "syntax" and "semantic," "zero" and "void" somewhat obscures Merrell's argument, it is interesting to think of Beckett's silence as an erosion of a compact form of proclamation, and as an opening of the discrete segmentation of a highly codified text. I think that Beckett's signifiers map out a discourse animated by a logic of change, and that silence can express the working of the temporal dimension as an essential component of discourse. After all, time itself is silent, and silence is time. Beckett's functional, structural, and thematic silences are antidotes to what de Man called "the fallacy of unmediated expression," because they actually mark the temporal dimension of speech.

Many of the readings of individual works produced in the 1970s and in the 1980s have registered with great sensitivity patterns of successive differentiations within each text. In this respect the role of the *Journal of Beckett Studies* has been crucial, for many of its contributors have opened the way to the exegesis of Beckett's late production. For example, John Pilling's "Review Articles" of *For to End Yet Again and Other Fizzles* and of *Company,*[96] and Peter Murphy's "Review Article" of *All Strange Away* provided keys for reading, very soon after the publication of these works. Structural similarities, perceived within the same work or in relation to others, have proven how important the working of *différance* is in the Beckett canon. As I have pointed out, these are works related to "a poetics of indigence" and they grow through subtraction and unwording; they can be better explained by introducing difference in a reconstructed context of reference, a context simultaneously held and released, given and denied, reconstructed when disappearing. This context should not "solidify," lest the text would be read merely pushing a little further the still maintained boundaries of its closure. As Murphy points out:

> *All Strange Away* does help to remove some of the 'strangeness' of the works which were written after it by clearly establishing the basic issues which they attempt to elucidate. More important than the use of phrases which will figure prominently in later works (for example, the first sentence 'Imagination dead imagine') is the delineation of a context, a set of 'signifieds,' to which the 'signs' of the later works (often regarded by critics as divorced from referents) are also drawn in the attempt to reveal the truth and meaning of the creative act.[97]

I believe that Beckett's texts are not totally "divorced from referents," even though the issue of reference remains problematic in them. In fact, an exact reference is often indeterminable, because of the intrinsic dynamism of the referents themselves, which keep changing in time, and thus really represent the dynamism of experience.

Susan Brienza has interpreted *Imagination dead imagine* in terms of an imaginative process which "does not depict" but produces its world "as it speaks,"[98] and James Hansford's exegesis of *Imagination dead imagine*, "As the story was told," and "La Falaise" has deconstructed Beckett's traces, showing how signs of separation are no sooner marked than effaced. Hansford's readings show very clearly how these later works destroy "the singularity of assertive statement," and how Beckett's prose in the 1970s is characterized by new epistemic coordinates ("seeing," for example), and structural traits (e.g., a different pronominalization). He takes into consideration essential components of Beckett's recent writing, such as the oscillations of "eye/I," "narrator/narrated," "inside/outside," and focuses on the multiple nature of description, structured as "tactile enquiry," "perceptual observation," and "geometric mapping."[99] Hansford's readings are systematic but not closed; they talk about a body of works whose cognitive problems are the ones we share in today's world.

In this synthetic survey, I should also mention some of the most important contributions to the understanding of Beckett, specifically, the book-length studies of many critics who have tried to capture the multi-faceted structural and thematic wealth of his writings. The very polyvalence of these expositions defies classification; however, I will present some of them, not without noticing the transformation of the "monographic" structure of earlier studies into a later "genre-oriented" exposition.

In his "Introduction" to *Samuel Beckett Now* (1969), Melvin J. Friedman presented an extremely interesting and articulate panorama of the state of criticism before Beckett's Nobel prize.[100] It is worth noticing how, at the time, the predominant interest of critics was focused on *Waiting for Godot;* we can infer that a great change of scholarship occurred in the 1970s. Friedman discusses in detail some important critical contributions with biographical and canonical preoccupations; Hugh Kenner's *Samuel Beckett: A Critical Study* (1961) and John Fletcher's *The Novels of Samuel Beckett* (1964)[101] are rightly presented as pathbreaking introductions to an author whose "unapproachability" was proverbial. Ruby Cohn's "close examination of Beckett's language, themes, and dramatic and fictional techniques" in *Samuel Beckett: The Comic Gamut* (1962) is linked by Friedman to Frederick J. Hoffman's "close examination of the relevant Beckett texts" in his *Samuel Beckett: The Language of Self* (1962).[102] "The premise of his book is that modern literature has moved from metaphysics to epistemology,"[103] says Friedman, who thus created a formula which anticipated the frame of reference of subsequent critical studies. Raymond Federman's *Journey to Chaos: Samuel Beckett's Early Fiction* (1965) "seems intent on defining the writer's fictional aesthetic,"[104] an endeavor that inspired much of the later body of criticism, starting with H. Porter Abbott. He focused primarily on the complexity of mimesis and linked what he calls the "dilemma of representation" to a study of the "form in terms of its effect on the reader." Porter Abbott discusses Beckett's early works (those written between 1940 and 1959), in relation to classical art and Beckett's own criticism.[105]

A remarkable interest in Beckett's forms leads Angela B. Moorjani to identify the central role of repetition in the Beckett canon. Repetition, she points out, is not only a thematic recurrence of certain narrative elements, but is a structural device which characterizes Beckett's "narrative game strategies," from *Murphy* to *Mal vu mal dit*. Far from sterile formalisms, Moorjani displays a consistent epistemological interest; she is well aware of the seriousness of the game, in spite of its relentless iconoclastic strategy. Significantly, at the end of her study she can say that in *Company:* "The first person is present—like nothingness and silence—only as what cannot be."[106]

Two relevant books, Niels Egebak's on Beckett's language and Dina Sherzer's on the structure of *The Trilogy,* appeared in the 1970s, and contributed to the analysis of Beckett's texts with a coherent semiotic approach.[107] The detailed study of language and levels of narration brought new light to significant problems concerning the narratives, and drew attention to new aspects of Beckett's works, such as linguistic functions, metalanguage, narrator role, and the dialectics of construction/deconstruction produced by writing.

It is interesting to note how the developments of methodology allowed formalization and explication of what was thought of as a puzzle only a few years earlier. It seems to me that the evolution of criticism can indicate how Beckett's works have often anticipated theoretical stances and epistemic models. Thus I believe that Beckett's "unworkableness" is at the leading extreme of the quest for knowledge in our times, and that his prompting obscurity leads to cognitive experimentation and progress. In this sense, the close reading of his later works compels a familiarization with the unknown, even when the exegetical effort seems to avoid theoretical issues. Explanation, presentation, description contribute to the development of ways of reading, even if such readings do not metacritically devise their own interpretive strategies.

Rubin Rabinovitz's work, mostly on early fiction, and Brian Finney's, on later fiction, trace a continuity of thought and motives throughout the works they examine. The accurate exploration of the entire canon carried out by Linda Ben-Zvi demonstrates the value of what she, perhaps too modestly, calls "abbreviated exegesis."[108] The development and value that she perceives in Beckett's art are clearly presented, by devising "analogical equivalents" in various works, so that the continuity of Beckett's world and aesthetic vision is no longer questionable, even for the non-specialized reader.

Judith E. Dearlove's *Accommodating the Chaos* (1982) is an extremely powerful study: each chapter enriches reading with fresh and profound critical suggestions regarding the canon, the central pseudo-dichotomies of Beckett's texts (both epistemic and aesthetic), the modification of "the voice and its words," and "the variety of strategies and chaos-accommodating forms" typical of Beckett's writing. Dearlove's starting and concluding point demonstrate the cohesiveness of her study which links Beckett's interest in a nonrelational art, to "the universal desire for relation." The entire book shows how

> Beckett accepts both the impossibility of a nonrelational art and the improbability of a relational one. Instead of denying the associations of traditional narratives, Beckett allows them to commingle with, but not supplant, the uncertainty and fluidity of nonrelational art. He employs conventions without being enslaved by their assumptions.[109]

Dearlove's attention to the use of allusion, affecting "Beckett's movement toward a 'minimalist' art," leads her to a brilliant hypothesis, one that cannot be avoided when approaching Beckett's later works:

> throughout his career Beckett increasingly shifts away from allusions and references to specific events, people, places and works, towards the evocation of archetypes and nonspecific, but nonetheless universal images.[110]

Although the issue of the universality of images needs further investigation, the centrality of nonspecific, "archetypal" images and patterns in the later Beckett is unquestionable. I think that *Company, ill seen ill said,* and *Worstward Ho* are exercises in iconic subtraction, emptying images of the "pictorial quality" that structures them. Thus, the more images vanish, the more representation appears as a primordial relational mechanism constituting consciousness and constructing the world.[111]

The critical scene has changed so much since Beckett's beginnings as an artist that it is no longer plausible to believe in a unity of intent in criticism. Critical presuppositions have drastically changed, and Beckett's texts have masterfully renewed their resistance to explanation. Though there is a certain convergence on the fundamental aspects of Beckett's dynamic art, Tom Driver's observations regarding Beckett's critics still sound humorously true and sufficiently provoking:

> He has devised his works in such a way that those who comment upon them actually comment upon themselves. One cannot say, 'Beckett has said so and so,' for Beckett has said 'Perhaps.'[112]

The Struggle with Beckett's "Verbal Oblique"

The main thesis behind the present study is that Beckett's writing constitutes a movement from representations to the representation of representation. Not only are specific images, phrases, narrative conventions, and structures constantly unworded throughout the canon, but by so doing, Beckett is probing into what today seems the elementary structure of our interpretation of reality or the simplest, basic mode of our being in the world.

Beckett's hermeneutics of experience is a continuous unraveling of what constitutes the liminal horizon of our interpretive being. The *limen* has indeed shown itself as a dynamic threshold every time that the iconic quality of symbols was subtracted from them, till the wavering structure of symbolization or representation could be expressed as the ineliminable, dynamic residuum that marks the human presence in the world. In other words, I investigate vehicles, structure, and function of "symbols" and images in a body of writings in which the manifest content of representation is always given only to be exceeded, and in which the destructurization of cognitive patterns becomes a successive cognitive pattern, in an incessant dynamism. Beckett the "nihilist" has swiftly moved from negation to subtraction, from binary oppositions to unmarked contraries, from silence to unsaying, or, to adopt his own words, from "over" to "*un*over," to the "not yet"—"yet again" of human experience. His work is intrinsically open: his communicative strategies question communication as they enact it; his subtractions transform words into echoes, and echoes into pure sound, still speaking; his endless combinations corrode the cultural marking of experience, and his impotence shows ineliminable creativity.

I hope I have avoided one of the most obvious risks of critical interpretation, a danger described by Aldo Tagliaferri as follows:

> The worst risk facing an exegesis of Beckett's work is not that of turning it into an endless analysis of an unending work, but of reducing it to the very things the word uses as a launching pad in order to demystify and expel: an ideology, rationalization and fetishism of the word itself.[113]

Starting with Chapter One, I intend to show how early cognitive orientations and textual teleologies are incessantly transformed by Beckett's writing strategies, and how new and unexpected ways of engendering meaning record these transformations, or produce them. The problematic relationship of "things" and "words," the representation of self and time, and the definition of the creative process, are basic issues in Beckett's works, but they are under constant reformulation, evolving according to an ever-changing awareness of the linguistic medium.

I want to show how Beckett's refusal of the traditional definitions of art leads him to go through several phases of meaning production, characterized by transgression (of realism), semantic reduction (of strata of meaning and implications), use of metalanguage (showing the conventions of discourse), and transformation of literary pseudo-referents into referents of literature. I will try to map out a "typology of meanings" in Beckett's narratives, with special regard to the changes occurring over the years in the process of meaning production. I have distinguished three phases: an early phase marked by a strong critical attitude toward realism and an acute awareness of the literary medium; a middle phase marked by the transformation of early anti-novels into a-novels, and a recent, "third" phase characterized by an epistemological use and conception of language. For example, if we recognize as an early question one formulated as: "with what authority does one speak?", we can see it become: "*who* speaks?" until, in the late Beckett, the question is transformed again, into an epistemologically crucial question: "does speaking need a subject?"

Beckett's "epiphanies" are of a linguistic, not a mythical or psychological order. By deconstructing the cultural encoding of meaning, his works ultimately show the linguistic order of reality, and the epistemic character of language. Charles Sanders Peirce's semiotic classification of signs and Roman Jakobson's definitions of linguistic functions directed me in indicating changes, both in the typologies of meaning of Beckett's works and in his meaning production.[114] I will discuss parody, incongruity, fragmentation, logorrhea, negation, and suspension as instruments of change, progressively transforming mimesis into diegesis. The inclusion of the present of reading in the narrative act is typical of Beckett's later works, when metanarrative techniques are no longer functional to the denunciation of literature as artifact. In the late Beckett the hermeneutical code becomes visible before the denotata of narration, pointing to an interpretive activity that precedes (self-)identification.

In the second chapter I exploit a number of suggestions deriving from linguistics and semiotics to discuss Beckett's use of the comic. Critical parody, referential incongruity, linguistic repetition, and nonsensical suspension are different narrative solutions that point to language as both epistemologically ineliminable and dubious. The comic in Beckett is the locus of doubtful discourse; it is the unsettling element, the agent of destabilization of cultural habits, and the arch-enemy of logocentrism. Comic effects are irresolvable semantic echoes, coming from no longer rigorous, closed statements: they show how difficult it is to control the movement of meaning. Beckett's early comic is parodic and intraliterary; it transgresses canonical discourse creating semantic/referential disjunctions. Later on, Beckett was to transform this still conceptual comic into an unresolvable incongruity: no reference can be retrieved, and the comic constitutes a mode of discourse that avoids actual negations. In the late Beckett, the comic of the absurd (which I have just described) becomes the absurd of the comic, because there is no disjunction possible, or, to use Beckett's words: "no two matters." As an early epistemology of suspicion became a practice of failure, comic freedom did not encounter the resistance out of which it grew, and the comic coincided with missaying, the unavoidable reality beyond the polarities of comedy and tragedy. Perhaps Beckett's late comic is sublime, "called into the mind by that very inadequacy itself which does admit of sensuous presentation."[115]

In Chapter Three, I relate Beckett's prose works to his recent theatrical pieces in terms of their structural and epistemic similarities. In fact, the coordinates of his universe remain essentially the same, to the point that they can be summarized as 1) the problem of the aesthetic reproduction of reality; 2) the dilemma of self-identification; and 3) the issue of temporality. The dramatic works of the 1970s and the 1980s can be seen as "un-representations" against "misrepresentations," because of their "unwording," because of their intrinsically reductive (not simply reduced) communicative strategy. Subtraction is, as in the prose, a real movement affecting visibility, against the false movement of mimesis which always implies a purely conceptual recognition of reality, more or less disguised. I believe that Artaud's idea of "the theater and its double" and Kierkegaard's notion of repetition somewhat anticipate Beckett's dramatic double, which is a complex, temporal, cognitive category. Repetition in Beckett's theater is more than a stylistic device: it is the engendering structure of our awareness of the immediate, a structure that allows the representation of phenomenalism, while avoiding the seduction of the referential fallacy.

In the theater Beckett exploits the mixing of iconic and verbal codes to develop the issue of the immediate, through the discrepancies of their articulations. The old "I say it as I hear it" of *How it is* becomes in the late plays an "I see it as I say it," because Beckett deconstructs the performative figurality of language, through the temporal literality of a theatrical performance. Linguistic figurality is shown as producing "reality effects" because theatrical "acts" are shown to be determined by a prescriptive reduplication of "facts," which are in turn the result of a previous interpretive repetition ("facts" are "interpreted events"). Beckett's enacted interpretations of reality, his simultaneous simulations, reveal the ineliminable interpretive articulation of phenomena (as events, as facts, or as acts) that presides over our knowledge of the world. Thus, the negative knowledge of Beckett's plays derives from the fact that since life cannot be reproduced, it is represented as displaying this impossibility. Minimal components of reality (breath, light, lips, eyes, voice, etc.) are used to show the impossibility of escaping interpretation and representation; even *they* are interpreted realities, whose interpretive nature is made manifest by the very difficulty the public encounters in interpreting them. Hermeneutical hypotheses are shown as shaping reality, and the simulation of reality is shown as the reality of simulation.

If literature deconstructs itself so as to designate life as immediate evidence, immediate evidence proves in turn to be the result of interpretive options. Gilles Deleuze's idea of difference and repetition, Foucault's conception of the "genitality of thought," and Derrida's "maps" of *différance* have guided my analysis of Beckett's critique of the fallacy of reference, which, typical of all of his work, acquires a visual specificity in drama. The elucidation of how life doubles the theater and the theater doubles life has certainly been at the core of my critical effort, since I feel that this double, the double of representation, enriches all of Beckett's most lucid, most unreliable, statements.

Part Two of this study offers close readings of Beckett's most significant prose works after his Nobel Prize. *Company* (1980), *ill seen ill said* (1981), and *Worstward Ho* (1983) provide a representative picture of Beckett's late production, or at least of the main problems engendered by his unwording, and of the structural and hermeneutical changes that have characterized his works since the early 1970s. Although each reading is centered around a specific text and proceeds with different hermeneutical preoccupations and methodological suggestions, I hope the homogeneity of these texts can be clearly perceived.

The reading of *Company* (in Chapter Four) addresses the implications of pronominalization and sees the text as a pronominal action through which the self is identified as "I." It is clear that Beckett's refusal of the Cartesian *cogito* derives from a conception of language as pervasive reality: the present state of self is always already a present stated, and the self can acquire the visibility of an "I" only by differing from itself. The tropology of the subject develops according to dialogical principles, so that the iconic image of the "I" is deprived of its monolithic configuration. The narrative articulation of the partial images of self shows a temporal dynamism which eventually leads to the unrepresentable *trace* of one, but plural, subject. Husserl's conception of the act-character of meaning and Lacan's description of the process of the self-visibility of self, have helped me bring out the coordinates of intentionality and image assumption, which are strictly related to language. The visibility of one-self in *Company* moves beyond a static mirror-image, and derives from the erosion of the conceptual nature of the pronominal "I." We are shown the temporal movement through which the "self" acquires a sense of totality, thanks to successive, dialogical reformulations of self-images. The suspended referentiality of *Company* actually reproduces a process of identification, by refusing to name a subject.

Chapter Five, a reading of *ill seen ill said,* deals with the problem of visibility within the epistemic perspective suggested by the text itself. Semiosis and representation are discussed insofar as the visible coincides with the figurations produced by language, even if the ontology of space is not the main concern of this discourse. Yet Beckett's suspended and fragmented mimesis develops a critique of seeing, correlating its exteriority ("landscapes") and interiority ("skullscapes").

The differentiation between what de Man calls "order" and "immediate Being" is made visible by a narrative in which fragmented icons and suspended reference represent the physicality of objects through textual anaphora, rather than through ecphrasis, that is, through linguistic repetition rather than through addition of vivid details. Beckett's narrative strategy displays the ineliminable role of saying in the determination of visibility.

It is my belief that the issue of reference is crucial for the understanding of this text, because here the power of the literary system is related to the semiotics of the natural world. When a discrepancy between "seen" and "said" is perceived, the temporal duration of things manifests itself as a component of the referent. Peirce's theory of signs, and in particular his idea of "interpretant," together with Derrida's formulation of the indefinite deferral of signifier, have helped in structuring the theoretical framework of my investigation of Beckett's concern about the translatability of the language of experience into the language of culture. In *ill seen ill said* we are shown that it is on the ground of duration, outside the boundaries of Platonic atemporality, that signs of a system can suspend their designative value, and express a signified which can either be used within the same system or assumed by a different one. It is thanks to the manifestation of a temporal discrepancy between designation and visibility, between interpretants and the object defined by them, that the seen and the said can appear as "ill." Beckett himself describes this process: "The already ill seen bedimmed and ill seen again again annulled."[116]

My analysis of the "illness" of the "seen"-"said" tries to describe the *loci* of its insurgence, because they differ, diachronically and structurally, in the process of semiosis. For example, while the seeing of an eye (led by language) identifies an object, the seeing of a mind's eye signifies a subject through that object. Thus, the fluctuation of reference becomes the expression of conflicting points of view, particularly as it is never inscribed into the absolute will of a narrative affirmation. Reference is produced as the result of a process of identification, not as the determination or illustration of a presumed thing-as-it-is, atemporally fixed. Thus I wish to demonstrate how literary diegesis in *ill seen ill said* is an instrument of investigation of the scope and extension of semiosis, and how much is yet to be known about our interpretations and, consequently, about our interpreted world.

Chapter Six, a reading of *Worstward Ho,* develops the recent Beckettian idea of the real as a process of inescapable *différance,* in which the involvement of perceiver and perceived leads to the unforgettable discovery of the diachrony of reference. Mimesis, for example, the use of language as literally representational, is defined as a pervasive "missaying" from the very beginning of the "novel," while the process of semiosis is progressively expressed as the inescapable mechanism of representation. In this light, Beckett's "unwording," theorized as early as 1937, can be seen as a process working with, but also against, intertextual mimesis, in order to show language as intimately, if figuratively, linked to the real world. In *Worstward Ho* Beckett's epistemic quest moves beyond narratives and regards language and reality, inasmuch as the latter is determined by the former. Beyond the intentionality of mental acts (which played a key role in *ill seen ill said*), and beyond the atemporal determinations of the linguistic system (which potentially determine endless representations), this novel develops toward the unreachable degree zero of representation, showing the in-eliminability of representation as *arché,* as the irreducible mechanism of our being in the world.

Well beyond a Gadamerian "hermeneutics of suspicion," and far from his expressive mistrust of the 1960s and 1970s, Beckett wrestles with, but basically accepts, the ambivalent character of language (which represents objects devoid of presence), and leads us to see the ineliminable residuum of our hermeneutical being. In this "latest" Beckett, the "showing" has given way to a "telling" radically indicative of the human experience. He proves that there can be "words without acts," but no acts without words, as the very intelligibility of phenomena is linguistic. Thus, the problem of presence in language is still faced in this late Beckett, even when the awareness of the law of the signifier no longer leaves any doubt as to the impossibility of directly expressing the speaking subject.

Worstward Ho shows that the very expressivity of language derives from its ineliminable figurality; but speech is not only figure or abstraction, but is also event, and in this a pure expression of phenomena. If in the 1950s Beckett flawed the compactness of any discourse "in order to get at the things (or the Nothingness) behind it,"[117] in the 1980s he no longer sees language as a "veil" but as an event, and figurality as an intrinsically temporal articulation, as symbolic ontology. In fact, *Worstward Ho* reminds us that even when the unseen becomes visible, it was already under every-body's eyes, except that the real compels no seeing, and thus can be defined as the radically ambivalent "nothing unseen—nothing to be seen." In this sense "missaying" is better than "saying well," because it reveals the strug-gle of figure and concept hidden by the *mot juste*.

The traditional ideal of mimetic adequacy (the myth of a good represen-tation) is totally abandoned in *Worstward Ho,* where Beckett is involved with a conscious and lucid exploration of semiosis, and where he seems to have accepted it, as a figurative but also ontologically diachronic engender-ing of meaning. As a consequence, the *via negativa* that Beckett theorizes invokes better failures, so that the trying (to express) can emerge as the specific component (of the event) of communication. Language use and linguistic manipulation no longer bear any illusions about the real power of words, but it is clear that their expressive inanity is, also, always an ontological excess. Thus, the "unwording" is pushed to the extreme; it becomes superlative, so that the failure of specific images can reveal the presence of the signifier (as defined by Lacan) and its pervasive epistemic role. Predictably, in *Worstward Ho* representation becomes the representation of representation, not as the result of metanarrativity or of literary self-reflection, but because the writing strategy of subtraction relentlessly deprives images of their iconic specificity, underscoring the cogency of representation itself. After all, the process of "voiding" happens in "real" life, where "everything is always endlessly ending."[118]

Beckett articulates with extreme lucidity the impossibility of totally escaping from representation and from interpretation, because he successively revokes every partial image of experience. The forward drive at the end of this "worst-ward" movement, that is, at the end of a superlative subtracting, points to an irreducible knot of the human condition: to the need for representation. Beckett lets it emerge as the unjustifiable, yet inescapable, need of humans; his early expression that there is "no desire to express, together with the obligation to express"[119] acquires a strikingly modern ring, in the light of a constructivist psychology and a hermeneutics of human experience which conceive the world as interpreted world.

Notes

1. Samuel Beckett, "Three Dialogues," originally published in *transition* (December 1949). Reprinted in *Disjecta: Miscellaneous Writings and a Dramatic Fragment by Samuel Beckett,* edited with a Foreword by Ruby Cohn (London: John Calder, 1983) pp. 138–45. Cited below as *Disjecta.* Quotation p. 145.

2. Samuel Beckett, "An Imaginative Work" in *Disjecta,* pp. 89–90. Quotation p. 90. The article, praising the novelist Jack B. Yeats, appeared first in *Dublin Magazine* (July–September 1936).

3. The best critical bibliographies of Beckett's works are Raymond Federman and John Fletcher, *Samuel Beckett, His Works and His Critics* (Berkeley: University of California Press, 1970) and *Samuel Beckett: Calepins de bibliographie,* Jackson R. Bryer, ed. (Paris: Lettres Modernes Minard, 1972). See also the list compiled by Robin J. Davis, *Samuel Beckett: Checklist and Index of His Published Works 1967–1976* (Stirling, Scotland: University of Stirling Library, 1979). For a bibliography from 1976 to 1982 see Breon Mitchell, "A Beckett Bibliography: New Works 1976–1982," *Modern Fiction Studies* 29, 1 (Spring 1983) 131–52. See also Cathleen Culotta Andonian, *Samuel Beckett: A Reference Guide* (Boston: G. K. Hall, 1989).

  For Beckett's biography, see Deirdre Bair, *A Biography: Samuel Beckett* (New York and London: Harcourt Brace Jovanovich, 1978).

For an ample collection of critical essays regarding Beckett's works from 1931 to 1977, see *Samuel Beckett. The Critical Heritage,* Lawrence Graver and Raymond Federman, eds. (London, Henley, and Boston: Routledge & Kegan Paul, 1979). Cited below as "Graver and Federman." In French see *Les critiques de notre temps et Beckett,* Dominique Nores, ed. (Paris: Les Editions Garnier, 1971).

4. Samuel Beckett, "Three Dialogues," p. 144.

5. See, for example, Maurice Nadeau, *Express* (26 January 1961) 25:

> After *The Unnamable* I naively imagined that Samuel Beckett would not be able to push further his quest, [. . .] After *The Unnamable* there were *Texts for Nothing, All that Fall, Embers,* and today the appearance of *How it is,* after which I would be tempted—had I not been taught by experience—to repeat the same adventurous prophecy.

See also Raymond Federman's authoritative comment in *French Review* (May 1961) 594–95:

> It seemed that after *L'Innommable,* Samuel Beckett had led the novel into some kind of impasse from which it could never emerge, unless by a repetition of what had already been done. And so one could expect a long silence on Beckett's part. Having reduced the essential elements of the novel—plot, characters, action, language—to their bare minimum, how could any writer push the experiment further? Yet with the recent publication of *Comment c'est,* Beckett once more manages to carry the form of the novel into a completely new and original no man's land.

Jean-Jacques Mayoux, *Mercure de France* (June 1961) 293–97, expressed a similar attitude:

> Reading *The Unnamable* one might have thought that it was impossible to go further in the negation of the story, in the rejection of characters, in the Catharian harshness of a retreat into the absolute.

All these critical contributions were translated and included in Graver and Federman; quotations appear respectively on pp. 224, 229–30, 232.

6. Samuel Beckett in an interview with Gabriel D'Aubarède, first published in *Nouvelles Littéraires* (16 February, 1961), now in English translation in Graver and Federman, pp. 215–17. Quotation p. 216.

7. The problem was formulated by Martin Heidegger, in "The Origin of the Work of Art," as follows:

> What could be more obvious than that man transposes his propositional way of understanding things into the structure of the thing itself? Yet this view, seemingly critical, yet actually rash and ill-considered, would have to explain first how such a transposition of propositional structure into the thing is supposed to be possible without the thing having already become visible. The question which comes first and functions as the standard, proposition-structure or thing-structure remains to this hour undecided. It even remains doubtful whether in this form the question is at all decidable.

Excerpted from *Poetry, Language, Thought* (New York: Harper and Row, 1971) and included in *Deconstruction in Context: Literature and Philosophy,* Mark C. Taylor ed. (Chicago and London: University of Chicago Press, 1986) p. 258.

8. Samuel Beckett, "German Letter to Axel Kaun," dated July 9, 1937, in *Disjecta,* pp. 51–54. English translation, pp. 170–73. Quotation pp. 172–73:

As we cannot eliminate language all at once we should at least [. . .] bore one hole after another in it, until what lurks behind it—be it something or nothing—begins to seep through; I cannot imagine a higher goal for a writer today. [. . .] On the way to this literature of the unword, which is so desirable to me, some form of Nominalist irony might be a necessary stage.

9. Talking about Proust's art, Beckett writes:

The only reality is provided by the hieroglyphics traced by inspired perception (identification of subject and object). The conclusions of the intelligence are merely of arbitrary value, potentially valid.

Samuel Beckett, *Proust* (New York: Grove Press, 1957) p. 64.

10. Samuel Beckett, *Proust,* p. 71. In his manuscript "Le Concentrisme" (probably written in 1930, now on permanent loan to the Beckett Collection of the University of Reading Library), Beckett expresses the same idea, but in relation to Mozart's art: "cet art qui, semblable à une résolution de Mozart, est parfaitement intelligible et parfaitement inexplicable." Quoted in *Disjecta,* p. 42.

11. Samuel Beckett, *Murphy* (London: John Calder, 1963).

12. Samuel Beckett, *Company* (London: John Calder, 1980) pp. 13–14.

13. Samuel Beckett, *Proust,* pp. 31–32.

14. *Ibid.,* p. 60.

15. *Ibid.,* pp. 53–54.

16. Samuel Beckett, "From an Abandoned Work" (1957) in *Collected Shorter Prose 1945–1980* (London: John Calder, 1984) p. 135.

17. Samuel Beckett, "That Time" in *Collected Shorter Plays* (London and Boston: Faber and Faber, 1984) p. 235.

18. *Ibid.*

19. Samuel Beckett, "From an Abandoned Work," p. 135.

20. Samuel Beckett, *Proust,* pp. 51–52.

21. Samuel Beckett, "Dream of Fair to Middling Women," written in 1932, in *Disjecta,* pp. 43–50. Quotation p. 43.

22. Samuel Beckett, *Proust,* p. 49. Beckett is actually quoting Calderon de la Barca's "La vida es sueño" in *Obras Completas* (Madrid: Aguilar, S. A. De Ediciones, 1951), Tomo I, pp. 221–55. Quotation p. 222.

23. Samuel Beckett, "Three Dialogues," p. 145.

24. Samuel Beckett, *Proust,* pp. 41–42.

25. Samuel Beckett, "That Time," p. 235.

26. Martin Heidegger, "The Origin of the Work of Art" in *Deconstruction in Context,* p. 265.

27. Samuel Beckett, "For to End Yet Again" in *Collected Shorter Prose,* p. 179.

28. Samuel Beckett, "First Love" in *Collected Shorter Prose,* p. 12.

29. Samuel Beckett, "Still" in *Collected Shorter Prose,* p. 184.

30. Samuel Beckett, *Proust,* p. 15.

31. Samuel Beckett, "First Love," p. 18.

32. Samuel Beckett, "Imagination Dead Imagine" in *No's Knife* (London: Calder and Boyars, 1967) p. 161. Emphasis mine.

33. Samuel Beckett, *ill seen ill said* (London: John Calder, 1982) pp. 12–13. See Chapter One, note 60.

34. Samuel Beckett, "La peinture des van Velde ou le Monde et le Pantalon" in *Disjecta*, pp. 118–32. The original quotation (p. 126) reads as follows:

La peinture d'A. van Velde serait donc premièrement une peinture de la chose en suspens, [. . .] C'est à dire que la chose qu'on y voit n'est plus seulement représentée comme suspendue, mais strictement telle qu'elle est, figée réellement. C'est la chose seule, isolée par le besoin de la voir, par le besoin de voire. [. . .] La boîte crânienne a le monopole de cet article.

35. Samuel Beckett, "For Avigdor Arikha" in *Disjecta*, p. 152.
36. This idea is expressed in Hans-Georg Gadamer's "Text und Interpretation" (1981) in *Text und Interpretation*, Philippe Forget, ed. (Munchen: Fink, 1984) pp. 24–55.
37. Samuel Beckett, *Proust*, pp. 64–67.
38. Although the transformation of hermeneutics from a technique of interpretation of specific texts (mostly juridical and religious) into a philosophical discipline may be said to have begun with Schleiermacher, it is only in recent times that it has more or less defined itself as a theory of dialogue. Interdisciplinary connections were essential for such a development, whereby ontology and epistemology are no longer regarded as totally separated. It is from this perspective that I use the term hermeneutics in the present study. Among the many contributors to this development of modern thought see Karl Otto Apel, *Towards a Transformation of Philosophy*, G. Adey and D. Frisby, trans. (London: Routledge & Kegan Paul, 1980); Hans-Georg Gadamer, *Truth and Method*, Garrett Barden and John Cumming, trans. (New York: Seabury Press, Continuum, 1975); *Philosophical Hermeneutics*, David E. Linge, ed. and trans. (Berkeley: University of California Press, 1976) and also "The Hermeneutics of Suspicion" in *Hermeneutics: Questions, and Prospects*, Gary Shapiro and Alan Sica, eds. (Amherst: University of Massachusetts Press, 1984) pp. 54–65; Clifford Geertz, *The Interpretation of Cultures* (New York: Basic Books, 1973); Jürgen Habermas, *Communication and the Evolution of Society*, Thomas McCarthy, trans. (Boston: Beacon Press, 1979) and *Theorie des kommunikativen Handelns*, 2 vols. (Frankfurt: Suhrkamp, 1981); Martin Heidegger, *Being and Time*, John Macquarrie and Edward Robinson, trans. (New York: Harper and Row, 1962), and *On the Way to Language*, Peter D. Hertz, trans. (New York: Harper and Row, 1982); Charles Sanders Peirce, *Philosophical Writings*, Justus Buchler, ed. (New York: Dover, 1955); Paul Ricoeur, *Hermeneutics and the Human Sciences*, edited, translated and introduced by John B. Thompson (Cambridge and Paris: Cambridge University Press and Editions de la Maison des sciences de l'homme, 1981), *Freud and Philosophy*, Denis Savage, trans. (New Haven, Conn.: Yale University Press, 1970); *The Conflict of Interpretations: Essays on Hermeneutics*, Don Ihde, ed. (Evanston, Ill.: Northwestern University Press, 1974), and *Time and Narrative*, Kathleen McLaughlin and David Pellauer, trans. (Chicago and London: University of Chicago Press, 1984); Richard Rorty, *Consequences of Pragmatism* (Minneapolis: University of Minnesota Press, 1982), and "Deconstruction and Circumvention," *Critical Inquiry* 11, 1 (September 1984) 1–23. See also Richard E. Palmer, *Hermeneutics: Interpretation Theory in Schleiermacher, Dilthey, Heidegger and Gadamer* (Evanston, Ill.: Northwestern University

Press, 1969); David Couzens Hoy, *The Critical Circle: Literature, History and Philosophical Hermeneutics* (Berkeley: University of California Press, 1978); and T. K. Seung, *Semiotics and Thematics in Hermeneutics* (New York: Columbia University Press, 1982) and *Structuralism and Hermeneutics* (New York: Columbia University Press, 1982).

39. The entire Derrida corpus can be seen as a modern, post-Heideggerian critique of metaphysics, starting from logocentrism. Among the most important works on the subject, see *Speech and Phenomena and Other Essays on Husserl's Theory of Signs,* David B. Allison, trans. (Evanston, Ill.: Northwestern University Press, 1973), *Of Grammatology,* Gayatri Chakravorty Spivak, trans. (Baltimore and London: Johns Hopkins University Press, 1976); *Dissemination,* Barbara Johnson, trans. (Chicago: University of Chicago Press, 1981), and *Margins of Philosophy,* Alan Bass, trans. (Chicago: University of Chicago Press, 1982).

40. Thomas S. Kuhn, *The Structure of Scientific Revolutions* (Chicago: University of Chicago Press, 1970). See in particular Chapter 5 for a definition of "paradigm"; Chapter 9 for a definition of "revolution"; and Chapter 10 for the consequences of revolutions on the formation of a new world picture.

41. From the interview with Gabriel D'Aubarède described in note 6. Quotation p. 217.

42. Samuel Beckett, *Proust,* p. 23.

43. *Ibid.,* p. 67.

44. From a conversation between Beckett and Tom Driver which appeared in *Columbia University Forum* (Summer 1961) 21–25. Reprinted in Graver and Federman, pp. 217–23. Quotations pp. 218–20.

45. Martin Heidegger, "The End of Philosophy and the Task of Thinking" in *On Time and Being,* Joan Stambaugh, trans. (New York: Harper and Row, 1972). Excerpted in *Deconstruction in Context,* pp. 242–55. Quotations pp. 243, 245, 242.

46. *Ibid.,* p. 246.

47. Maurice Blanchot, review of *The Unnamable, Nouvelle Revue Française* (October 1953) 678–86. English translation in Graver and Federman, pp. 116–21. Quotation p. 119.

48. Samuel Beckett, *Proust,* p. 63.

49. *Ibid.,* p. 56.

50. *Ibid.*

51. *Ibid.,* p. 62.

52. *Ibid.,* p. 57.

53. The effects of the creative process are described by Beckett himself as "the expression of an inward and active variety, but a multiplicity in depth, a turmoil of objective and immanent contradictions over which the subject has no control." *Ibid.,* p. 32.

54. *Ibid.,* p. 6.

55. Barbara Johnson, *The Critical Difference* (Baltimore and London: Johns Hopkins University Press, 1980) pp. x–xi.

56. See in particular Gadamer's *Truth and Method* and *Philosophical Hermeneutics* and Derrida's *Of Grammatology, Dissemination,* and *Writing and Difference,*

translated with an Introduction and Additional Notes by Alan Bass (London: Routledge & Kegan Paul, 1978).

57. John Pilling, "Editorial," *Journal of Beckett Studies* 6 (Autumn 1980) 5.

58. *Ibid.*

59. "La réalité que les romans de Beckett cherchent à représenter ne se laisse pas réduire à cette esthétique de modelage et d'élucidation qu'a été toute esthétique traditionelle." Olga Bernal, *Langage et fiction dans le roman de Beckett* (Paris: Gallimard, NRF, 1969) p. 155. Translation mine. On the issue of "explicable/inexplicable," see Chapter Six: "La déchirure des formes."

60. "*L'innommable* est une conscience et non pas un sujet dont on affirme quelque chose, à qui on attribue quelque chose. Le narrateur est ici un simple *préposé* symbolisant l'homme privé des catégories d'être du langage." *Ibid.*, p. 152.

61. "Cette écriture réussit à dissoudre ces trois fonctions essentielles du langage: descriptive, énonciative et prédicative." *Ibid.*, p. 151. Translation mine. A similar idea is expressed by Fernande Saint-Martin in *Samuel Beckett et l'univers de la fiction* (Montréal: Presses de l'Université de Montréal, 1976). See in particular "Langage et fiction," pp. 14–15.

62. "Penser c'est empêcher qu'un être se conçoive et se fixe dans un pronom et un verbe." *Ibid.*, p. 163.

63. Samuel Beckett, *Proust*, p. 4.

64. *Ibid.*, p. 10.

65. "En prenant la parole l'écrivain ne pouvait se soustraire à la règle de son travail: révéler, faire voir qu'il y a sens et cohérence. Cette tradition subit dans le travail de Beckett une épreuve si périlleuse qu'écrire et s'effondrer devient un seul et même geste. A mesure que ce travail avance, il abandonne toutes formes du savoir qui pourraient le conduire à des certitudes instauratrices d'ordre." Olga Bernal, "Samuel Beckett: l'écrivain et le savoir," *Journal of Beckett Studies* 2 (Summer 1977) 59–62. Quotation p. 59. Translation mine.

66. Samuel Beckett, "German Letter," pp. 172–73.

67. Ruby Cohn, *Samuel Beckett: The Comic Gamut* (New Brunswick, N.J.: Rutgers University Press, 1962) p. 283. On Beckett's humor see also Maurice Nadeau, "Samuel Beckett: l'humour et le néant," *Mercure de France* (August 1951), translated and reprinted as "Samuel Beckett: Humor and the Void" in *Samuel Beckett: A Collection of Critical Essays,* Martin Esslin, ed. (Englewood Cliffs, N.J.: Prentice-Hall, 1965) pp. 33–36.

68. Although these words referred specifically to *Company*, I think they can be applied to the entire Beckett canon. See John Pilling's "Review Article: *Company* by Samuel Beckett," *Journal of Beckett Studies* 7 (Spring 1982) 127–31. Quotation p. 130.

69. Georges Bataille, Review article on *Molloy*, *Critique* (May 15, 1951) 387–96. English translation in Graver and Federman, pp. 55–63; Blanchot, review.

As to the definition of "misreading" and of "strong texts" see Harold Bloom, *The Anxiety of Influence: A Theory of Poetry* (New York: Oxford University Press, 1973) and *A Map of Misreading* (New York: Oxford University Press, 1975). For a recent discussion of "the language of transcendence and the transcendence of language" in Beckett, see his "Introduction" in *Samuel Beckett: Modern Critical Views* (New York: Chelsea House, 1985) pp. 1–5.

For the influence of Blanchot on modern critical thought, and on the "Yale School" in particular, see Donald G. Marshall "History, Theory, and Influence: Yale Critics as Readers of Maurice Blanchot" in *The Yale Critics: Deconstruction in America,* Jonathan Arac, Wlad Godzich and Wallace Martin, eds. (Minneapolis: University of Minnesota Press, 1983) pp. 135–55. Quotation p. 55.

70. Georges Bataille in Graver and Federman, pp. 62–63.

71. *Ibid.,* p. 57.

72. *Ibid.,* p. 63.

73. The expression "literature of exhaustion" derives from John Barth's seminal essay "The Literature of Exhaustion," *The Atlantic,* 220, 2 (August 1967) 29–34, to which subsequent theorization relates more or less directly. For example, Ronald Sukenick's emphasis on the purely artificial nature of art, in light of the initial discovery that art is not a direct reflection of reality, seems to map out a type of literature that ignores the nature of Beckett's self-questioning, not merely self-reflecting, texts. See his "Thirteen Digressions" in *The Death of the Novel and Other Stories* (New York: Dial Press, 1969). Also Ihab Hassan's "paracriticism" does not seem to account for Beckett's specific complexity, because of the attempt to link Beckett to postmodernism when the very notion of postmodernism is not sufficiently defined (or perhaps definable). In his *The Literature of Silence: Henry Miller and Samuel Beckett* (New York: Alfred A. Knopf, 1967), he is very sensitive to the avant-garde anti-literary aspects of Beckett's art, but he seems to elude the meaning of Beckett's texts when he compares them to mathematical tautologies. Beckett's silence is not a void, but a voi*ding* of language, and I do not think that it necessarily implies, as Hassan suggests, the end of history and the literal exhaustion of art. See also his "Joyce, Beckett, and the Postmodern Imagination" in *Triquarterly* 34 (Autumn 1975) 179–200, *The Dismemberment of Orpheus: Toward a Postmodern Literature* (New York: Oxford University Press, 1971), *Paracriticism: Seven Speculations of the Times* (Urbana: University of Illinois Press, 1975), and "The New Gnosticism: Speculations on an Aspect of the Postmodernist Mind," *Boundary 2,* 1, 3 (Spring 1973) 547–69. See also Paul Bové, "The Image of the Creator in Beckett's Postmodern Writing," *Philosophy and Literature* (Spring 1980) 47–65.

For a discussion of postmodernist aesthetics, see Charles Altieri, "From Symbolist Thought to Immanence: The Ground of Postmodern American Poetics" in *Boundary 2,* 3 (Spring 1973) 605–41 and Hal Foster, *The Anti-Aesthetic: Essays on Postmodern Culture* (Washington, D.C.: Bay Press, 1983).

74. Blanchot, review, p. 116.

75. *Ibid.,* p. 119.

76. *Ibid.,* p. 120.

77. Edwin Muir, *Listener* (4 July 1934) 42. Reprinted in Graver and Federman, pp. 42–43.

78. Ruby Cohn, *Samuel Beckett: The Comic Gamut,* pp. 182–207. Reprinted in *Samuel Beckett: Modern Critical Views,* H. Bloom, ed., pp. 83–101. Quotations p. 98.

79. Ruby Cohn, *Back to Beckett* (Princeton, N.J.: Princeton University Press, 1973) p. 271.
80. Among the French critics who related Beckett's works to existentialism see Huguette Delye, *Samuel Beckett ou la philosophie de l'absurde* (Aix-en-Provence: La Pensée Universitaire, 1960).

    Among those who related it to Christianity see André Marissel, *Samuel Beckett* (Paris: Editions Universitaires, 1963); Jean Onimus, *Samuel Beckett* (Paris: Desclée de Brouwer, 1967); and Louis Perche, *Beckett, l'enfer à notre portée* (Paris: Le Centurion, 1969). Among the English-speaking critics to discuss Beckett's religious vision see Josephine Jacobsen and William Mueller, *The Testament of Samuel Beckett* (New York: Hill and Wang, 1964); and Declan Kiberd, "Samuel Beckett and the Protestant Ethic" in *The Genius of Irish Prose,* Augustine Martin, ed. (Dublin and Cork: The Mercier Press, 1985) pp. 121–30.

    Among French critics who dedicated full-length studies to Beckett's works see Ludovic Janvier, *Pour Samuel Beckett* (Paris: Minuit, 1966), and *Beckett par lui-même* (Paris: Seuil, 1969); Gérard Durozoi, *Beckett* (Paris: Bordas, 1972); Vivian Mercier, *Beckett/Beckett* (New York: Oxford University Press, 1977). See also Janvier's article: "Place of Narration / Narration of Place" in *Samuel Beckett: A Collection of Criticism,* Ruby Cohn, ed. (New York: McGraw-Hill, 1975), pp. 98–110.
81. See in particular Hugh Kenner, *Samuel Beckett: A Critical Study* (New York: Grove Press, 1961) and *A Reader's Guide to Samuel Beckett* (London: Thames and Hudson, 1973); Richard N. Coe, *Beckett* (Edinburgh and London: Oliver and Boyd, 1964); John Fletcher, *Samuel Beckett's Art* (London: Chatto and Windus, 1967), and *The Novels of Samuel Beckett,* 2nd ed. (London: Chatto and Windus, 1970).
82. Many scholars have expanded this field of studies in different directions. All of them proceed according to a personal approach, and develop their investigations in different ways. However, the need for brevity compels a synthesis here; I trust that the title of these contributions is in itself indicative of significant differences. See Michael Robinson, *The Long Sonata of the Dead* (London: Rupert Hart-Davis, 1969); Edith Kern, *Existential Thought and Fictional Technique: Kierkegaard, Sartre, Beckett* (Chicago: University of Chicago Press, 1970), and "Black Humor: The Pockets of Lemuel Gulliver and Samuel Beckett" in *Samuel Beckett Now,* Melvin J. Friedman, ed. (Chicago: University of Chicago Press, 1970); David H. Hesla, *The Shape of Chaos: An Interpretation of the Art of Samuel Beckett* (Minneapolis: University of Minnesota Press, 1971); Hans Joachim Schulz, *A Hegelian Approach to the Novels of Samuel Beckett* (The Hague: Mouton & Co., 1973); Steven Rosen, *Samuel Beckett and the Pessimistic Tradition* (New Brunswick, N.J.: Rutgers University Press, 1976); Edouard Morot-Sir, "Samuel Beckett and Cartesian Emblems" in *Samuel Beckett: the Art of Rhetoric,* E. Morot-Sir, H. Harper, and D. McMillan III, eds. (Chapel Hill: North Carolina Studies in the Romance Languages and Literatures, 1976); Eric P. Levy, *Beckett and the Voice of Species: A Study of the Prose Fiction* (Dublin: Gill and Macmillan, 1980); Hélène L.

Baldwin, *Samuel Beckett's Real Silence* (University Park: The Pennsylvania State University Press, 1981); Lance St. John Butler, *Samuel Beckett and the Meaning of Being: A Study in Ontological Parable* (New York: St. Martin's Press, 1984); *and Samuel Beckett: Humanistic Perspectives,* Pierre Astier, Morris Beja, and S. E. Gontarski, eds. (Columbus: Ohio State University Press, 1983).

Although no systematic study has been made from a psychoanalytic or psychological point of view, Guy Christian Barnard's *Samuel Beckett: A New Approach* (London: Dent, 1970) emphasizes the role of schizophrenia in Beckett's works, and A. Alvarez in his *Beckett* (New York: Watts, Fontana, 1973) criticizes him on the ground of having turned depression into a category of thought.

83. Reception theory may be said to have gained importance through the works of Hans-Robert Jauss and Wolfgang Iser. See Jauss, *Aesthetic Experience and Literary Hermeneutics,* Michael Shaw, trans. (Minneapolis: University of Minnesota Press, 1982), and *Toward an Aesthetic of Reception,* Timothy Bahti, trans. (Minneapolis: University of Minnesota Press, 1982); Iser, *The Implied Reader: Patterns of Communication in Prose Fiction from Bunyan to Beckett* (Baltimore and London: Johns Hopkins University Press, 1974), *The Act of Reading: A Theory of Aesthetic Response* (Baltimore and London: Johns Hopkins University Press, 1978), and "Indeterminacy and the Reader's Response" in *Aspects of Narrative: Selected Papers from the English Institute,* J. Hillis Miller, ed. (New York and London: Columbia University Press, 1971).

84. Wolfgang Iser, *The Implied Reader,* p. xiv. See also "The Pattern of Negativity in Beckett's Prose," *Georgia Review* 29, 3 (1975) 706–19. Reprinted in *Samuel Beckett: Modern Critical Views,* pp. 125–36.

85. The term is used in Jonathan Culler's *Structuralist Poetics: Structuralism, Linguistics and the Study of Literature* (Ithaca, N.Y.: Cornell University Press, 1975). For a discussion of reading conventions see also Stanley Fish, *Is There a Text in This Class? The Authority of Interpretive Communities* (Cambridge, Mass.: Harvard University Press, 1980).

86. Lawrence Harvey, *Samuel Beckett: Poet and Critic* (Princeton, N.J.: Princeton University Press, 1970) and "A Poet's Initiation" in *Samuel Beckett Now,* Melvin J. Friedman, ed., pp. 171–84. See also Thomas J. Taylor, "That Again: A Motif Approach to the Beckett Canon," *Journal of Beckett Studies* 6 (Autumn 1980) 107–116.

87. Stanley E. Gontarski, "The Intent of Undoing in Samuel Beckett's Art" in *Samuel Beckett: Modern Critical Views,* pp. 227–45. Quotation p. 229. "The shift from *Watt* to the trilogy is from a mannerist (never wholly mimetic) work to a diagenetic one, where *action* is lodged within discourse," p. 238.

88. James Knowlson and John Pilling, *Frescoes of the Skull: The Later Prose and Drama of Samuel Beckett* (London: John Calder, 1979). Quotation p. 190. See also Knowlson's *Light and Darkness in the Theater of Samuel Beckett* (London: Turret Books, 1972), *Samuel Beckett: An Exhibition* (London: Turret Books, 1971); and Pilling's *Samuel Beckett* (London: Routledge & Kegan Paul, 1976).

89. Jacques Derrida, "Force and Signification" in *Writing and Difference,* p. 8.

90. Michel Foucault, *The History of Sexuality: An Introduction,* Robert Hurley, trans. (New York: Vintage Books, 1980) p. 27.

91. Maurice Blanchot in Graver and Federman, pp. 116–17.

92. Northrop Frye writing on *The Trilogy, Hudson Review* (Autumn 1960) 442–49. Reprinted in Graver and Federman, pp. 206–14. Quotation p. 214.

93. David Lodge's analysis of *Ping* appeared in *Encounter* (February 1968) 85–89. Reprinted in Graver and Federman, pp. 291–301. Quotation p. 301. This brilliant reading can be indicative of a new tendency in Beckett criticism: as the beginning of a critical production focused on individual works, which was to expand in the 1970s and 1980s. See, for example, Rubin Rabinovitz on *Murphy,* Lawrence Harvey on *Watt,* Eric P. Levy on *Mercier and Camier,* Judith E. Dearlove on *How it is,* and Dougald McMillan on *Worstward Ho,* in *On Beckett: Essays and Criticism,* S. E. Gontarski, ed. (New York: Grove Press, 1986), which also contains a number of valuable readings of individual plays. See also James Leigh, "Another Beckett: An Analysis of *Residua*" in *The Analysis of Literary Texts: Current Trends in Methodology,* Randolph D. Pope, ed. (Ypsilanti, Mich.: Bilingual Press/Editorial Bilingue, 1980) pp. 314–30; and Julia Kristeva, "Le père, l'amour, l'exile," *L'Herne* 31 (1976) 246–52. Reprinted in *Desire in Language: A Semiotic Approach to Literature and Art,* Leon S. Roudiez, ed. and trans., with Thomas Gora and Alice Jardine (New York: Columbia University Press, 1980) pp. 148–58.

94. E. M. Cioran, "Encounters with Beckett," *Partisan Review* XLIII 2 (1976) 280–85. Reprinted in Graver and Federman, pp. 334–39. Quotation p. 336.

95. Floyd Merrell, *Deconstruction Reframed* (West Lafayette, Ind.: Purdue University Press, 1985). See in particular chapter seven, "Beckett's Dilemma: or, Pecking Away at the Ineffable" for the delineation of a modern epistemological background against which Beckett's texts could be placed. For a clarification of his use of the terms "syntactic" and "semantic," see in particular pp. 183–84.

96. John Pilling, "Review Article: *Fizzles,* by Samuel Beckett," *Journal of Beckett Studies* 2 (Summer 1977) 96–100; and "Review Article: *Company,* by Samuel Beckett," *Journal of Beckett Studies* 7 (Spring 1982) 127–31.

97. Peter Murphy, "Review Article: *all strange away,* by Samuel Beckett," *Journal of Beckett Studies* 5 (Autumn 1979) 99–113. Quotation p. 99. Murphy's discussion of Beckett's late realism as being connected to contiguity and metonymy seems particularly suggestive; see p. 113. See also his "The Nature of Allegory in *The lost ones,* or the Quincunx Realistically Considered," *Journal of Beckett Studies* 7 (Spring 1982) 71–88.

98. Susan Brienza, "'Imagination dead imagine': The microcosm of the mind," *Journal of Beckett Studies* 8 (Autumn 1982) 59–74. See in particular p. 70.

99. James Hansford, "*Imagination dead imagine:* The imagination and its context," *Journal of Beckett Studies* 7 (Spring 1982) 49–70. Quotations p. 55 and p. 61. See also his "Seeing and saying in 'as the story was told'," *Journal of Beckett Studies* 8 (Autumn 1982) 75–93; and "'Imaginative transactions' in 'La Falaise'," *Journal of Beckett Studies* 10 (1985) 76–86.

100. Melvin J. Friedman, "Introduction" in *Samuel Beckett Now,* pp. 3–30.

101. Hugh Kenner, *Samuel Beckett: A Critical Study;* John Fletcher, *The Novels of Samuel Beckett.*

102. Ruby Cohn, *Samuel Beckett: The Comic Gamut;* Frederick J. Hoffman, *Samuel Beckett: The Language of Self* (Carbondale: Southern Illinois University Press, 1962). Quotation from Friedman's "Introduction," *Samuel Beckett Now,* p. 8.

103. Friedman, *ibid.*

104. *Ibid.*, p. 10.

105. H. Porter Abbott, *The Fiction of Samuel Beckett* (Berkeley: University of California Press, 1973). Quotation p. 1.

106. Angela B. Moorjani, *Abysmal Games in the Novels of Samuel Beckett* (Chapel Hill: North Carolina Studies in the Romance Languages, 1982). Quotations p. 61 and p. 136.

107. Niels Egebak, *L'écriture de Samuel Beckett: contribution à l'analyse sémiotique des textes littéraires contemporains* (Copenhagen: Akademisk Forlag, 1973); Dina Sherzer, *Structure de la Trilogie de Beckett* (The Hague: Mouton, 1976).

108. Rubin Rabinovitz, "Style and Obscurity in Samuel Beckett's Early Fiction," *Modern Fiction Studies* 20 (1974) 399–406, *The Development of Samuel Beckett's Fiction* (Urbana: University of Illinois Press, 1984); Brian Finney, *since 'how it is'. a study of Samuel Beckett's later fiction* (London: Covent Garden Press, 1972); Linda Ben-Zvi, *Samuel Beckett* (Boston: Twayne Publishers, 1986).

109. Judith E. Dearlove, *Accommodating the Chaos: Samuel Beckett's Nonrelational Art* (Durham, N.C.: Duke University Press, 1982). Quotation p. 128.

110. Judith E. Dearlove, "Allusion to Archetype," *Journal of Beckett Studies* 10 (1985) 121–133. Quotation p. 121.

111. I apologize for inevitable omissions, and I prompt the scrupulous reader to examine the Beckett bibliographies quoted in note 3.

112. Tom Driver, in Graver and Federman, p. 223.

113. Aldo Tagliaferri, "Beckett and Joyce" in *Samuel Beckett: Modern Critical Views,* p. 252.

114. Charles Sanders Peirce, *Collected Papers,* Vol. 4 (Cambridge, Mass.: Harvard University Press, 1966); Roman Jakobson, *Selected Writings,* Vol. VI (The Hague-Paris-New York: Mouton, 1971–1981).

115. Immanuel Kant, *Critique of Judgement,* James Creed Meredith, trans. (New York: Oxford University Press, 1973). Quoted in *Deconstruction in Context,* p. 36.

116. Samuel Beckett, *ill seen ill said* (London: John Calder, 1982) p. 48.

117. Samuel Beckett, "German Letter," pp. 51–54. Translated pp. 170–73. Quotation p. 171.

118. "Ici tout bouge, nage, fuit, revient, se défait, se refait. Tout cesse, sans cesse." Samuel Beckett, "La peinture des van Velde." Quotation p. 128.

119. Samuel Beckett, "Three Dialogues." Quotation p. 139.

Part One

1. Typologies of Meaning in Beckett's Narratives

The Framework of Narrative Changes

"I can't go on. I'll go on". This seemingly contradictory statement which ends *The Beckett Trilogy*[1] is in fact a perfect formula to indicate how Beckett has worked since 1934. By admitting that he could not conform to tradition ("I can't go on"), he has succeeded in showing for so many years what a truly contemporary artist could be ("I'll go on"). Furthermore, this paradoxical declaration seems to underscore the fact that Beckett knew that he had reached, with the accomplishment of each of his works, the furthest expressive limit conceivable within the literary universe. Each one of his narrative pieces breaks boundaries: even to define narratives as radical transgressions fails to describe the aesthetic and epistemological power of his creative innovations.

Beckett has experimented with a variety of media and forms, comprising drama and the cinema, poetry and prose, plays and criticism. Yet, in spite of the variety of genres and media, when his artistic production is viewed in retrospect, a unifying motivation in his "multi-medial" choices can be traced: namely, his coherent attempt to achieve a radical negation at the core of the usual production of sense. Be it because of a need to show unnoticed sediments of meaning, or presuppositions on which utterances grow, be it because of a need to deny uncritically accepted cultural foundations (either celebrating or denying the power of language), he has contributed to the development of the awareness of the relentless evolution of semiosis in the Western world, and has confronted the endless flux of the phenomenology of meaning with a series of equally endless and lucid subtractions.

The practice of subtraction has implied for him a demystifying will, which shares with phenomenology a methodology of reduction, but which totally avoids transcendental systematization. Subtraction is the only way through which residua and traces can recapture and display their unrepresentable value, the value of a real linguistic movement. Beckett's many segnic reductions and referential demystifications have produced one of the most striking corpora of traces in the twentieth century, a century in which traces (as opposed to signs) have gained semiotic and epistemological dignity through philosophical critiques of logocentrism from Heidegger to Husserl to Derrida.[2]

In an interview with Israel Shenker in 1956, Beckett declared:

> I'm working with impotence, ignorance. I don't think impotence has been exploited in the past.[3]

In fact, before the epistemological revolutions of the twentieth century, Beckett and his modernist predecessors had inherited a more or less "romantic" conception of art, which saw it as the realm of personal expression, indulging creativity and rhetorical profusion. With Beckett, however, verbal art fully assumes the developing critical awareness of its relationship to the experience of truth; and it is reasonable to see that the "exploitation of impotence" better than the application of verbosity would enhance the exploration of this problematic relationship. If a verbal excess could multiply the ambivalences of the role of language in the experience of truth, verbal penury would on the contrary reduce them, leaving before our eyes the ineliminable residua of the implications between language and truth. Georges Bataille pointed to this "exercise in subtraction" in a famous article on *Molloy,* where he described and acutely interpreted Beckett's narrative solutions:

> This is not a school's manifesto, not a manifesto at all but one expression, among others, of movements that go beyond any school and that want literature finally, to make language into a façade, eroded by the wind, and full of holes, that would possess the authority of ruins. [. . .]
>
> This frantic progress toward ruin that animates the book, which, being the author's attack on the reader, is such that not for an instant is the latter given the leisure to withdraw into indifference—could it have been produced if so persuasive a conviction did not originate in some powerful motive?[4]

Bataille goes so far as to suggest the nature of that motive as

> a parody of meaning, perhaps, but finally a distinct meaning, which is to obscure within us the world of signification. Such in fact is the blind purpose of this brisk narrative. [. . .] Thus literature necessarily gnaws away at

existence and the world, reducing to nothing (but this nothing is horror) these steps by which we go along confidently from one result to another, from one success, to another.[5]

At the time in which Bataille was writing, a strong "hermeneutics of suspicion"[6] (which had developed earlier, probably starting with Kierkegaard and Nietzsche), was typical of philosophical thought. To perceive that the "authority of ruins" is stronger in Beckett than a superficially dogmatic negation of the authority of language was to acknowledge his originality. Time has shown that, beyond the demystifying attitude of a hermeneutics of suspicion, there is a constructive aspect of linguistic experience, a temporal shape of linguistic determinations which, inescapably (even if single ones are incapable of providing a foundation), maps out the evolution of a gnoseological struggle and structures historically our experience of truth.

Maurice Blanchot, writing about *The Unnamable,* asked some of the questions that have remained essential for an understanding of Beckett; they anticipated that Beckett's works would be more and more caught in (and expressive of) the problematics of writing and presence:

What is this void that becomes the voice of the man disappearing into it? Where has he fallen?

Blanchot also provides a tentative answer:

perhaps we are approaching that movement from which all books derive, that point of origin where, doubtless, the work is lost, the point which always ruins the work, the point of perpetual unworkableness with which the work must maintain an increasing initial relation or risk becoming nothing at all.[7]

As a result, once we see the perpetual unworkableness of Beckett's works, we also see how they deny the very possibility of "play," unless we admit that "play" is a synonym for "life," and thus we are to face the terror or the nausea or other emotional and physical sensations present in an actual dramatic situation, one from which we cannot escape.

The fundamental dichotomy between words and things (*verba et res*) becomes a recurrent theoretical questioning in the Beckettian corpus, insofar as his texts exist ambiguously, not totally detached from either one of the terms of that opposition. Beckett discovers language to be very powerful and seemingly mystifying; but it is the impossibility of getting rid of it which will found his subsequent, tenacious investigation for reasons of acceptance, beyond a demystifying practice. Beckett does not end his *recherche* with the "rituals of negation" of earlier avant-garde writers; on the contrary, his use of negation and subtraction conveys a cognitive passion that deals with, and fully assumes, the ambiguity of pseudo-reference in the literary text:

> At the end of my work there's nothing but dust—the namable. In the last book—'L'Innommable'—there is complete disintegration. No 'I,' no 'have,' no 'being.' No nominative, no accusative, no verb. There's no way to go on.
> The very last thing I wrote—'Textes pour rien'—was an attempt to get out of the attitude of disintegration, but it failed.[8]

As soon as disintegration becomes nothingness, as soon as it turns into an ontology of the void, Beckett changes that "namable" (that "dust") into a "trace," and his writing connotes itself as process, showing the presence of thinking, not the structure of thought.

In Beckett's use of the cinema we can recognize a similar structural purpose. His *Film* (1964) manages to get out of disintegration while illustrating a theme which will occur again and again in his works: the inanity of vision and the essentially "corrupted" epistemology that derives from it. He is interested in reformulating Berkeley's formula, not in exemplifying it; *Film* reproduces the experience of being as being perceived; it does not demonstrate it. Even the "General" introduction to the published script glosses the proverbial *"Esse est percipi"* with what cannot possibly sound like a mere explanation, since the text moves from a desire of non-being rather than from the desire to anchor being to some irrefutable evidence:

> Search of non-being in flight from extraneous perception breaking down in inescapability of self-perception.

This premise is followed by a somewhat exemplifying "stage direction":

> In order to be figured in this situation the protagonist is sundered into object (O) and eye (E), the former in flight, the latter in pursuit. It will not be clear until the end of film that pursuing perceiver is not extraneous, but self.[9]

This elaborate reinterpretation of Berkeley's formula also captures the ambivalent duplicity of the subject-instrument Beckett chose to investigate:

his "non-being in flight." In fact, the inescapability of self-perception points to language, as it is achieved through the alienation of the subject in language. We are shown that experience is achieved through language, and can be treasured only as linguistic experience. Presence, then, can only be recognized in the movement of signs, that is, in the presence of traces which diachronically articulate visibility and self-perception. So, while the cinema is used to criticize vision, language expresses the power of time and the value of silence. As it is only in relation to silence as constituting a limit, if invisibly, that the granite surface of naming can break down and acquire a desirable relativization, Beckett himself asks:

> Is there any reason why that terrible materiality of the word surface should not be capable of being dissolved, like for example the sound surface, torn by enormous pauses [. . .] so that through whole pages we can perceive nothing but a path of sounds suspended in giddy heights, linking unfathomable abysses of silence?[10]

It is clear that Beckett is moving on the way of what he calls the "literature of the unword,"[11] as he is choosing to leave behind any starting point, be it of his own choice (something like a "personal" style) or imposed on him (by the tyranny of linguistic "common usage"). His reductions keep indicating the intrinsic fallacy of believing in "free thinking" without seeing the weight of "starting points." This concern with linguistic presuppositions will lead him to concentrate on the communicative circuit rather than on a specific message or on linguistic description, starting where the self surrenders in order to speak. At some point Beckett will declare: "once a certain degree of insight has been reached [· · ·] all men talk, when talk they must, the same tripe."[12] However, the actual flow of words, that is, their specific movement, can indicate the shortcomings of language, as well as give rise to the hypothesis or trace of a subject, which is other than merely namable, referential, or thematic (other than "the same tripe"). Thus, the Beckettian gnoseological quest implies the urgency of working on, and with, all the available means of communication, so that the metamorphosis of meaning can show a variety of aspects and alternatives of representation. In fact, I think that in retrospect we can see that aesthetic representation in Beckett comes to coincide with a linguistically based hermeneutics of experience, and that the ineliminable (yet ambivalent) nature of representation emerges as the pervasive horizon of human experience.

If we attempt to define Beckett's peculiar contribution to the evolution of the novel in our century, and if we focus on the functional value of his narrative structures in relation to recent and current ideological and epistemological issues, we can come up with a classification of his works into three main phases, which may be diachronically arranged.

In this chapter I intend to describe the complexity of the semiotic process at work in the corpus of his prose works, from early "parodies" to late "texts," some of which are characterized by the return to the use of English, rather than French, after a "suspension" of over fifty years. The scope of this chapter on typologies of meaning is introductory and orientative; it aims at sketching a background against which one can place the extremely innovative works published after 1970. As we shall see, typologies of meaning never stopped changing; from one text to the following, experiment and innovation were continuously sought and achieved, even if the entire corpus of Beckett's writings can be seen as a sort of homogeneous connective tissue that bridged and linked together works that only apparently seem very different and unrelated.

The design behind all of Beckett's works concerns the discovery and investigation of the linguistic nature of experience. If it takes so many expressive forms, it is because the variety of linguistic experience is manifold, especially when language usage, rather than metalanguage or linguistic description, constitutes both the instrument and object of investigation.

Of all the many possible classifications of the Beckett canon, a tripartite subdivision seems to capture the evolution of a narrative movement concerned at first with the life/literature, mind/body dualisms, then with subjective epistemological limitations, and finally with the unavoidable dialectics of interiority and exteriority. Although every classification is bound by the relativistic choice of a point of view, I think that this one can account for the essential continuity of Beckett's writings, because the main object of each phase is determined within the common horizon of a hermeneutics of experience linguistically based. I believe that a strong theoretical and emotional continuity links the linguistic suspicion and ironical demystifications of the first phase (up to the 1960s) to the solipsistic critique of the mind in a second phase (up to the mid-1970s), finally culminating in the most recent dialectics of criticism and acceptance of linguistic visibility (in the 1970s and 1980s). If the epistemological value of language is suspected and denied at first, the very ineliminability of traces witnesses to the power of a persisting formulation, and to the strength of an oblique diachronical meaning whereby the problem of reference re-acquires legitimacy. It seems to me that, in the late Beckett, exteriority and interiority are seen as semiotic determinations of different interpretants, that is, as different outcomes of signs interpreting other signs. The experience of truth resides in the temporal movement of signs, in the evolving presence of language as the foundation of visibility. The still disturbing awareness of the impossibility of a control of meaning no longer legitimizes a dualistic perspective, nor the absoluteness of negation. On the contrary, communication emerges as the only means to come to terms with reality, as the only linguistic practice that can construct and inhabit the (interpreted) world.

The Early Phase: Fighting Against the "Professors' Tastes"

The early phase of Beckett's production shows that he started out fully aware of the medium he was working with, and of the literary tradition in which he was moving. Yet, it also shows that he was constantly attempting to discard and defy the forms he had inherited and used. Basically, he was refusing the set of implications that would express a consent to the definition of "Literature" given by tradition. Beckett no longer believed that the aim of the writer was to create images of life; in fact, he was opposed to the creation of "mimetic images," inasmuch as they do not reveal precisely the fact that they *are* images, and accurately conceal their figurative, conventional quality. He, on the contrary, wanted to create images of the "invisible images," so that he could constantly remind the reader that genres are essentially a convention, and literature a place where words "take their parts" before they actually relate to things.

The thematic expression of this critique resulted in a series of dualistic images (of art and life, of the body and the mind, of internal and external worlds). The opposition between art and life could not be stated any more forcefully than through his desecrating parodies, nor could the distance between language and the world be represented as any more unfathomable. *The Trilogy* is significant in this respect, as it starts with the desire to complete an account of reality (but certainly not with a desire to account for it, as in Victorian "novels of ideas"), and ends with the project of getting rid of words altogether. It is no surprise that in both "Proust in Pieces," and "Recent Irish Poetry" (under the pseudonym Andrew Belis), Beckett lucidly and angrily attacks the conventions of traditional realism:

> Uniformity, homogeneity, cohesion, selection scavenging for verisimilitude (the stock-in-trade exactly of the naturalism that Proust abominated), these are the Professor's tastes.[13]

And again:

> What further interest can attach to such assumptions as those on which the
> convention has for so long taken its ease, namely, that the first condition of
> any poem is an accredited theme, and that in self perception there is no
> theme, but at best sufficient *vis a tergo* to land the practitioner into the correct
> scenery, where the self is either most happily obliterated or else so improved
> and enlarged that it can be mistaken for part of the *décor*? None but the
> academic.[14]

At this stage, Beckett was particularly interested in demystifying the
thematizations of self-perception. He saw that narratives did not capture
the flux of consciousness, and that the efficacy of realism depended on exag-
geration or obliteration. The relationship of consciousness with various
forms of speech would then constitute the focus of his subsequent investigation, past the acknowledgement of the merely fictional nature of the narrative portraiture of consciousness itself. Beckett started experimenting
with forms of impersonality in narration; significantly, when Dylan Thomas
wrote about *Murphy,* he chose "the story" as the subject of his sentence:

> the story never quite knows whether it is being told objectively from the
> inside of its characters or subjectively from the outside.[15]

It is important to note that Thomas pointed to the absence of a firm
realistic convention, as in fact, the *enjeu* of this writing innovation is the
telling of the story, rather than the creation of unforgettable adventures or
characters. Beckett is seeking a way of telling a story that could demystify
the telling of stories, independently from their more or less surprising
"content."

It is perhaps worth noticing here that a wide gap separates the early
Beckett from Joyce, in that their treatment of consciousness obeys two
radically different teleologies. Joyce aimed at rendering the conventions of
the interior monologue so pliable and transparent that the effect created by
the narrative should be the immediacy of consciousness. Beckett, on the
other hand, aimed at denouncing the monologue as a mystifying, "lyrical"
convention. Beckett, like Joyce, was looking for a form to accommodate the
chaos of human experience, but he refused to identify it in the improvement
of a realistic convention. Rather, he kept his distance from both Joyce and
the acknowledged masters of the "stream of consciousness" tradition. He
rejected the lyricism as well as the subtleties that rendered their artifacts

invisible, and kept connoting literary conventions as "mind manacles." On the subject, we should keep in mind Beckett's own words:

> Must we wring the neck of a certain system in order to stuff it into a contemporary pigeon-hole, or modify the dimensions of that pigeon-hole for the satisfaction of the analogymongers?[16]

If we see a narrative convention behind the image of a "pigeon-hole," we can understand Beckett's criticism against a mechanism incapable of capturing the complexity of a "system" (namely, the variety of feelings and mental states), bound to be modified only "for the satisfaction of the analogymongers." Obviously, this also means that Beckett was aware of his own individuality even before being "analogized" with Joyce. Yet, the "analogymongers" must have been still around when he stated quite forcefully in a letter to Sighle Kennedy:

> I simply do not feel the presence in my writings as a whole of the Joyce & Proust situations you evoke. If I were in the unenviable position of having to study my work my points of departure would be the 'Naught is more real . . .' and the 'Ubi nihil vales . . . ' both already in *Murphy* and neither very rational.[17]

These apparently nihilistic "points of departure" actually hide a creative strength and a lucid awareness of the fact that entire systems of presuppositions enter, more or less unnoticed, literary representations. Beckett opts for a literature in which "nothing is valid" enough to be a real foundation of knowledge, a real basis for the experience of truth. So, unlike most writers, he starts working in the direction of progressively reducing the strata of implications of a work of art, with the dissolution of traditional narrative structures, and then with the breaking down of ordinary linguistic linkage. His early works, which include *More Pricks than Kicks* (1934), *Murphy* (1938), and the somewhat different *Watt* (written 1942, published 1953), and the later ones, such as *Molloy* (1951), *Malone meurt* (1951), and particularly, *L'Innomable* (1953), *Nouvelles et textes pour rien* (1955) and *From an Abandoned Work* (1956), are characterized by the presence of a structural and linguistic passion which aims not only at ridiculing canonical forms and at reducing allusions to a minimum, but also at transcending the semantic dichotomies which ruled over the selective principle (and the axiologies) of traditional narratives. Remember, for example, the humorously provocative statement: "'Yes or no?' said Murphy. The eternal tautology."[18]

Progressively, Beckett's words drift away from the things to which they refer, and in a more manifest way than in the usual creation of pseudo-reference conveyed in literary discourse. His writing is more than a mere destruction of traditional narratives: it is a critique of traditional typologies of meaning. In this respect, semantic negations and subversions reveal strong cognitive tensions, and are endowed with epistemological value.[19] Beckett's words on the page point to the existence of the insurmountable gap between reference and any literary form. Consider, for example, the opening sentence in *Murphy:*

> The sun shone, having no alternative, on the nothing new. Murphy sat out of it, as though he were free, in a mew in West Brompton.[20]

The structural linkage of narrative syntagms[21] in these sentences produces a surprising and parodic effect, due to the evidence that meaning viewed in relation to facts is irrelevant to the development of meaning in the narrative. The sun shines with no alternative, a useless specification from the point of view of fiction, but an essential fact in reality. Furthermore, we are told that Murphy is sitting "out of it." At this point, it is legitimate to ask what the narrator "really means" when he says "out of it" (rather than "in the shade," for example). Why is the narrator talking about the sun, since Murphy's story is not particularly related to it? The only answer to these traditional questions about life-like representations can be that it is because this narrator wants the reader to question narrative logic and narrative sequences. In fact, the specification "The sun shone, having no alternative" also challenges the most elementary principle of traditional narrative economy, and brings the reader to see the enunciation of this obvious fact, the enunciation being not obvious at all in most narratives. Actually, the only real alternative in a novel concerns the being or not-being said, since in narratives, we can only find the actualization of possible alternatives. "Having an alternative" is an impossibility which, however, constitutes the original repression from which narrative verisimilitude can ensue. Through this intricate, demystifying parody (of the world in discourse and of realism and truth in literature), Beckett leads us to perceive that "sentences constituting a literary discourse have no referent."[22] Later, the awareness of pseudo-referents will constitute the further step for the development of his suspicion, which becomes more radical in the solipsistic critique of his later novels. There, as we shall see, linguistic mistrust will culminate in a struggle with language and in a pervasive tension toward silence.

In one of the excerpts from "Dream of Fair to Middling Women," Beckett thematicizes, through the protagonist's words, the narrative goal of his early phase of novelistic production:

'I shall write a book' [Belacqua] mused, tired of the harlots of earth and air [. . .] a book where the phrase is self-consciously smart and slick, but of a smartness and slickness other than that of its neighbours on the page. The blown roses of a phrase shall catapult the reader into the tulips of the phrase that follows.[23]

Although the project is for the creation of metanarratives ("where the phrase is self-consciously smart"), the example of "blown roses" transformed into "the tulips of the phrase that follows" tells us that Beckett has not totally rejected "realism," but is envisioning a critical transformation of it. This prelude to the critical self-reflexivity of his subsequent texts is reinforced by Beckett's description of his plan for the reader:

the experience of my reader shall be between the phrases, in the silence, communicated by the intervals, not the terms, of the statement [. . .] his experience shall be the menace, the miracle, the memory of an unspeakable trajectory.[24]

By keeping this sort of programmatic statement in mind, we can easily summarize the development of Beckett's poetics: from the rejection of pseudo-referents ("the terms of the statement"), to the development of a metanarrative awareness ("between the phrases"), to the final acknowledgement of the value of traces ("the memory of an unspeakable trajectory"). These various phases reveal a very different and ever-changing interest in the production of meaning: from suspicion to negation, and then to a tentative acceptance of its narrative genesis. In the famous letter to Axel Kaun, which I have already quoted to describe Beckett's fight against the "terrible materiality of the word surface," he confirms the plan for successive stages of intervention in his writings:

On the way to this literature of the unword, which is so desirable to me, some form of Nominalist irony might be a necessary stage. But it is not enough for the game to lose some of its sacred seriousness. It should stop.[25]

As we can see, Beckett is saying that literature should coincide with a practice culminating in silence. After a phase in which he wants to find "the method by which we can represent this mocking attitude towards the word," he wants to end the game, to bring the literature of the *un*word to its radical extreme. However, in front of the ineliminable residua which remain even within an achievable silence, Beckett will reshape his idea of a "literature of the unword," into the idea of an "unwording." This means that he will move towards a conception of literature that should be able to deconstruct itself (as much as possible) in its own making. In fact, this is what happens in the third phase of Beckett's production, when the process of meaning expresses the presence of language (as communication) and also the fact that the present is penetrated by the linguistic system.

On the way to this later realization Beckett exploited "nominalist irony" (so that the literary "game" would lose "its sacred seriousness"), and expressed a tension towards silence which, for a long time, appeared to him as the only warrant of truth. It is clear that at this stage Beckett thought of silence as an absolute, as a perfect antidote to literary falsifications, but it is also true that this dualistic conception opposing silence with word would be abandoned as soon as the polarization of experience revealed itself as a conceptual fallacy in the expression of one's experience of truth.

Beckett was fully aware of the originality of his unwording project, and he expresses this awareness both in a comparison with Joyce and in the definition of his "poetics of indigence." In fact, he tried to describe his difference from Joyce, as well as in relation to tradition:

> In this dissonance between the means and their use it will perhaps become possible to feel a whisper of that final music or that silence that underlies All.
> With such a program, in my opinion, the latest work of Joyce has nothing whatever to do. There it seems rather to be a matter of an apotheosis of the word.[26]

And:

> Fortunately, it is not a matter of saying something that has not yet been said, but to say over and over again, as often as possible, in the most reduced space, what has already been said.[27]

Beckett's original task is in the semantic exploitation of subtraction, in the pursuit of what he once called the "pure interrogation, rhetorical question less the rhetoric."[28] The difference between this narrative strategy sustaining a "poetics of indigence" and Joyce's poetics, was only suggested, but conceptually very clear for Beckett already in 1929, when in his "Dante . . . Bruno. Vico . . Joyce" he acknowledged the presence of "direct expression—pages and pages of it"[29] in Joyce's *Work in Progress*. Implicitly

Beckett admits that he is far from achieving "direct expression" both because he does not aim at expressing immediacy and because he does not want to connote the forms he is using with apparent naturalness. Although in both Joyce and Beckett there is no divorcing form from content, their works demand the recognition of two very different types of semiosis: one working through excess and the other through subtraction; one a "direct expression," an apotheosis of multiplying signifiers, the other eroded, "post-literary," that is, an essentially "indirect expression." The typology of meaning in Beckett involves a degree of self-reflexivity as memory of what is gone, as record of what is left; the typology of meaning in Joyce involves self-reflexivity as abolition of the arbitrariness of signs. Joyce multiplies the allusions of onomatopoeia; Beckett erodes expressive correlations of meaning and "motivated" forms.

When Beckett describes contemporary reactions to Joyce's prose he is actually reporting about a traditional way of reading that constitutes the major interlocutor for his own writing. In other words, he uses Joyce's works to elucidate a modern alternative of reading that seemed significant to him:

> You complain that this stuff [Joyce's] is not written in English. It is not written at all. It is not to be read—or rather it is not only to be read. It is to be looked at and listened to.[30]

By doing so, Beckett points to the intrinsic excess of Joyce's signs, and to a happy, typically Joycian "materiality of the word," a kind of metamorphosis through and by which

> When the sense is sleep, the words go to sleep. (See the end of *Anna Livia*). When the sense is dancing, the words dance. [. . .] the sense which is for ever rising to the surface of the form and becoming the form itself [31]

Joyce's verbal "transubstantiation" (whereby when the meaning is "dancing," "the words dance") results in the futility of "conceptual" reading. It is interesting to note that Beckett points to "apprehension" rather than to "reading" in order to describe the phenomenological and gnoseological adventure brought about by a Joycian text, in which

> inner elemental vitality and corruption of expression imparts a furious restlessness to the form [. . .] There is an endless verbal germination, maturation, putrefaction, the cyclic dynamism of the intermediate.[32]

Fascinated by the generative aspect of Joyce's typology of meaning, Beckett reveals his own interest in the movement of signs. The vitality of semiosis attracts him, even if he will never accept in his works the "dynamism of the intermediate," that is, the single specifications of referents. Joyce's "intermediate concreteness" is quite different from Beckett's "conceptual erosion." Their texts demand a different type of aesthetic vigilance, one based on concurrence and synesthesia, the other based on memory and subtraction; one exploiting vividness, the other repetition. In Joyce the sign becomes an icon; in Beckett it becomes a referent of Literature, an index as opposed to a symbol.[33] So, both of their typologies of meaning run counter to conceptualization, since narrative semiosis is in both of them a process of transformation rather than the establishment of definitions. The acknowledged literariness of Joyce's artifacts does not need to be reassessed, but it is important to note that the "rites" of Literature survive also in Beckett's works, literature no longer being the realm of fiction but the index of fiction. Beckett's enunciation establishes a new relationship of signification, a relationship in which literature is shown more than meant. The pervasiveness of self-reflexive structures pointing to the presence of literature will be more marked in Beckett's second phase, in the many epiphanies of his a-novels.

The Second Phase: "That's All Words [. . .] There is Nothing Else."

As I have already said, the distinctive feature of the second phase of Beckett's prose production is to be found in his "negative" and "self-reflexive" structures, which radicalize the desecrating traits of his earlier production, transforming the earlier "anti-novels" into "a-novels." In fact, the most evident feature of these later texts is in the endless impediments that obstruct narration, so that the reader is more aware of the fact that he or she has a literary narration in front of him or her, rather than being involved in the development of the story.

One of the most obvious signs of the will to objectify the presence of literature was Beckett's pervasive choice of a foreign tongue (even if he had started using French much earlier).[34] In fact, all the works written in the 1960s and the majority of those written in the first half of the 1970s produce an evident negation of narrative spontaneity, which is certainly facilitated by the systematic refusal of one's own mother tongue.

Furthermore, these works seek to undo the phenomenology of meaning resulting from cultural encoding; they do not allow all those associations which are not proper to the strict linguistic meaning of a word, the one provided by a disciplinary definition. Here again, Beckett's intent towards language moves in a direction opposite to the one taken by Joyce while using his "mythical method." If we adopt Roland Barthes's description of language as

> a corpus of prescriptions and habits [. . .] It is not so much a stock of materials as a horizon [. . .] merely a reflex response involving no choice, the undivided property of men, not of writers; it remains outside the ritual of Letters,[35]

we can see how radically the use of a foreign language can affect the phenomenology of meaning, inasmuch as it becomes the result of a choice, not of habit. The fact of using a foreign language (a choice at the level of enunciation, and regarding the code), allows Beckett to probe more deeply into the relationship between reality and language, and to radicalize his refusal of allusions. Because of a certain lack of familiarity, the structure of a foreign language allows him to point out the conventional nature of the "naturalness" (or presumed "inevitability") of the structure of reality, which comes through essentially as the result of linguistic structuring. A conscious, normative use shows the fact that reality is determined according to just one of many possible descriptive conventions, and thus that it would change with a change of code. In this sense we can say that Beckett needed to achieve the negation of cultural encodings (of habitual, repressed hyperdeterminations) so that he could show the pervasiveness of language. The powerful compelling presence of a "reflex without choice" no longer can go unnoticed, but can be perceived as existing before the existence of style. Again in his "German Letter" of 1937 Beckett writes:

> It is indeed becoming more and more difficult, even senseless, for me to write an official English. And more and more *my own language appears to me like a veil* that must be torn apart in order to get at the things (or the Nothingness) behind it. *Grammar and Style*. To me they seem to have become as irrelevant as a Victorian bathing suit or the imperturbability of a true gentleman. *A mask*. Let us hope the time will come, thank God that in certain circles it has already come, when language is most efficiently used where it is being most efficiently misused.[36]

If one's mother tongue is a "veil" and grammar and style are "a mask," then a foreign language could unmask conventions, preparing the demystifying way to a linguistic practice in which language is most efficacious

when most efficiently misused. These epistemological considerations investing the efficient use of language lead Beckett to plan his unwording
strategies as follows:

> As we cannot eliminate language all at once, we should at least leave nothing
> undone that might contribute to its falling into disrepute. To bore one hole
> after another in it, until what lurks behind it—be it something or nothing—
> begins to seep through; I cannot imagine a higher goal for a writer today
> [. . .] In this dissonance between the means and their use it will perhaps
> become possible to feel a whisper of that final music or that silence that
> underlies All. [. . .] Only from time to time I have the consolation, as now,
> [Beckett is writing in German] of sinning willy-nilly against a foreign lan-
> guage, as I should like to do with full knowledge and intent against my
> own—and as I shall do—Deo juvante.[37]

Linguistic practice coincides with a critical usage, and the "highest goal
for a writer today" is defined in terms of an epistemological questioning of
the value of language, given that language cannot possibly be eliminated
altogether and that the "final music" or "silence that underlies All" could
not otherwise be perceived. A transgressive practice represents the means of
getting to the affirmation of an epistemological desire, and the practical
procedure of "sinning" against a foreign language becomes an educational
experience inasmuch as it precedes the sinning against one's own.

The significant consequence ensuing from such a critical linguistic
choice shows that the *Trilogy* and the works written in those years tend to be
equally a-topical and a-typical, because virtually no evocation of context is
produced or allowed, and also no difference in the nature of meaning is
activated (for example as allegory, anagogy, symbolism, etc.). Meanings are
exact (definitional) and fictional: they are the meanings produced by words
extraneous to any context except the narrative one. Furthermore, Beckett
often activates semantic co-textual incongruities, which cannot even be
reduced, because of the impossibility of shifting meanings onto another,
qualitatively different level (from a literal to a figurative one, for example).
The narrative context is the only site of a struggle of a seemingly literal
meaning, that no longer can acquire referential value, having so obviously
become part of fiction. Narrative meanings remain stuck to their odd
linguistic exactness and neutrality, while lexical simplicity, elementary syntax, and concise sentence patterns reinforce the abstinence from allusion,
creating a fully understandable, but equally disquieting text. It is perhaps
suitable to describe Beckett's own texts with the comparison he used in his

manifesto on "Le Concentrisme" in the 1930s: "this art which, like a Mozart resolution, is perfectly intelligible and perfectly inexplicable." Here Beckett warned the reader against the temptation of "hardening the idea" ("solidifier l'Idée"), lest art should degenerate into "*vaudeville*."[38]

Starting with *The Unnamable* Beckett's prose works move in a "negative" direction, against the solidification of all themes and ideas. The typology of meaning of these narratives is structurally very different from his previous works, to the point that we may say that we are forced (once and for all) to leave the domain of fiction for that of metafiction. In fact, these "novels" focus on "forms of content," not so much because these forms represent the specificity of Literature (as a "special" type of discourse),[39] but because Beckett has become painfully aware of the pervasiveness of language: "That's all words, never wake, all words, there's nothing else."[40]

However, far from expressing a formalistic interest for the description of words and literary structures, Beckett is always ready to remind us that "my life, we're talking of my life."[41] He is convinced that we are trapped in the radical impossibility of doing without words: "the voice quaqua on all sides,"[42] but this disquieting evidence bears no signs of fascination with verbal mannerism. Ruby Cohn has often underscored the existentialist scope of Beckett's stories, and significantly, Hugh Kenner has noted:

> If Beckett's comedy derives from mathematics and system, from the impingement of system, and notably systematic forms of discourse, on experiences to which they seem inappropriate, it is to our quickening sense of persons imprisoned inside all this system that his works owe their grip on our attention. Persons stir because every word is an utterance. Patterns close because all discourse has shape.[43]

The experience with words appears to Beckett as a most crucial *Erfahrung,* as an experience providing the most radical modification of the subject, insofar as words do not represent (only) a conceptual mediation, but the experience of the world. As a consequence, Beckett's "epiphanies" are essentially of a linguistic order, and they invest the relationship of language and reality. His wish for silence, so often openly stated at this point of his production, utters a wish for liberation from the unavoidable working of words (which always exceed the subject), and includes a wish of liberation from memory of words that, preceding the subject, have interpreted the world before him or her. It seems to me that at this stage Beckett is basically oppressed or angry at the power of language. Only later, in the third phase of his production, will he recognize that words interpret but also re-present the world, and that the movement of representations implies the liberating recognition of subjective traces. In the late phase of his narrative production Beckett will in fact accept language as a problematic but open horizon in which the cogent, ineliminable hermeneutics of human experience can take place, in the light of the transience of linguistic forms and of the event-like quality of our experience of truth.

In the second phase of his narrative *recherche,* Beckett's "to be or not to be" does not regard ontology, but the unfathomable risk at the end of the word. Silence is posited, still somehow idealistically, as a limit, as the ambivalent risk of oblivion that, however, makes linguistic choices possible. The *locus* of silence will be Beckett's "garden of Eden" for a long time, not insofar as it represents some origin but because it indicates the possibility of existing without foundation, beyond consent and visibility. This attitude towards silence is a prelude to Beckett's subsequent sense of language as communication, that is, to his perception of language as an undescribable, unutterable, subjective process of a posteriori traces. Silence is still the background of this linguistic experience, and will also become one of the images of time, a time in which the traces of human experience endlessly take form.

As I have said earlier, in order to express the nature and value of silence, Beckett used basically negative structures; one of them is a lucidly chosen logorrhea, a form of unlimited blabbing, whereby the excess in the flow of words brings them to the verge of total (primitive?) insignificance. Through their narrative multiplication (but there comes another, if unasked, question: "who multiplies them?") words destroy their clarity and correctness which normally serve to hide in the linguistic process those determinations of reality which enslave the unaware language user. In *From an Abandoned Work* (1957), *Comment c'est* (1961, *How it is,* 1964), *Imagination morte imaginez* (1965, *Imagination Dead Imagine,* 1966) and in *Bing* (1966, *Ping,* 1967), *Assez* (1966, *Enough,* 1967), *Sans* (1969, *Lessness*) as well as in *Le Dépeupleur* (1971, *The Lost Ones,* 1972) Beckett's negative narrative structures play against the efficiency of language, waging a war against its efficacious power. This struggle obviously invests and affects literary language. In relation to this chosen linguistic inanity, David Lodge asks a very relevant question:

> Is it, in effect, seeking the extinction of literary culture by denying from within the epistemological function of the literary medium itself (*i.e.,* language)?[44]

It is obvious that the implied answer to this question could have been affirmative, except that it was expressed by Beckett in the emotional form of literary iconoclasm, rather than as a philosophical concept. Instead of decreeing a "metaphysical" death of Literature (which he never decreed), Beckett articulated a process which challenged the epistemological function of the literary language while using it. Besides, his critique of the epistemological function of the literary medium confirmed his awareness of the pervasiveness of language, an awareness that disclosed the path to his subsequent, critical acceptance of language as communication.

The other Beckettian "negative" technique combined with logorrhea can be seen in the narrative multiplication of pseudo-referents, up to the point where a single meaning can be identified and yet no specific meaning assessed, because of a web of multiple ambivalences. For example, the encounters with animals in *From an Abandoned Work* devoids the "white horse," "marmosets," and "stoats" of their referential value, as they are named in a narration that devoids the significance of their specificity. The reader cannot even decide whether the story concerns a precise day (badly remembered in different versions of the same story) or a number of different days, given that the narrator and the narrative create the ambiguous image of "that far day any far day."[45]

This flow of denials and contradictions affects also the profile of the protagonist-narrator, who appears to be totally unreliable and powerless, having no knowledge and no insight into what he is reporting. Let us consider another example in *From an Abandoned Work:*

> The questions [about the story] float up as I go along and leave me very confused [. . .] questions that when I was in my right mind [presumably not now, then, when he is speaking] would not have survived one second, no but atomized they would have been [. . .] did I kill my father? and then, Did I ever kill anyone? That kind of way, to the general from the particular I suppose you might say.[46]

Here the disintegration of authorial knowledge goes beyond the destruction of a traditional character (a hero turned into an anti-hero), and also beyond the discrediting of a traditional narrator. Implicitly, it poses fundamental questions of a semiotic and hermeneutical kind, such as "who speaks?", "does speaking need a subject?", "what is the truth of a fictional statement?"; and also "is the intrinsic structure of language responsible for inevitably ridiculous (because "atomized") questions?" and "is the deductive method a methodological absurdity?". These questions are encoded in what is being said; they are part of what is actually being said, even if they are precise formulations of what is normally concealed in a narrative. In this sense, they become the cogent ob-scenity (in a strict and perfectly etymological sense) of Beckett's writing, an "off-scene" which, combined with the unreliability of the first-person narrator, reveals the presence of fiction, probing deeply into the epistemology and premises of narratives.

The lack of harmony (which is often an inherent semantic contradiction, peculiarly typical of Beckett's narrative statements), becomes the negation of a "normal" phenomenology of meaning, one ensuing from a congruous relationship between the content of a linguistic utterance and its utterance, and between the content of a message and its enunciation. After his denial of language as an expressive system of semantic potential, Beckett challenges also the semantic value of the enunciation. In a traditional novel those who speak do know, or at least they seem to know, because their authority is one of the oldest conventions on which fiction builds its credibility. In Beckett, however, the content of an utterance is so much in contrast with the imaginable traits of the subject of the enunciation, or the narrator is so discredited by what he says, that the credibility of fiction is seriously challenged. Paradoxically, language seems to reacquire its epistemological value only in the process of questioning itself. The arbitrariness of semantic codification in narration is shown, not only because language as a system of cognitive potential is misused, but also because the introduction of the act of the enunciation in some utterances shows that the enunciation itself can only be extraneous to a diegetic narration (and is normally excluded from it). Even if it is true that the enunciating act has no power to encode a "final" meaning, yet it can show the meaninglessness of a narrative message. This is why, in order to accomplish a radical negation of the mythology of fiction, Beckett will include the modalities of the enunciation as part of the narrative utterance, so that their traditional exclusion from fiction appears as one of many fictional conventions. The whole of *Ping*, for example, indicates the occurrence of rhythm (a form of the enunciation), because a recurrent element ("ping") works both as a referent and as an index of time, being a described punctuation mark, which thematizes and produces a pause:

Bare white body fixed ping fixed elsewhere.[47]

As David Lodge has pointed out:

"Ping" itself is the most ambiguous word in the text precisely because it is the one least defined by any referential or structural function in ordinary usage.[48]

It is obvious that this phenomenology of meaning works towards the destruction of the story, not only because its denotata are eroded, but also because narrative axiology, that is, the establishment of value, does not maintain a valid coherence. For example, Beckett often refuses to exercise any selection upon the subject-matter of the story, or to attribute any importance to specific events (very important in reality, but very marginally related). Thus, again, the narrator appears as an idiot who compulsively follows his own line of thought, which becomes the "chain" of the plot. This fictional innovative convention allows the mapping out on the page of the way in which language works, and this indication actually seems the only "true" story that Beckett is interested in telling.

The increase of meaning in these novels is linked to a diminished relevance of the denotata, and conative and poetic functions of language replace the referential one.[49] By saying this, I intend to emphasize the importance of the speaker's attitude in Beckett, not only because it contradicts traditional renderings of the story-teller, but also because it is revealed by repetition and symmetry, formal devices which underline the presence of literature. The novel shows its nature of artifact and its intrinsic conventionality; language itself is connoted as a doubtful source of authority in relation to truth. Thus, especially at the end of his second narrative phase, Beckett's novels have an essentially critical function, and are rooted in a gnoseological paradox: they aspire to meaninglessness beyond inevitable meaning, and they keep saying that they are longing for silence while they are "speaking." In a way, Beckett wants to reach what is missing by destroying what he has; he wants language to get closer to reality by destroying some linguistic conventions; and he wants to produce anti-novels, being past the gratifications of parodies. However, he does not seem interested in meta-narratives, something which would only illustrate and name the process of writing (but from an exteriority). On the contrary, he wants to indicate the presence of writing, so that something is changed in the essence of literary communication.

As a consequence, a different attitude is developed towards, and demanded from, the reader: his or her awareness is called upon to witness a production of meaning, the process of its being produced. The understanding of the text is no longer separable from the process of reading, as much as concepts are not separated from the process in which they are produced. The climax of this use of language will be reached in Beckett's latest works, where an earlier epistemological critique of language is transformed into a radical hermeneutics of human communication.

The Latest Phase: "Time Truth to Tell Still Current."

The third phase of Beckett's narrative production is characterized by a recurrent mixture, in each text, of diegesis and mimesis. In fact, it seems that Beckett no longer considers it legitimate to question language without being aware of its inevitability (of its presence in such questioning), and that he no longer thinks it possible to conceive of narratives apart from narration. As a consequence, the extradiegetic narrator (i.e., the traditional omniscient observer) comes closer and closer to a configuration as subject of the enunciation (of the story), and the narratee seems to coincide with an actual reader.[50] Sentences like "Imagination dead *imagine*.", "From where she lies she sees Venus rise. *On*.", "A voice comes to one in the dark. *Imagine*"[51] indicate the uncertain boundaries of a new narration and dramatize the diegetic self-reflexivity of Beckett's earlier anti-novels.

The latest phase of his writings is marked by the dominant dramatic (mimetic) quality of his typology of meaning, since the position of the interlocutor is encoded as a part of the narrative (which, in fact, becomes a "narrative performance"). Furthermore, the story includes the hermeneutical code of reading as one of its visible narrative meanings. By saying this, I mean to underline the act-character of meaning in these narratives, which allow no paraphrase because part of their meaning is the process of meaning occurring in them. Meaning exists phenomenologically, by direct temporal apprehension, and as such it is mirrored in these "novels," where concepts and abstractions exist only as inevitable mediations, rather than as formulas of some a priori meaning or abstract knowledge. Even hermeneutical hypotheses are inscribed in the narrative as meanings of the narrative, as the constitutive components of meaning, as elements of a self-reflected communicative process.

If we adopt Paul Ricoeur's description of narrative interpretation,[52] we can see that what he calls "the pre-understanding of the world of action" (that is, our "capacity for identifying action in general, by means of its structural features") does not constitute the preliminary requisite for the understanding of these Beckettian narratives. On the contrary, against our usual reading habits, a suspension of that understanding is required, because the *Einstellung,* the disposition, of the Beckettian message is oriented toward "symbolic mediations" (that express an undefinable or undefined action) rather than toward the clarification or development of referential elements (constituting an action). The great exegetical difficulty investing Beckett's latest works derives from the secondariness of an understanding of actions in relation to the primary importance of an understanding of the rules of narration. This narrative understanding constitutes the preliminary competence required of the reader, in order for him or her to "make sense" of the narrative (not of the story). Beckett inverts the dependence of narrative understanding from the pre-understanding of the world of action, and makes the construction of a hermeneutical code a prerequisite for the subsequent elucidation of narrated actions; here clarification will not necessarily produce a coherent unit, according to the traits established for the definition of an action. The evidence of a hermeneutical code is a precondition for the subsequent understanding of a *fabula,* especially when actions have lost the structural traits that would identify them as actions. For example, all the Beckettian works written in the 1980s are characterized by a pervasive use of impersonality, and yet the reader can reconstruct actions because of a perceived narrative logic. The point is that Beckett does not imitate actions but constructs them, through narrative articulations. He imitates the process in which we define an action in reality, not the action as the result of a definition. A narrative process of determinations and specification constitutes a Beckettian action, without the need to determine it according to the conformity of predetermined structural traits. Thus, a new hermeneutics of experience is expressed by a narrative in which we do not know what is happening because we cannot recognize it. However, we can see here a narrative movement of linguistic mediations that suspend definition but also produce the evidence of successive determinations. Far from metalanguage and poetic functions, the Beckettian message reveals the world as constructed by linguistic residua. The self-reflexivity of these texts mirrors our own construction of experience, and reproduces our need for hermeneutical codes. For example, we shall never know exactly what happens in *ill seen ill said,* but we see our need to make sense of "it," and this is the epistemological "epiphany" of this irreducibly ambiguous story.

Furthermore, the stories of the so called *Second Trilogy* (including *Company,* 1980; *ill seen ill said,* 1981; and *Worstward Ho,* 1983) are thematically similar, as they insist on auditory and visual perceptions. Each of these works develops in detail one aspect of our being in the world, but always in a way that does not let the reader forget about the linguistic constructions that, in fact, establish the world. The time in which these constructions develop is made to coincide with the time in which the narrative develops, and the story is constructed from fragments of defined actions, much in the same way in which phenomena are given shape and order by the elements of the linguistic system. In this sense we could say that Beckett is showing us that if life cannot become art, art discovers itself as being life, inasmuch as language is present in it as ongoing communication: the text is in the reading, even if the reading is not in the text.

Not surprisingly, in these late "novels," images of time are no longer iconic (narrative, pseudo-referential), but un-iconic, expressive of the time being. The distinctions between facts of the story and the facts of "making sense," grow progressively thin, like the distance between narrator and reader. Sometimes the narrator acts upon the narratee through impersonal description, for example, illustrating the movements that an actual reader could be performing with his eyes. Ambiguity regards the subject of the action, indeterminably oscillating between the protagonist of the story and the reader himself. We can find this sort of mirroring-metanarrative in *Still* (written in 1973), for instance, where the narrative frame of reference could be read to include the contextual act of reading:

> Eyes open again while still light and close again in what if not quite a single movement almost.[53]

In his earlier works Beckett underlined the fact that the "observer infects the observed with its own mobility";[54] in his third phase he dramatizes this fact, emphasizing the phenomenology of linguistic mediations.

Narrative meanings indicate that, although the foundation of the subject is (still) lacking, there are different ways of being absent from oneself. There is even the "fable of one fabling of one with you in the dark," a "fable" of "company"[55] in which the "I" comes to terms with his multi-faceted representations. At the end (of the fable and of fabling) they are mastered into an identity, exactly as the reader masters the meaning of "one character" (only referent of many signifiers). In *Company,* re-membering constitutes the "happy ending" of the story and of the interpretive task of the reader: "And you as you always were. Alone".[56] The character has literally been impersonated, or, more precisely, his *Bildung* has been enacted as well as told. Only at the end of the novel is the meaning "one person" accomplished, and it is so because the reader has found a hermeneutical code through which the character can acquire visibility.

Also *Still, ill seen ill said,* and *Worstward Ho* point to the existence of the contextual matrix of meaning, that is, to the presence of reading, which is, if not more, just as important as any thematic pseudo-reference or "expressive device."[57] In fact, not only does the reader have to discover the hermeneutical code before he or she can "make sense" of the denotata, he or she must also acknowledge that the denotata are part of a process of meaning (of their meaning). Beckett's late epiphanies reveal that the narrative enigma concerns the "content," also to the extent in which interlocutors act as constituents of it. This is an absolute novelty in the typology of meaning in a novel, since dramatization in narrative had previously invested only the "gesture-phrase" of character and narrator,[58] not the one of reader.

With Beckett, ellipsis in description has gone beyond the context pointed out by the narrative, onto the context implied by the establishment of a hermeneutical code, including specific hypotheses implied at various stages of the interpretive cycle. Hypotheses are (or are not) confirmed by the text, but they certainly become part of the construction of a global narrative meaning. Reference is reintroduced in these novels, but not as the specificity of denotata. However detailed, the significant insistence on the description of positions and gestures should not connote the specificity of reference as the ultimate or dominant level of meaning in the narrative. As we have seen, reference itself depends on linguistic mediation and diachronic interpretation. A determination matters because it implies the enunciation, a position of the addressee and a temporal specification within the hermeneutical cycle. It is almost as if the proliferation of descriptive details in the text wanted to prevent readers from pausing to conjecture about the story, so that they are then free to see how they take part in constructing what is being said. Specifically, the meaning of place develops into the questioning of the reader's own place in the narrative, and the meaning of reference becomes the meaning of a process that determines reference through successive selections of specific traits in different hermeneutical hypotheses. The shift from the thematic level onto one of a performative self-reflection suspends both the referential function and the parodic hyper-realism of certain motifs, and traces an actual working of the communicative model. Often this model has a double addressee—character and reader—but they are not always simultaneously addressed. A narrative voice and a sort of temporal ontology in which meaning is "processed"

appear as essential components of the global, although by no means exhaustive, narrative meaning. The temporal determinations of voice replace
the traditional mimetic portraiture of things, and traces rather than signs
map out, only a posteriori, the process of meaning.

The massive dominance of the present tense, a perfect figure of time to
indicate the enunciation, shifts the diegetic discourse typical of narratives
into the mimetic discourse typical of drama.[59] Thus, time of narration and
time of enunciation tend to coincide. See for example "A voice comes to
one in the dark. *Imagine*"; and "The cabin. Its situation. *Careful. On*. At the
inexistent centre of a formless place"; and again *"Time* truth to tell *still
current"*.[60] The implicit dialogue somehow manifested between an implied
narrator and an addressee indicates the presence of a problematic yet active
communicative level in the novel, and underscores the intrinsic dialogic
quality of its language, a trait which is not normally foregrounded in
literature.[61]

It is worth remembering that the dialogical quality of Beckett's texts
involves not only the plurality of interpretants determining reference,
but also the reader, whose position is undeniable even if he or she obviously cannot fully "express a position." Therefore, his or her "word"
remains essentially unuttered, and a final meaning essentially unachieved
and unachievable. This radical openness of the narrative is reinforced by
the "dramatic" use of a dichotomy between "true/false" or "reality/
appearance," which indicates the existence of narration as an arti/fact,
because the narrative uses "mimetic" elements as equivalent to "mythic"
ones.[62] This means that the traditional binary opposition between
"mythic" and "mimetic" becomes untenable, and that "allegiance to the
mythos" is made to coexist with "allegiance to reality."[63] In fact, as we said,
the story and the story-telling flow into one another: "From where she lies
she sees Venus rise. *On*. From where she lies when the skies are clear she
sees Venus rise followed by the sun. Then she rails at the source of all life.
On."[64]

Beckett's discourse in his recent works does not choose just one of the
options for its narrative modes; mythic and mimetic modalities are made to
coexist in the same speech act, and communication becomes the meaningful
focus of meaning. Beyond the sight of the referential elements of the story,
the visibility of the world is at stake, as the narrative dialectics of interiority
and exteriority make us acknowledge the presence of inevitable and constructive, ever-changing and precise linguistic articulations. Here the novel

has truly become dramatic, because fiction implies itself as a referent of communication.

Notes

1. Samuel Beckett, *The Beckett Trilogy: Molloy, Malone Dies, The Unnamable* (London: Picador-Pan Books, 1979, first published 1959) p. 382.
2. See the Introduction for suitable references and for a bibliography (in particular notes 38 and 39).
3. Israel Shenker, "An Interview with Beckett," *New York Times,* May 5, 1956, Section II, 1, 3. Graver and Federman, pp. 146–49. Quotation p. 148. See also Chapter Six.
4. Georges Bataille, Review article on *Molloy, Critique* (May 15, 1951) 387–96. English translation in Graver and Federman, pp. 55–63.
5. *Ibid.,* pp. 59, 63.
6. For a contextual definition of the expression "hermeneutics of suspicion" see the Introduction and Hans-Georg Gadamer's "The Hermeneutics of Suspicion" in *Hermeneutics: Questions and Prospects,* Gary Shapiro and Alan Sica, eds. (Amherst: University of Massachusetts Press, 1984). See also Paul Ricoeur, *Freud and Philosophy: An Essay on Interpretation* (New Haven, Conn.: Yale University Press, 1970).
7. Maurice Blanchot, review of *The Unnamable* in *Nouvelle Revue Française* (October 1953) 678–86. English translation in Graver and Federman, pp. 116–21. Quotations pp. 117, 120.
8. Israel Shenker, "An Interview with Beckett," p. 148.
9. Samuel Beckett, *Film* (New York: Grove Press, 1969) p. 11. This work was written in English in May 1963 and produced in 1964 by Evergreen Theatre, Inc., directed by Alan Schneider. Also published in *Eh Joe and Other Writings* (London: Faber and Faber, 1967) and in *Cascando and Other Short Dramatic Pieces* (New York: Grove Press, 1968).
10. Samuel Beckett, "German Letter to Axel Kaun," dated July 9, 1937. This letter, which is very important for the understanding of Beckett's poetics, is included (both in the original and in translation) in *Disjecta,* pp. 51–54. English translation pp. 170–73. Quotation p. 172.
11. *Ibid.,* p. 173.
12. Samuel Beckett, *Murphy* (London: Picador-Pan Books, 1973, first published 1938), p. 37.
13. Samuel Beckett, "Proust in Pieces," review of *Comment Proust a composé son roman* by Albert Feuillerat, *Spectator* (June 23, 1934), reprinted in *Disjecta,* p. 64.
14. Samuel Beckett, "Recent Irish Poetry," *The Bookman* (August 1934), signed with the pseudonym Andrew Belis. Reprinted in *Disjecta,* pp. 70–76. Quotation p. 71.

15. Dylan Thomas in *New English Weekly* (17 March 1938) 454–55, also in Graver and Federman, p. 47.
16. Samuel Beckett, "Dante . . . Bruno . Vico . . Joyce" in *Disjecta*, p. 19.
17. Samuel Beckett, letter to Sigle [sic] Kennedy, June 14, 1967, in *Disjecta*, p. 113.
18. Samuel Beckett, *Murphy*, p. 27.
19. In his discussion of "mimesis" as the ruling concern in the creation of meaning at a textual level, Paul Ricoeur points out:

    > Whatever the innovative force of poetic composition within the field of our temporal experience may be, *the composition of the plot* is grounded in a *pre-understanding* of the world of action, its meaningful structures, its symbolic resources and its temporal character. [. . .] their enumeration follows an easily established progression. First, if it is true that plot is an imitation of action, some *preliminary competence* is required: the capacity *for identifying action* in general by means of its structural features [. . .] Next, if imitating is elaborating an articulated significance of some action, *a supplementary competence* is required: an aptitude for *identifying* what I call *the symbolic mediations* of action [. . .] Finally, these symbolic articulations of action are bearers of more precisely temporal elements, from which proceed more directly the very capacity of action to be narrated and perhaps the need to narrate it.

    Time and Narrative, Kathleen McLaughlin and David Pellauer, trans. (Chicago: University of Chicago Press, 1984) p. 54. Emphasis mine.
20. Samuel Beckett, *Murphy*, p. 5.
21. I use the word "syntagm" as defined by Robert Scholes in his "Glossary of Semiotic Terminology" in *Semiotics and Interpretation* (New Haven, Conn. and London: Yale University Press, 1982). "Syntagm refers to a word's relation to other words (or a grammatical unit's relation to other units) within a particular speech act or utterance," p. 149.
22. Oswald Ducrot and Tzvetan Todorov, *Encyclopedic Dictionary of the Sciences of Language,* Catherine Porter, trans. (Baltimore and London: Johns Hopkins University Press, 1979) p. 260.
23. Samuel Beckett, "Dream of Fair to Middling Women," written in 1932, in *Disjecta*, pp. 43–50. Quotation p. 49.
24. *Ibid.*
25. Samuel Beckett, "German Letter," p. 173.
26. *Ibid.,* p. 172.
27. "Heureusement il ne s'agit pas de dire ce qui n'a pas encore été dit, mais de redire, le plus souvent possible dans l'espace le plus réduit, ce qui a été dit déjà." Samuel Beckett, "Peintres de l'empêchement," originally entitled "Le Nouvel object," 1948, in *Disjecta*, pp. 133–37. Quotation p. 133. Translation mine.
28. Samuel Beckett, "Intercessions by Denis Devlin," *transition* (April–May 1938), in *Disjecta*, pp. 91–96. Quotation p. 91.
29. Samuel Beckett, "Dante . . . Bruno . Vico . . Joyce," pp. 19–33. Quotation p. 26.
30. *Ibid.,* p. 27.
31. *Ibid.*
32. *Ibid.,* p. 29.
33. Robert Scholes, "Glossary," pp. 144, 146.

    > In Peirce's theory of signs any given sign is iconic to the extent that it signifies by virtue of some resemblance or similitude between the sign and what it stands for. [. . .] In

Peirce's semiotic theory every sign has an object to which it refers, but the object need not have a physical existence [. . .] icons and indices are defined by their relation to their referents, symbols by their place in a conventional or arbitrary system.

34. Some examples of works written in French include *Mercier et Camier,* written in 1945 and published in 1970; *L'Expulsé,* published in December 1946–January 1947; *La Fin* and *Le Calmant,* published in 1955, together with *Texts for Nothing,* 1950, as *Nouvelles et textes pour rien;* and *Premier Amour,* written in 1945, but published in 1970.

35. Roland Barthes, *Writing Degree Zero,* Annette Lavers and Colin Smith, trans., preface by Susan Sontag (New York: Hill and Wang, 1968) p. 9.

36. Samuel Beckett, "German Letter," p. 171. Emphasis mine.

37. *Ibid.,* pp. 172–73.

38. "Cet art qui, semblable à une résolution de Mozart, est parfaitement intelligible et parfaitement inexplicable" in "Le Concentrisme," paper read to the Modern Language Society of Dublin, probably written in 1930; in *Disjecta,* p. 42.

39. See Maria Corti, *An Introduction to Literary Semiotics,* Margherita Bogat and Allen Mandelbaum, trans. (Bloomington: Indiana University Press, 1978) p. 5, for the notion of literature

as a *conditio sine qua non* of literary communication [in which] the hyper-sign function of the literary text is fully realized in the general process made possible by the existence of literary conventions and codifications (behind which stand the socioideological codes).

Furthermore (p. 19),

Inside every historical sign system there exists a hierarchy of cultural codifications well-known to the sender and to the addressee of a message [. . .] The destruction of the level of signedness of a period, that is, the desemiotization of a cultural system, leads necessarily, as Lotman has demonstrated, to a new and different type of semiotization, and therefore of communication.

As a consequence, the artist, and this is particularly evident in Beckett, is one who:

on the one hand, has the rigorous destiny of ingathering the deep, indecipherable obscurity of the real and, on the other, of connecting in a new way the signs emitted by the referents in the cultural and ideological world of his own age—a process through which he participates in the social nature of literary structures.

40. Samuel Beckett, *The Beckett Trilogy,* p. 381.

41. Samuel Beckett, *How it is* (London: John Calder, 1977, first published 1964) p. 141.

42. *Ibid.,* p. 140.

43. Hugh Kenner, in *Spectrum* (Spring 1961) 3–20; reprinted in Graver and Feder-man, p. 239.

44. David Lodge, in *Encounter* (February 1968) 85–89; reprinted in Graver and Federman, pp. 291–92.

45. Samuel Beckett, "From an Abandoned Work" in *Collected Shorter Prose,* p. 132.

46. *Ibid.,* p. 133.

47. Samuel Beckett, "Ping" in *Collected Shorter Prose,* p. 149.

48. David Lodge in Graver and Federman, p. 300.

49. In describing the constitutive factors of verbal communication, Roman Jakob-son defines six corresponding functions of language. The *referential* or "de-notative" function results from

> an orientation toward the context (the context being the referent) of a message. [. . .] The so called *emotive* or "expressive" function, focused on the addresser, aims a direct expression of the speaker's attitude toward what he is speaking about [. . .] Orientation toward the addressee, the *conative* function, finds its purest grammatical expression in the vocative and imperative. [Furthermore,] there are messages primarily serving to estab-lish, to prolong, or to discontinue communication, to check whether the channel works. [. . .] This set for contact, or in Malinowski's term *phatic* function may be displayed by a profuse exchange of ritualized formulas [. . .] Whenever the addresser and/or the addressee need to check up whether they use the same code, speech is focused on the code: it performs a *metalingual* (i.e. glossing) function. [. . .] The set (*Einstellung*) toward the message as such, focus on the message for its own sake, is the *poetic* function of language. [. . .] The poetic function is not the sole function of verbal art but only its dominant, determining function, whereas in all other verbal activities it acts as a subsid-iary, accessory constituent.

Roman Jakobson, "Linguistics and Poetics" in *Selected Writings* Vol. III: *The Poetry of Grammar and the Grammar of Poetry,* edited with a preface by Stephen Rudy (The Hague, Paris, New York: Mouton, 1981) pp. 18–51. Quotations pp. 22–25.

50. For a discussion of the typology of narratees, see Gerald Prince, "Introduction to the Study of the Narratee" in *Reader-Response Criticism: From Formalism to Post-Structuralism,* Jane P. Tompkins, ed. (Baltimore: Johns Hopkins Univer-sity Press, 1980) pp. 7–25.

51. These are the opening sentences of *All Strange Away* (1976), *Company* (1980), and *ill seen ill said* (1981).

52. Paul Ricoeur, *Time and Narrative;* see also note 19.

53. Samuel Beckett, "Still" (written in 1973) in *For to End Yet Again and Other Fizzles* (London: John Calder, 1976) p. 19.

54. Samuel Beckett, *Proust* (New York: Grove Press, 1957) p. 6.

55. Samuel Beckett, *Company* (London: John Calder, 1980) p. 88.

56. *Ibid.,* p. 89.

57. One of the basic concepts of formalist poetics, the "device" was defined in relation to the "material" by Victor Shklovskii in "Art as Device," 1917, and in the last articles of *Poetika,* 1919. It was developed later by Boris Eikhenbaum in "How Gogol's 'The Overcoat' is Made" in *Poetika,* 1919. See *Gogol from the Twentieth Century,* Robert A. Maguire, ed. and trans. (Princeton, N.J.: Prince-ton University Press, 1974). Describing the historical evolution of the formal-ists' critical inquiry, Mikhail Mikhailovich Bakhtin writes:

> The formalists did not isolate the construction of the poetic work as the primary object of study. They made "poetic language" the specific object of their research. [. . .] It was with the problem of plot [*siuzhet*] that the formalists completed the transition from poetic language to the poetic construction of the work. [. . .] The basic definitions of the two components of the poetic construction—"material" and "device"—were devel-oped in the process of this vacillating transition from the language system to the study of the construction of the work. These concepts were to replace "content" and "form."

M. M. Bakhtin and P. M. Medvedev, *The Formal Method in Literary Scholarship*, Albert J. Wehrle, trans. (Cambridge, Mass.: Harvard University Press, 1985) pp. 78–79.

58. Andrej Kodjak, "Dramatization in Narrative Texts" in *The Structural Analysis of Narrative Texts*, Andrej Kodjak, Michael J. Connolly, Krystyna Pomorska, eds. (Columbus, Oh.: Slavica Publishers, 1980) pp. 96–111.

59. Robert Scholes includes the term "Mimesis" in his "Glossary" (pp. 145–46):

> Holding its traditional sense of imitation or representation, this term is now used in two more specific senses. Opposed to diegesis, it means enactment of what is represented as opposed to imagination of the events based on a verbal text [. . .] In another context, mimesis is opposed to semiosis. Here, mimesis is the attempt to take language as literally representational. When this is impossible—as in metaphor, metonymy and other figures of speech—the interpreter must move from mimesis to semiosis. That is, the reader must give up trying to move from words to things and must accept the principle of unlimited semiosis, moving from word to word, sign to sign.

60. Samuel Beckett, *Company*, p. 7 (emphasis mine); *ill seen ill said* (London: John Calder, 1982) pp. 8, 13–14 (emphasis mine). This work was first published in Paris as *Mal vu mal dit*, 1981.

61. For a discussion of dialogue and the novel, see Mikhail Bakhtin, *Problems of Dostoevsky's Poetics*, R. W. Rotsel, trans. (Ann Arbor, Mich.: Ardis, 1973). Here Bakhtin defined the "polyphonic novel," asserting that Dostoevsky was its creator, since "The plurality of independent and unmerged voices and consciousness and the genuine polyphony of full-valued voices are in fact characteristic [of his works]." While discussing dialogical relationships Bakhtin pointed out (pp. 4, 151, 152, 153) that they are

> extra-linguistic phenomena [. . .] not reducible to logical or concrete semantic relationships, which are in and of themselves devoid of any dialogical aspect. In order for dialogical relationships to arise among them, they must clothe themselves in the word, become utterances, and become the positions of various subjects, expressed in the word. [. . .] in order to become dialogical, logical and concrete semantic (*predmetno-smyslovye*) relationships must be embodied, *i.e.* they must enter into a different sphere of existence: they must become a word, *i.e.* an utterance, and have an author, *i.e.* the creator of the given utterance, whose position is expressed. [. . .] in all of them the word has a double-directness—it is directed both toward the object of speech, like an ordinary word, and toward another word, toward another person's speech.

62. For a definition of the terms used here see Robert Scholes and Robert Kellogg, *The Nature of Narrative* (New York: Oxford University Press, 1966); they discuss "historical, mythic, and fictional plot forms" as well as the "plot forms usually adopted by mimetic narrative." They point out (pp. 229, 235) that

> With respect to plot the mimetic is the antithesis of the mythic [and that] with the coming of the twentieth century, plotting in narrative became dominated by time as it never had been before [. . .] plots began to be developed which were based on rearranging time so that the resolution became not so much a stasis of concluded action as a stasis of illumination, when the missing pieces of the temporal jigsaw puzzle were all finally in place and the picture therefore complete.

63. *Ibid.*, p. 13.

64. Samuel Beckett, *ill seen ill said*, p. 7. Emphasis mine.

2. Comic Strategies in Beckett's Narratives

The Comic: Modern Definitions and Beckettian Articulations

In the course of his endless reformulations of the basic question: "Do we know what writing is?" Mallarmé once answered:

> It is, this insensate game of writing, to arrogate to oneself, on the basis of a doubt [. . .] some sort of duty to recreate everything, through some reminiscences, in order to assess that we are right where we should be (because, let me say this apprehension holds an uncertainty).[1]

It seems to me that this interpretation of writing includes, among other things, an indication of the *locus* of the comic in modern literature, inasmuch as a radical "virtue of the doubt" lies at the core of it. After all, the modern comic indicates, through a vast range of formulas, but always with a certain degree of uncertainty, where we could be, rather than questioning where we should be, or rather than indicating where we are.

Of the many possibilities one might use to approach an investigation of the comic,[2] I decided to consider it as a *locus* of doubtful discourse. As such, we can easily find it in all of Beckett's works, and it is my intention to discuss it analytically. His comic strategies keep changing throughout his production, but they always reflect a basic, modern uncertainty, whether they express transgressive wit, scornful suspicion, helpless irony, or radically open humor. In my analysis I will rely, methodologically, on suggestions that come from linguistics and semiotics, and draw evaluative conclusions about the pervasiveness of the comic in Beckett's narratives. The field of investigation is obviously very vast, and depends on what aspect of the umbrella concept "the comic" one wants to consider. I expect to approach only part of it, formulating suggestions that derive from a close consideration of some Beckettian texts.[3] It is easy to anticipate that Beckett's comic strategies evolve throughout the years, not only because they involve different targets and reveal different axiologies of discourse, but also because his discursive structures change radically, as they accommodate higher degrees of uncertainty. Different themes and an ever-changing discourse successively involve cognition and value, revealing significant historical changes in epistemological and ideological presuppositions.

If we keep in mind Umberto Eco's analysis of "the frames of comic freedom," we can profitably adopt his double, essential distinction, between narrative and discursive comic.[4] In fact, chronologically, in Beckett we can find, first, changes that produce a "frame-breaking freedom" *out of* narrative structures (regarding the "material" of the story), and then a "compromise frame" produced *within* narrative structures (and involving discourse). For a clarification of the specificity of Beckett's comic strategies, it is probably worth recalling also Teun A. Van Dijk's definition of "frame" as a type of information determined by context,[5] so that it is clear that the freedom ensuing from the comic is a contextual transgression, or a contextual penetration-separation. In either case the role of the context is essential for the determination of comic effects. The transgression is narrative when traditional narrative structures (specifically, the *fabula*) constitute its *inter*textual context; the discursive penetration-separation occurs when a degree of self-reflection is involved, and literary discourse is the *intra*textual context of rupture (with no guarantee as to the reestablishment of the integrity of meaning, and thus with no guarantee as to the success of a transgressive power). The use of the term "compromise" seems accurate from a cognitive point of view, because, when transgression exhausts its denunciating power, that is, when demystification is too limited a horizon of investigation, the word "compromise" can convey the power of suspension, as the foundation of the reliability of a serious critique. We should talk about compromise when the mere inversion of bipolar opposites cannot describe the comic effects produced by these discursive strategies, which often involve the self-reflexive quality of the text and always exceed the parodic use of codes.

Eco's theoretical distinction, and specifically his opposition between humor and the comic, emphasizes the difference between the comic at the level of the *fabula* and humor at the level of *discourse,* in a way that should be remembered, even if in my analysis I use the term comic as covering a wider semantic area:

Semiotically speaking, if comic (in a text) takes place at the level of *fabula* or of narrative structures, humor works in the interstices between narrative and discursive structures; the attempt of the hero to comply with the frame or to violate it is developed by the *fabula,* while the intervention of the author, who renders explicit the presupposed rule, belongs to the discursive activity and represents a metasemiotic series of statements about the cultural background of the *fabula.*[6]

In the shadow of Eco's distinction we can outline three phases in the evolution of the comic in Beckett's prose works from the 1930s to the 1980s. I will briefly define these phases; that is, I will illustrate the reasons for my tripartite classification of the comic as parodic, metanarrative, and discursive, and I will then provide a number of textual instances, which will be analyzed in detail.

The first phase is parodic, interliterary, and exhibits a marked relation to previous texts, which are contra-dicted. This means that a literary tradition with its canonical traits and structural characteristics is assumed, but only in order to be denied, that is, in order to be transposed at the level of the *fabula.* The methodological suggestions of some Russian Formalists seem particularly useful in describing such "parodies." I cannot totally accept Tynianov's early formulation of the principle of construction of a literary text as solely determined by the literary system. I simply cannot agree to a total subordination of the "material" to the "form," or the total dependence of the narrative content on the formal level of discourse. However, his "late" description of "syn-function" and "auto-function,"[7] as simultaneous relations of the constructive function of the elements in a work, helps me to foreground the literary use of Beckett's culturally comic "sememes";[8] that is, they help me to characterize his formalized portions of meaning as culturally stable comic motifs. In fact, the "auto-function" links the extraliterary level of what is told to a traditionally literary way of telling. In other words, Beckett's first phase is defamiliarizing (in relation to literary motifs), and relies on crystallized comic sememes, culturally comic from the beginning.

A distinction between the culturally comic and the literary comic probably finds its theoretical roots in Cicero's *De Oratore,* where he established a marked opposition between *facetia in re* (the comic pertaining to things) and *facetia in dicto* (the comic pertaining to saying). This basic opposition has been reinterpreted for hundreds of years. For example, in recent times, Pierre Guiraud has distinguished between *mot d'esprit* and *jeu de mot.*[9] Violette Morin has spoken of "referential disjunction" and "semantic disjunction,"[10] Jean Cohen of "verbal comic" and "non-verbal comic,"[11] and Umberto Eco of "situational games" and "verbal games."[12] I would like to point out that these oppositions should not be interpreted as expressing a radical antithesis between a hypothetical pre-verbal reality and the presence of a linguistic system, but that the pertinence of each term should be grasped only within the contexts of texts that establish the opposition, because neither of the terms can ever be pre-verbal. As Eco himself has emphasized, all the comic occurs only within a sign system, and the opposition between "situational" and "linguistic" is tenable only within a chosen system.

Comic ambiguity in Beckett's early narratives generates a fairly stable semantic contrast, a blatant contextual disjunction (referring to what is and what should be, or to what is and what seems, etc.), so that, in spite of a transgressive frame, a conceptual resolution can always be achieved, and without exploiting the specificity of the signifiers involved. By saying this, I mean to emphasize the non-specifically discursive quality of the comic motifs in this early phase, and to stress the fact that comic transgressions produce a closure of meaning, often in the form of an opposition or contradiction. In Violette Morin's terminology, we can say that comic instances in Beckett's early works are often *jeux de signes* (sign games) rather than *jeux de mots* (verbal puns), even when those "signs" are characterized by a contextual literariness. Besides, literature can be, and in Beckett often is, one among the many targets aimed at by this type of transgressive narrative. Yet, as Morin points out, we can ignore the fact that signs are signs, and we are subdued by referential seduction:

> most of the time signs are obliterated by the referential elements of the narrative: gesture, action, feeling, whose different meanings or polysemy feed the [comic] disjunction.[13]

In his first phase Beckett is not very different from many other comic writers. His originality can at most be found in the choice of his targets, often allusively literary, and always presupposing intellectual refinement and a certain "superior" detachment.

The second phase of Beckett's narrative comic is metanarrative, because "interdiscursiveness" ("interglossia") is systematically exploited in it, in order to produce a metanarrative parody of any discourse on the world.[14] In this phase the comic relies on the logical figures of speech, such as antithesis, irony, antanaclasis, etc., and therefore it is more dependent on the awareness of the presence of signs than before. However, it is still possible to achieve a clear resolution of meaning, which often implies a negation or a contradiction of the truth of a received (non-comic) text. In this phase, the author's comic competence corrodes the meaning of the a priori knowledge of the world expressed by narrative motifs, and foregrounds the existence of a "notation." Demystification animates a "battle of books" that uses the complexity of literary artifacts to denounce dogmatic discourse, passive reception, and canonical excellence.

At this stage, repetition and contiguity produce linguistic connections, which "make sense" while being, at the same time, absolutely incongruous at the level of the story. Often, the relation of discourse to the referential context produces the comic disjunction. Individual occurrences, specific episodes, random observations do not fit into the long-term plan of a narrative, and the whole notion of plot is challenged, in the light of a "ridiculous" story and a ridiculous narration. The narrator's manifest ignorance (of "reality") and his incompetence in dealing realistically with the thematic level reinforce the reader's incredulity and highlight the presence of a ridiculing discourse and of a ridiculed reference. What is foregrounded in these Beckettian texts is the axiological contradiction established within the narrative, rather than the logical contradiction established within a referential system.[15] As Raymond Federman has forcefully pointed out:

> Fiction [. . .] need not agree with reality, with the truth of an event, particularly when it is explicitly presented as subfiction, when it points to itself as being reported secondhand, as being an invention of the characters' imagination.[16]

This "disagreement" of fiction and reality takes the form of a comic disjunction in many of Beckett's works in the 1940s and 1950s. This second phase of Beckett's comic simply does not let us forget the fact that we are in the presence of literature, or at least in the presence of signs, and the consequence of this awareness produces the double effect of rendering suspect an art whose shortcomings are amusing, enjoyable even if they are ridiculed. The metaliterary scope of this type of comic is obvious, as this literary production grows on the shortfalls of literary self-reflection. It seems to me that Beckett is as close here as he will ever be to postmodernist writers, and to their demystifying irony.

The third phase of Beckett's production of the comic is essentially discursive ("humorous" according to Eco's terminology) and highly problematic, because it does not produce a resolution of meaning. This type of comic fulfills the function of "irony" as described by Geoffrey Hartman, as that "rhetorical [. . .] limit that prevents the dissolution of art into positive and exploitative truth."[17] In the case of the comic the limit is discursive rather than rhetorical, but it performs the same function. By making impossible a semantic closure, the comic can show the limits of discourse as never before. Comic strategies move to the limits of a metasemiotic frame, to the borders of a cognitive experience where the gnoseological opposition between "true" and "false" can be assumed only as *différance*. The irreducible figurality of language appears, revealing the fragility of the opposition between "reality" and "appearance," between the real and "how say its contrary?"[18]

If the power of logocentrism can (seemingly) attribute existence to whatever is said, then the new epistemological role of the comic suspends logocentric determinations, even at the cost of leaving its old demystifying role behind. The comic becomes a *locus* of a radically doubtful discourse; it is a self-reflexive suspension of meaning, producing a logocentric indecision, thanks to sophisticated metasemiotic statements. The comic assumes extremely modern tones, past romantic irony and devoid of enthusiastic iconoclasms. It still serves corrosion, but instrumentally, with no illusion as to the power of effectively moving beyond the suspicion that animates it. The comic has to doubt itself, as the cogent co-occurrence of "saying" and "missaying" becomes progressively indisputable. Significantly enough, in the third line of a recent prose work (*Worstward Ho,* 1983), Beckett writes: "From now say for be missaid," thus warning the reader, once for all, as to the actual, or incumbent, transformation of the irony of the absurd into the absurd of irony.

In the light of the impossibility of a totally "sense-less " or of a purely "meaning-full " writing, the comic of discourse can be seen as an "insensate" excess, which manages to indicate a will to mean differing from the meaning perforce produced. The "must" of meaning, that is, the impossibility of escaping meaningfulness, is articulated in such a way as to indicate a counter-will-to-mean. The comic play reveals the presence of an insensate choice, the residuum of a trace (of a will), and the insistence of the unutterable upon the letter of the uttered. At this stage the comic preserves suspension and irresolution until they become astounding indications of the limits of the work of art, even as "conscious tautology." The Russian Formalists were of course the "forefathers" of many of these conceptions of art. More recently Ronald Sukenick has indicated a programmatic attitude which has found counterparts and supporters in many late modernist and postmodernist writers and critics. His point of view is worth discussing in relation to Beckett, as he writes:

If art is not reflection of reality, then the last reflection to get rid of is self-reflection. The fate of Narcissus is to drown in contemplation of himself. The way out of the dilemma of Narcissus lies in the work of art as artifice. As artifice, a work of art is a conscious tautology in which there is always an implicit (and sometimes explicit) reference to its own nature as artifact—self-reflexive, not self-reflective. It is not an imitation but a new thing in its own right.[19]

It seems to me that this "way out of the dilemma" drastically sacrifices the value of fiction in relation to reality, disregarding a relationship that Beckett does not dismiss, in spite of his lucid iconoclasms against literature, and naturalistic literature in particular. On the contrary, the progressive movement of his writings indicates a belief in the impossibility of "freezing" art into an artifice, as well as the uselessness of such an endeavor if it were possible. Rather than accepting its self-reflexivity as the foundation of its being "a new thing in its own right" (as many writers did in the 1970s), and rather than endorsing the realistic conception of a work of art as imitation, comic strategies in Beckett's recent works deconstruct the production of meaning, while they reflect (on) the problematic presence of a notation in the text. The aesthetic function of a work of art always implies the irreducibly double nature of "Narcissus's dilemma." Beckett's latest texts deconstruct themselves through a work involving both referential and formal structures, but with no interest for the production of a closed "artifice." In fact, even the "solidity" of formal elements is bound to undergo the metamorphosis of the text's work on itself, so that the truth of the text rests in the *process* of meaning (that is, the text's work), rather than in the perfect closure of tautology. If we think of it as a process, the meaning of text cannot become totally transparent, or simultaneously "conscious" and "tautological," as suggested by Sukenick.

In his third phase Beckett seems to express the experience of truth as linguistic procedure, so that his self-reflexive texts are instruments of a cognitive endeavor that wants to analyze language while using it. The comic as suspended disjunction provides an opening on contextual reality, a reality which has been disclosed as linguistically structured and inclusive of the reality of fiction. Comic structures and strategies become instruments of a play of *différance,*

which prevents any word, any concept, any major enunciation from coming to summarize and to govern from the theological presence of a center the movement and textual spacing of differences.[20]

Whether parodic, metanarrative, or discursive, Beckett's comic runs counter to a tautological conception of art and the closure of texts; it emphasizes the *production* of signs rather than the formalization of sign systems or the semantic content of any specific utterance. His main concern is gnoseological, and his literary practice is a denunciation of the text as artifact rather than the establishment of a ludic discourse. The comic in Beckett's prose works reveals itself as a progressive means of destabilization of cultural habits of sign production, as he moves from a hermeneutics of suspicion to a praxis of denunciation, and finally opens onto a deconstructive practice closely connected with the problematics of communication. In this respect we can say that Beckett was very close to a tradition of Surrealists and Dadaists, inasmuch as their primary goal was the radical destruction of traditional sign productions based on crystallized associations. However, he soon moved away from them, showing the fact that the maximum of incongruity, that is to say, the "absolutely improbable," could coincide with both counter-reality and anti-art effects. His recent comic strategies, imbued with the problematics of communication, are far from Surrealistic and Dadaist "ready-made"[21] and equally far from postmodernist ironic *bricolage;* they can be seen as a precious device, or rather, as a precious work, against *clôture,* against the closure of any text.

Beckett's comic has succeeded in denying the textuality of thought, and in indicating its suspensive fragmentation, its cogent differences, its endless contradictions, and its polymorphic movements.

The First Phase: Co(n)textual Incongruity and Interliterary Parodies

At the beginning of Beckett's career as a novelist, comic effects were largely pursued in his works, and their intrinsic "frame-breaking freedom" involved the levels of content, which, to some extent, coincided with the thematics of traditional novels. In his early works, such as *More Pricks than Kicks* (1934) and *Murphy* (1938), the prohibition of "spelling out the norm"[22] involves primarily the *fabula,* and only secondarily discourse, as we shall see.

In spite of many apparently metanarrative observations, the comic in this first phase is not metaliterary, because it assumes literature and narratives only qua objects, that is, as parodic targets. The comic characterization of both Belacqua and Murphy and of their friends, and the account of their "adventures" indicate the existence of a double incongruity: one regarding the actions told and one regarding the canonical forms chosen to describe them. Comic descriptions are parodies of traditional ways of telling a story, parodies of a *Divina Commedia* or of the *Bildungsroman,* for example, but they are not subversions of the ways in which a story could be told. The comic play does not posit the issue of narrative unreliability, but simply exploits the comic effects of an allusive literary game. Rather than probing into the aesthetic notion of adequacy of expression, these narratives amusingly illustrate some limits of traditional mimesis.

The comic of this first phase is closely related to the canonic notion of genre, a specific determination which is kept as the background or as the model for parodic transgression. A metanarrative denunciation, really challenging the notion of genre, and a critical investigation, involving discourse, will take place in Beckett's second phase of comic production, when comic strategies ridicule and erode essential aspects of traditional narratives (such as the notion of narrative authority, authorship, or the foundation of textual coherence).

The interliterary quality of motifs in the first phase of Beckett's production, and the pronounced rhetoric of most of his statements (whether descriptive or introspective), indicate the presence of a "background entailment,"[23] that is, of a situational or referentially literary contextualization. The comic effect of certain sentences can be explained in relation to the *topoi* of literature, but not as an essential transformation of the traditional production of meaning in narratives. The crucial distinction made by linguists, between the meaning of a sentence and the interpretation of an utterance, lies at the core of an explanation of comic effects. However, I want to stress, first, that the difference between meaning of a sentence and interpretation of an utterance does not imply the rejection of a literal meaning, as some rhetoricians maintain. Together with Deirdre Wilson and Neil Smith, I would rather describe this difference in terms of "certain further propositions in the interpretation of an utterance which are *not* supplied by semantic rules alone."[24] In other words, comic effects can be explained in terms of an addition to, rather than an abolition or rejection of, the literal meaning. The previous discussion on the importance of context, and particularly of Violette Morin's notion of disjunction, should make it clear that some sort of referential meaning has to be grasped before any utterance can be understood as comic. Contrary to a superficial impression, semantic synonymity is likely to disrupt comic effects rather than foster them. It is syntax or intonation (in the case of oral communication) that provides the bifurcation of meaning, a disjunction from which the comic effect can ensue. After all, jokes cannot be explained while they are told; that is, a synonymical insistence does not enact a comic effect, whereas a bifurcation of meaning can produce it.

Now let us proceed with the analysis of a passage taken from *More Pricks than Kicks,* in which Belacqua prepares his lunch:

> The stump of the loaf went back into prison, the crumbs, as though there were no such thing as a sparrow in the wide world, were swept in a fever away, and the slices snatched up and carried to the grill. All these preliminaries were very hasty and impersonal. [. . .] He laid his cheek against the soft of the bread, it was spongy, and warm, alive. But he would very soon take that plush feel off it, by God, but he would very soon take that fat white look off its face. He lowered the gas a suspicion and plaqued one flabby slab plump down on the glowing fabric, but very pat and precise, so that the whole resembled the Japanese flag.[25]

The detailed description of the actions of the protagonist is combined with a pervasive use of hyperbole ("The crumbs [. . .] were swept in a fever away," "He laid his cheek against the soft of the bread," he "plaqued one flabby slab plump down"), and the level of the *fabula* develops towards the creation of a ludic outcome, because of the contextual incongruities produced at the semantic level. Linguistic tropes, such as the metaphor of the biscuit tin and of the grill (as "prison" and "glowing fabric"), and the personification of bread ("warm," "alive," with "a fat white look" on "its face"), create a semantic incongruity, which is carried even further by referential tropes, such as litotes ("as though there were no such thing as a sparrow") and the simile of the Japanese flag (built on an analogy which lacks referential consistency).

In this passage, as in many others, comic effects secondarily relating to discourse could also be seen in the explicit authorial intervention, lingering on the description of the action after its completion: "all these preliminaries were very hasty and impersonal." In fact, the comic quality of this statement is not bound to the context of the protagonist's actions, but involves the narrative level, and more specifically the traditional axiology of novels. Such "hasty preliminaries" take a long time to be described, and the narrative insistence on details is unjustified in the light of the insignificance of these actions. However, this axiological contradiction points to referentially suspect statements, so that the implicit critique of traditional forms of narration becomes comically interesting. In other words, we could say that the comic of this description "slips" from the contextual level of the illustrated actions to the co(n)textual level of the production of signs. The comic effect derives from a stylistic disproportion, and invests a narrative "excess."

Furthermore, if we reinterpret the "preliminaries" along the lines of a metanarrative reading, that is, as the preliminaries of a *description* (concerning Belacqua's lunch), this author's intervention would point to a verbal skill which is "hasty" because of its hyperbolic, cumulative rhythm, but which is, ironically, as far from being objective or accurate as Belacqua's actions are from being "impersonal." In this sense, irony (at the level of the *fabula*) and humor (at the level of discourse) co-occur in the same passage. A sort of double parallel, a narrative isotopy, links ridiculed actions to a ridiculous narration, and the contextual frame of reference is irreducibly double: both referential and discursive. Incongruity takes place at the level of both the narrated and narrating content, so that realism is challenged even though the traditional formal structures of narration are not abolished.

As I have said, we must look at Beckett's subsequent works (roughly, wait until the 1950s) to find a systematic erosion of narrative structures. A gradual but unmistakable shift in emphasis (from narration to discourse) takes place when the narrator emerges as a problematic entity, thanks to a very ironical challenging of his traditional role. At this point the reader can legitimize a comic reading only by focusing on the relation between enunciation and message, between an utterance and the referents of a statement. Often, in this phase, the comic derives from the contrast of appearance and reality, or rather of intention(s) and result(s), in statements produced by a voice which is problematically external (or internal) to the narrated event.

However, we must remember that before being metanarrative or discursive Beckett's comic is essentially parodic, particularly in the first phase of his narrative production. As Bakhtin forcefully reminded us:

> The most ancient forms for representing language were organized by laughter—these were originally nothing more than the ridiculing of another's language and another's direct discourse.
> [. . .] All these parodies on genre and generic styles ("languages") enter the great and diverse world of verbal forms that ridicule the straightforward serious word in all its generic guises.[26]

Beckett's comic, in what I have called the first phase of his artistic production, is mostly the parodic double of classical epics and narratives, and is often endowed with the axiological contradictions deriving from a double desire: that of ridiculing traditional axiologies and that of creating an alternative set of meanings at the referential level. So, in *More Pricks than Kicks* we can find, together with referential incongruity, a denunciation of what Raymond Federman calls "the mimetic pretensions of fiction." In fact, we can see that in these short stories the comic quality of the *fabula* anticipates a subsequent modality of the comic, which will focus on the presuppositions of story-telling, and on the incongruity deriving from the substitution of referents with signs (rather than from the substitution of referents with referents as in the first phase). For example, the detailed description of Belacqua's lunch is introduced by an interesting remark, following the description of his hearing "midday strike."

Then he ventured to consider what *he had to do next*. There was always something that one *had to do next*.[27]

The working of the antiphrase allows the reader to be alert to the apparent synonymity, but actually enjoy the difference, in the identical syntagms "had to do next." This constitutes a perfect example of a "disjunction," because the narrative is in fact bifurcated through the semantic exploitation of a narrative polysemy deriving from repetition. The *fabula* presents a comic situation due to the fact that Belacqua's dilemma involves the "large obligation" of cooking lunch, but the reduplication of identical signifiers ("had to do next") points also to the discursive level, and therefore to what Roland Barthes calls the "presence of Art" and the "ritual of letters."[28] Repetition points to the existence of a narrative conjugation, "in proportion as existence becomes fate, and soliloquy becomes a Novel."[29] In this case the comic derives from breaking the archi-genre rule of not indicating the rules of narration (specifically, here, the rule of "what next"). Events are "for the narrative"; in order to be understood they have to become a plausible sequence, rather than remaining erratic and "real." This type of narrative specification alludes to the fact that imitation obeys the rule of intelligibility, which, however, does not inhere in phenomena. The economy of narration invades the sense of duration, transforming present and imminent future into an unavoidable determination. Thus, the comic here takes place at both the narrative and discursive level. Belacqua's struggle against "what he had to do next" is comic in relation to his constitutional laziness (at the level of the *fabula*), but the subsequent generalization "there was always something one had to do next" subtly involves the narrator, who has to go on articulating the story as a sequence of events. So, the awareness of this "next," ensuing from repetition, transforms the borders of narration with a metanarrative awareness (produced at the level of discourse).

Also in *Murphy* we find some comic effects involving both the level of the *fabula* and of discourse. It is significant to note that the comic climax is reached precisely by transcending the comic quality of narrated events, towards some sort of parody of the rules of traditional story-telling. One of the many examples in the text reads as follows:

> Not the least remarkable of Murphy's innumerable classifications of experi-
> ence was that into jokes that had once been good jokes and jokes that had
> never been good jokes. What but an imperfect sense of humour could have
> made such a mess of chaos. In the beginning was the pun. And so on.[30]

The thematization of the comic as an instrument to achieve a rule-breaking freedom (expressed through a negation, as "making a mess of chaos") sets Beckett quite close to Surrealists and Dadaists, as their concept of *humour noir* made them sophisticated connoisseurs of chaos. Here, Beckett's narrative indicates the danger of confounding comic reference (*fabula*) with the actual occurrence of a comic inference. This confusion would be a fatal mistake, one that "ontologizes" the comic and is satirized in the statement "In the beginning was the pun." Furthermore, thematic reference to time ("had once been / had never been"), indicates the existence of a temporal factor that specifically affects the comic exploitation of both referential and linguistic tropes and devices. Beckett's homage to the tradition of *humour noir* underlies this thematic dichotomy between jokes "that had once been good jokes" and "jokes that had never been good jokes," those that break an existing rule and those in which the disjunction never produced the frame breaking, or rule breaking, inference. When jokes become a "classification of experience" they inevitably make a "mess of chaos," because the concern with the *fabula* compels ignorance of the actuality of sign production, which could be the generative mechanism of a discursive comic. In this example, the *fabula* is comic because of the denotation of devices ("jokes") as a classification of experience. However, chaos would be better represented by a mode of discontinuity and a linguistic suspense brought about by the quality of discourse. Discourse can "enact" the chaos described by the *fabula;* the *fabula* can only thematize the chaos of discourse.

Furthermore, even when reality as such is not implied by a life-like portraiture, narrative structures can point to a discursive activity in a comic way. In those cases, our literary competence, that is, our ability to connect the worlds of fiction and experience, is challenged by pointing to the linguistic nature of literature, which is not normally foregrounded in narratives.

Out of the many Beckettian instances of a comic remark pointing to the discursive level, let us take an example from *First Love:*

> I returned to the bench for the fourth or fifth time since I had abandoned it, at roughly the same hour, I mean roughly the same sky, no, I don't mean that either, for it's always the same sky and never the same sky, what words are for that, none I know, period.[31]

In this brief passage, the use of antiphrase progressively cancels out "reality," or rather drives the narrative away from it, leaving the reader aware of narration and, in the end, only in the presence of signs ("period"). At first the entailment of the signifier "the same" is exploited for the creation of a comic referential contradiction, which devaluates the specificity of referents ("hour," "sky"). Then the level of the *fabula* explicitly thematizes, through a rhetorical question, the role of language in relation to reality and the existence of a discursive level in every "account" of experience ("what words are for that"). Here the comic is referentially open, as it denounces both the intrinsic insufficiency of language (lacking words) as well as the shortcomings of the speaker (who does not know them). Finally the verbalization of a diacritical mark ("period"), expressing what would otherwise be a simple pause of discourse, constitutes a complex comic instance. On one hand, the content of the message ("period") constitutes an admission of impotence on the part of a speaker, who gives up his metalinguistic thoughts. On the other hand, however, he can appear in the narrative as an agent of discourse (rather than as a character) and as a transgressor of narrative rules. Comic relief here derives from the fragmentation of a compact text, as the interstices of a pause reveal the presence of a subject of discourse who has decreed it, against any naturalistic plausibility. Furthermore, the complexity of this comic effect is such that, together with the break in this expressive *logomachia* between subject and language (expressed by "period"), we also, ambivalently, enjoy the release from metanarrative, and the pleasure of a return to the power of fiction.

As this passage shows, the problem of the correspondence of words with things, and of narration with reality, that is, the issue of reference, is essential for an appreciation of the self-reflexive quality of Beckett's narratives. Even metanarrative remarks imply a conception of the work of art which goes beyond tautology and "formal objectivity"; rather, Beckett's narratives point to the invisible social presuppositions underlying sign

systems. The collective existence of common principles of sentence formation is challenged in these novels by naming and showing the unconscious
knowledge that underlies social rules.

Let us consider some examples that defy presupposed grammatical sharing, and also the "common features" of novelistic utterances. In *First Love*
we find a thematized critique of a semantic incongruity which is then
produced in the same paragraph a couple of sentences later and exemplified
in relation to spatial reference:

> I was so unused to speech that my mouth would sometimes open, of its own
> accord, and void some phrase or phrases, *grammatically unexceptionable,* but
> entirely *devoid if not of meaning,* for on close inspection they would reveal one,
> and even several, at least *of foundation* [. . .] I heard her steps in the kitchen
> and then the door of her room close *behind* her. Why *behind* her?[32]

The perfection of grammar is denounced as misleading in the articulation of experience when sentence formation is not linked to reference. The
subtle opposition between "meaning" and "foundation" underscores the
discrepancy between meaning and will-to-mean. The conflict of the *vouloir
dire* of the text (unavoidable meaning) with the mean*ing* of the subject of
the enunciation, points to a discrepancy that shakes the belief according to
which grammatical features are inherent to phenomena. It is obvious that
Beckett from the time he began writing was concerned with our habits of
sign production. The second part of this example reinforces the denunciation of our naif assumption that language imitates reality, through a metalinguistic question following description: "I heard . . . the door of her
room close *behind* her. Why *behind* her?"

From the example we have quoted we can see that when he was writing
First Love, in the 1940s, Beckett was already pointing to the fact that sign
production affects our associations and expectations regarding the world of
phenomena, in spite of any presumed referential objectivity. He knew that
the articulation of signs and their systemic value determine the visibility of
reality, and that we often confound the visibility generated by a linguistic
system with the structure of reality.

"Delayed continuous communication": The Critical Irony of Linguistic Games

In a subsequent phase, Beckett's narratives do not need to presuppose the
world. They "only" presuppose a linguistic ontology which will be put

under constant scrutiny and challenge. As a consequence, the comic is generated not so much by referential incongruity as by breaking associative habits related to the production of signs. While pointing to habits of sign production, Beckett exploits the self-reflexiveness of codes as a form of entailment which produces a comic effect. This new phenomenology of communication will include the comic as a critical technique, and the presence of language will be highlighted in all of his works.

In *Enough* (*Assez*, 1966), for example, a thematic nucleus develops as the description of a communicative performance, but with such an accurate taxonomy of possible alternatives that description itself loses referential unity and simply enumerates the variety of articulations of the same narrative motive. Rather than developing as a sequence referentially oriented, narrative becomes a mere "ordered entailment," which produces comic effects investing narration:

> He sometimes halted without saying anything. Either he had finally nothing to say or while having something to say he finally decided not to say it. [. . .] Other main examples suggest themselves to the mind. Immediate continuous communication with immediate redeparture. Same thing with delayed redeparture. Delayed continuous communication with immediate redeparture. Same thing with delayed redeparture. Immediate discontinuous communication with immediate redeparture. Same thing with delayed redeparture. Delayed discontinuous communication with immediate redeparture. Same thing with delayed redeparture.[33]

As we can see, narration folds on itself so that the presence of language can be self-reflected and denounce the presence of narrative conventions, through an uncommon listing of narrative alternatives. The comic derives from the fact that what is realistic in reality is shown to become absolutely improbable in narrative. The pedantry of the listing demystifies the narrative artifact, and yet discourse grows so monstrously on itself that it produces a total obliteration of the referential level. The reader stops thinking about the protagonist and laughs at the referential incongruity generated by this discursive excess, not without some desire for the resumption of the story.

At this point of his development as a writer Beckett systematically exploits the discrepancy between message and enunciation, and between narration and discourse. His comic is then produced beyond the parody of the narrative structures canonized by tradition, and moves into metanarrative denunciation. If the aim of the bourgeois writer was the creation of mythologies of life, that is, the production of mimetic images of life, the aim of Beckett's comic is the creation of images of those invisible images.[34] He has to show discourse because traditional writers hide it; his words drift away from the things to which they refer, and irony and humor provide the means to achieve such distancing. The comic derives from the fact that language is used to destroy the invisible linguistic games that preside over narration. Yet, narration has to be destroyed by its own rules, and any metanarrative realism can only point to the existence of an inescapable linguistic paradox. The representation of discourse seems, at some point, the only true story that we can tell, but discourse is condemned to insignificance and to an end, once it has achieved its denunciation, since it has left behind any link with reality.

In *From an Abandoned Work* (1956), for example, a disquieting comic is produced by the visibility of referentially incongruous hyperdeterminations of reality that occur through correct language use:

> Nor will I go out of my way to avoid such things, when avoidable, no, I simply will not go out of my way, though I have never in my life been on my way anywhere, but simply on my way.[35]

Mere discursive growth deletes "clarity" and correctness; word multiplication does not provide clarification; rather, the semantic value of reference is checked back by an evidence of the pseudo-referentiality of literary language. As de Man says:

> This gives the language considerable freedom from referential restraint, but it makes it epistemologically highly suspect and volatile, since its use can no longer be said to be determined by considerations of truth and falsehood, good and evil, beauty and ugliness, or pleasure and pain.[36]

Furthermore, the sense of pseudo-reference is reinforced by a series of denials and contradictions at the narrative level, which connote the narrator as a totally unreliable authority, at least according to traditional standards.

Beckett's "poetics of indigence" seems to imply here a lucid willingness to avoid presuppositions that take for granted the analogy between the linguistic model and the world of phenomena. Comic verbosity, necessarily excessive in order to be self-reflexive, serves an epistemological imperative, insofar as the ineffectual imitation of reality in an incongruous story reveals the myth according to which signs are motivated, and language imitative. This Cratylian fallacy, applied to literariness, is denounced by a metanarrative comic in which we are shown the dependence of the *fabula* on the tyranny of discourse.

For example, the story of an encounter with a horse, one of the main episodes of *From an Abandoned Work,* allows the mapping out of a linguistic coherence achieved at the expense of referential congruity:

> This is the only completely white horse I remember, what I believe the Germans called a Schimmel, oh I was very quick as a boy and picked up a lot of hard knowledge, Schimmel, nice *word* for an English speaker. The sun was full upon *it,* as shortly before on my mother.[37]

Again, narration shifts its referential focus from reality to language, from a "white horse" to the (German) word for a white horse. Even justifying this narrative digression on the ground of a psychological motivation, whereby the narrator's memory operates on the level of a signifier ("Schimmel"), comic incongruity develops because of the unusual narrative concatenation. The referential quality of "it" is highly ambiguous, and the comic ensues from the awareness of a referential fallacy: that of taking fictional statements as accurate representations of a reality that, as a matter of fact, was never "there" (but is there as a matter of discourse).

All of Beckett's narratives in this second phase of his production of the comic deny the possibility of an epistemic reassurance as to the nature of reality conveyed by words. Instead, he is interested in showing how language works in fiction as a mirror of its misfunctioning in reality. Thus, the indeterminations of what cannot be said emerge through the imperfections of a narrative language that, thanks to rhetorical manipulations, can allude to them, at the expense of its pervasive denotative power. In this respect, the comic provides an interesting form of displacement, a form of provisional negation of an assumed linguistic solidity which had been assumed precisely because of its accurately disguised fictional quality.

Sometimes hyper-realistic specifications are expressions of a linguistic obsession with correctness, and provide the ground for a metanarrative denunciation of mimetic presuppositions. Let us consider another comic example, this time regarding narrative rules about implied meaning:

> My stick of course, by a merciful providence, I shall not say this again, when not mentioned my stick is in my hand, as I go along. But not my long coat, just my jacket.[38]

In the course of time, Beckett's comic repeatedly invests epistemic issues centered on language. In the 1960s, the issue of presence begins to be articulated through subtle comic displacements. For example, we can find an epistemologically humorous statement such as body fixed ping fixed elsewhere. Traces blurs signs no meaning.[39]

This narrative fragment thematizes the insurmountable distance be-tween the body and body representations, by calling to our attention the semiotic power of "traces" (signs of "actuality," signs of the present) which can corrode "signs" (stable crystallizations of a sign system). Besides, this discursive activity enacts a pause, by introducing the verbalization of a pause, so that the minute in which the pause occurs coincides with its denotation. "Ping," the mark of a pause, is the actual "trace" of the pause, but, ironically, it seems to yield no meaning at all. Besides, "ping" coincides with a present during which the body is "fixed elsewhere," as there is no possibility of a pause in reality, no break in the present, in spite of the linguistic sign of a pause.

Thus we learn that traces are the most faithful "signs" of a transient present and that, even though they seem devoid of meaning, they are the instruments of its temporal articulation. This type of comic critically probes into the issue of the tenability of a specific reference, in the light of the temporal processing of meaning. Thus, it is not a simple parody of codified discourses but an exploitation of the relevant semantic differences that can originate from *use* (*emploi*) or *citation* (*mention*) of the same words, or segments of discourse, or even entire sentences.[40] The contiguity of use and citation of certain expression in the same text can express a meaningful difference; that is, it can show the work of the text, the text's constant differing from itself.

In spite of its denunciation of novelistic artifacts, Beckett does not seem interested in the production of an anti-novel, so much as he is interested in practicing and showing a radically different use (or conception) of lan-guage, a use that could eventually bridge the gap (de facto insurmountable) between narration and reality, between language and presence. Beyond the creative parody of traditional literary forms, a comic logorrhea deconstructs discourse in its own making, bringing words to exhibit their actual impo-tence, that is, their insignificance outside discourse.

In this second phase of his production of the comic Beckett does not criticize any specific discourse, through the parody of its structures or the reversal of its values; rather, the "meaning to say nothing" takes the place of the "meaning to say well," and the effort to achieve this "innocence" finds the text ironically:

entangled in hundreds of pages of a writing simultaneously insistent and elliptical, imprinting [. . .] even its erasures, carrying off each concept into

an interminable chain of differences, surrounding or confusing itself with so
many precautions, references, notes, citations, collages, supplements . . . [41]

In this respect, a linguistic description of the mechanism of irony is
probably too insufficient to describe the strategies of Beckett's epistemic
criticism. However, a modern description of irony can clarify the limits of
its previous "figurative" interpretation, which is misleading since in irony
no "literal" meaning is ever abandoned in favor of a "figurative one," for the
simple reason that irony involves the transferring of meaning, and not its
rejection. However, an inferential mechanism linking use and citation
(either explicitly or implicitly) can explain ironic effects, when semantic
discontinuity is exhibited as a disjunction linking the message and the discourse. Inference explains much better than a figurative theory the Beckettian comic in this second phase of his production, especially since this comic
is based on demystifying metanarrative and metalinguistic observations.
The old dichotomies "true/false" and "reality/appearance" are posited
within the text: the context is the text itself, rather than a contextual frame
of reference. In other words, the text ironically mirrors the production of
signs which constitutes it, so that the question of reference involves signs.

In this phase, the freedom ensuing from a frame-breaking and rule-
breaking activity involves both narration and discourse, often pointing to
the existence of "signs," "no meaning," and a "ping elsewhere always."[42]
The semiotic nature of "Ping" is determinable both as a referent of a pause
and as the meaning of a pause, depending on a discursive or narrative
perspective. Thus, the comic involves also the difference between written
word and voice, between "writing" and "*phonē*." The play of a signifier
such as "ping" is crucial in relation to the issue of writing and presence.
"Plato said of writing that it was an orphan or a bastard, as opposed
to speech, the legitimate and high-born son of the 'father of logos'."[43]
The actual occurrence of a diacritical mark as a sign in the text ("Ping")
indicates that "Meaning must await being said or written in order to inhabit itself, and in order to become, by differing from itself, what it is
meaning."[44]

The comic here involves acknowledgment of the difference between
written word and silence, a difference which emerges as one of the meanings of the text, thanks to an ironical confusion. "Ping" expresses a fragment of silence within the verbal chain, a fragment which can emerge and
can be recognized thanks to the linguistic system. Language, however,
betrays silence, inasmuch as silence speaks, in "ping." On the other hand,

the visibility of silence would be betrayed by silence itself, and the ping-pause could not be expressed as meaning: "imploring ping/silence/ping over."[45]

It seems clear that in this second phase comic slippage does not affect realistic reference but the production of signs as referents of language (of the linguistic system). Furthermore, the metanarrative quality of statements radically points to the alternative between writing and presence. The new core of the comic goes far beyond inference between homogeneous (if incongruous) semantic series. By transforming discourse into the mirror of narrative mimesis, it points to the fiction of fiction, and the presence of the letter, "of the first letter, if the alphabet, and most of the speculations which have ventured into it, are to be believed."[46]

The Humor of "no matter":
Comic Freedom Against Logocentrism

The latest Beckettian humor (for we can no longer speak of parody or irony, according to the terminological distinction proposed earlier, and based on imitative transgression and inference) is definitely beyond "Sky earth the whole kit and boodle,"[47] but not beyond the awareness of language and a linguistically based hermeneutics of experience. Using Beckett's own words, we could say that it takes place at the level of

> No matter. No matter how. Such the confusion now between real and how say its contrary? [. . .] No matter now. Such equal liars both. Real and how ill say its contrary? The counter-poison.[48]

The dialectic which once might have involved "reality" and "appearance," and then the (small) "true" and the (great) "false" of language, becomes now the dialectic of "real" and "how say its contrary?" because the epistemological presuppositions at work involve reality, as awareness of linguistic visibility.

The third phase of the Beckettian comic is then perforce discursive, as the reality of "ill saying" overlaps and even coincides with reality itself. In other words, the role of language cannot be thematized while forgetting that it is language that allows such thematization. Thus, even counter-realistic effects do not glorify verbal art, but they radicalize the question of the relationship between things and words, connoting them both as a problem, as "equal liars." At this stage of Beckett's production the "counter-poison" can be found only in a self-reflective narrative suspension, not in a simple rejection or in a simplifying glorification of language. The antidote to language is the actual use of it in a critical linguistic praxis. Inasmuch as it provides a suspension, comic elation also can help to counter-check the "lie" by making it appear as a lie, thus devoiding it of its power. Demystification is instrumental rather than final, as language cannot be dismissed lightheartedly, in view of its actuality, in view of its presence, of its eliminable use.

The openness of Beckett's comic and the semantic irresolution of his statements at this stage of his writing production cannot be approached by simply counting on mechanisms of semantic inversion, nor is it possible to advocate the "context" as an instrument of final clarification. In fact, the context is always linguistic, at least when it is identified as the ground of interpretation. Thus these comic semantic inversions or displacements involve signs, rather than referents. Furthermore, even if a determination of context were possible the ensuing reduction of ambiguity would still not solve the problem of the identification of a specific reference, as part of what is being said is the way in which it is said. So the *form* of the message would necessarily have to be part of the context, a context that remains ambivalent, open, simultaneously referential and constituted by the formal messages of the text.

We have to conceive comic effects as echoes of statements, susceptible of being re-read rather than subverted, so that we can understand comic freedom as a liberating experience, breaking the dogmatism of close, logocentric statements. We do not even need to identify reference to enjoy the comic, and we could even ignore the exact meaning of the structure of statements if we do not relate it to the referents that constitute them.

However, thanks to these groundless referents, we can see the working of language and perceive the actuality of linguistic expressions. See for example a passage taken from "He is Barehead" where neither referential precision nor structural traits are as relevant as the connotation of the processing of meaning:

> *But see* how *now,* having turned right for example, instead of turning left a little further on he turns right again. *And see* how *now again,* yet a little further on, instead of turning left at last he turns right yet again. And so on until, instead of turning right yet again, as he expected, he turns left at last. Then for a time his zigzags resume their tenor, deflecting him alternately to right and left, that is to say bearing him onward in a straight line more or less, but no

longer the same straight line as when he set forth, *or* rather as when he suddenly realized he was forth, *or perhaps after all the same.*[49]

As we have seen, when the field of tension, the *Spannungsfeld* as Goethe called it,[50] involves narration, the comic becomes metanarrative. But in this case it is metanarrative in the sense of reflecting back onto itself the generative process of meaning in the text, not of adopting a point of view that is external to the narrative. The comic is no longer conceivable as some sort of "understatement," since the statement itself gets deconstructed (through the stating). The cogent elusiveness of the "tongue-in-cheek" is replaced by the manifest evidence of a devaluation of any closed statement, critically conceived as an unavoidable metonymy of the language system. Comic relief derives from the introduction of a difference where words seemed to have implied an unavoidable determinism, either as referents, reflecting the structure of an "objective" reality, or as material signifiers.

It is interesting to note that it is often through repetition, which indicates the notation in the narrative, that comic effects are produced at this stage. Beda Alleman points out that often "it is through repetition that the sentence acquires its ironical transparence."[51] Yet I must stress that Alleman's conclusions are contradicted by Beckett's most recent literary practice, since he does not "give up such signals," that is, does not renounce the use of ironical repetition, but uses repetitions as a device which reflects the "becoming" of meaning (rather than signal the comic). Repetition allows the re-presentation of reference not only as the pseudo-reference of literary discourse, but also as an expression of the duration intrinsic to reference itself. Repetition is probably the most important feature of Beckett's production since the 1970s, because it allows the expression of temporality without recourse to the diegetic marks typical of traditional narratives. It fosters a transformation of diegesis into mimesis, inasmuch as it enacts a double whereby description cannot be closed or limited to narrated features. Repetition connotes narration as a process and makes duration a meaning of the text; in this way it questions not only the atemporality of descriptions but also the borders of textuality.

Through repetition we can clearly see that the status of narrative implies a systematic citation of elements of the cultural system, rather than their more common *emploi* in relation to phenomena, their use in ordinary communication. The breaking of linguistic frames through repetition opens the way to an endless play of difference, without the need of strong binary oppositions. As Barbara Johnson puts it:

Reading, here proceeds by identifying and dismantling differences by means of other differences that cannot be fully identified or dismantled. The starting point is often a binary difference that is subsequently shown to be an illusion created by the workings of differences much harder to pin down.[52]

In Beckett's *Worstward Ho* (1983) a sentence such as "Say for be said. Missaid. From now say for be missaid"[53] implies a definition of unlimited semiosis, whereby every cultural unit is interpreted by cultural units with no need for an original *Grund*. The comic derives from the acceptance of missaying as the mode of discourse, but also from seeing that discourse keeps changing and does not close on its impotence (comic relief). It seems to me that Beckett is actually pointing out the fact that no contextual selection of formalized portions of meaning (no contextual selections of sememes), will ever offer an effective alternative to the universality of missaying. Yet that also means that endless alternatives will be given, and that they can acquire a liberating effect as semantic movement in which the value of specific choices can be diachronically retrieved.

In *Worstward Ho* the ultimate power of language is challenged by the boundary perspective of the penultimate opposition: the difference between "somehow" and "nohow." It is penultimate because it can only take place in time, and so long as there is time there is a "somehow" or the *thought* (the missaying) of a "nohow":

Blanks for nohow on. How long? Blanks how long till somehow on? Again somehow on. All gone when nohow on. *Time gone when nohow on.*[54]

The comic freedom achieved through these humorous repetitions is of an essentially epistemic nature, as it calls to our attention the content and structure of previous statements, questioning them as the presuppositions and instruments of a present knowledge. The entire history of knowledge can thus be described as a series of "better failures":

All of old. Nothing else ever. Ever tried. Ever failed. No matter. Try again. Fail again. Fail better.[55]

Unusual pseudo-oxymorons such as "unworsenable void," "boundless bounded," and "At most mere minimum. Mere most minimum,"[56] and surprising tautologies such as "Never since first said never unsaid,"[57] call for a transformation of reading into rereading. Semantic innovation is linked to a system of improbability in the production of signs that compels a return of reading, as a suspension of meaning is achieved within the system that generates them.

This modern comic, essentially discursive, ensues from a long questioning of language (from) within the frame of language. The enjoyment of a position "At bounds of boundless void"[58] connotes language as formal diachrony, as a persisting system: "Nohow less. Nohow worse. Nohow naught. Nohow *on*."[59]

Beckett's "poetics of indigence" mirrors a cogent linguistic indigence, epitomized in a fragment like "Said nohow on"[60] which, however, emphasizes the presence of time as the unutterable horizon of language. No matter how, and no matter what can be said, reality goes on, beyond the control of language. Comic relief is produced by an image of temporal permanence ("on"), after a rigorous experience of subtraction and demystification has shown us that there is no guarantee for any positive gnoseological revelation. The "on" takes us beyond the fear of fearful rules: "Try better worse another stare when with words than when not."[61] The "better-worse" of words is their presence: words in use are words in time, as close to life as they can be.

Words in Action: The Temporal Changes of an Epistemic Comic

If we look at Beckett's achievements in relation to the evolution of his comic strategies, we can acknowledge the fact that they evolved reflecting the major philosophical and aesthetic avant-garde movements of our century. Yet, in doing so, Beckett has been primarily, if perhaps surprisingly, faithful to his own gnoseological and aesthetic quest, and it is that quest which has led him through most original positions. Should we take Molloy's words to be descriptive of Beckett's art, we can define his relentless *recherche* in terms of a specific oscillation: "I mean that *on reflection, in the long run* rather, my verbal profusion turned out to be penury, and inversely."[62]

At the time of the Surrealist conception of *humour noir*, which relied on the extensive use of negation, we can see Beckett's unimitative "verbal profusion" enacting similar negations, mostly against the conventions of codified literary genres. Like many Surrealists and Dadaists, Beckett is fully aware of the importance of the medium, so that he tries to create images of words, and demystifying images of literary language (somewhat similar to Magritte's famous *picture* of a pipe accompanied by the inscription "ceci n'est pas une pipe"). His novels in the 1940s and 1950s produce images of the invisible images which constitute novels; through parodies and negations Beckett denounces linguistic and narrative conventions that are naively believed to be mimetic images of life. As we have seen, Beckett's beginnings as a narrator are marked by a pervasive use of the comic, articulated through strategies which point to the substantial difference between life and novels. His words, indeed a profusion of words and codes, constantly drift away from both the things to which they refer and the traditional literary models which had transformed narration into mythologies of life.

From the beginning of his career Beckett shared with T. S. Eliot and Joyce a very modern notion of culture, based on the interaction of texts. However, unlike them, he has been interested in showing how even the plurality of forms is an inescapable "hereditary" necessity rather than the foundation of free thinking and personal expression. His comical displacement of canonical forms expresses a bound negation within a compelling common heritage. This can explain why parodistic modes were so common in his early production.

However, when Hugh Kenner, talking about *The Unnamable,* wrote: "He means too that man is man by virtue of speech, and that all speech is an echoing of echoes,"[63] he called to our attention the presence of a relativistic horizon in Beckett's narratives, even if they grow within an inescapable tradition. The early Beckettian parodies are echoes of a well-learned tradition whose face values are reversed rather than revered, and furthermore, his interpretation of speech as echo and of texts as echoes of echoes is confirmed by the subsequent development of Beckett's comic strategies, which move past referential functions into textual self-reflexivity.

The reality of language is at stake in the comic reduplications of the second phase of Beckett's production, and his metanarrative remarks can be grasped as the effect of an epistemic irony that connotes the text as a locus of oblique meaning. Comic strategies establish unusual, defamiliarized, and metanarrative relations between fact and expression; the text works on itself as it develops, unveiling the artifacts on which it grows. This is probably why Kenner talks of Beckett's texts as words in action: "Whether cryptic or copious talk in the Beckett universe is generally a mode of behavior, like Watt's oscillatory walk or Molloy's extraordinary performance with the sixteen stones."[64] The performative quality of Beckett's texts is understandable as a metanarrative practice, whereby "A few dozen expressions permuted with deliberate redundancy accumulate meaning even as they are emptied of it."[65] These lucid expressions build up into a self-reflexive devaluation of artistic devices, not without a passion for truth and for an epistemological investigation of the power of language. If, in *Waiting for Godot*, "Lucky's style dehumanizes man through mechanized mockery of his rational and progressive accomplishments," it seems to me that it is so because the notion of "humanity" is at stake, together with a traditional idea of progress and a critique of acritical rationality. After all "the play's point about words is not that they mean nothing—nothing is silent—but that meaning shifts, breaks and repeats."[66]

> When reading Beckett one must constantly guard against imposing on the fiction one's own notions of order, truth, plausibility, and reality [. . .] Too often we are guilty of reading paradoxes into Beckett's fiction because we cannot accept what cancels itself as it creates itself—that which is contrary to common sense, or that which points to itself (even though ironically) as paradoxical.[67]

The essence of the paradox is, to adopt Raymond Federman's definition, "a split between two levels of narration—between the truth of fiction and the lie of fiction."[68] In Beckett's narratives the exploitation of the two levels, as constant oscillation from one to the other, helps to indicate how greatly he differs from some postmodernist writers, especially in the third phase of his narrative production.

Beckett's comic deconstructs "saying" as an inescapable "missaying," with no conceptual solutions or reductions of the contradictions that generate it. On the contrary, the postmodern thematizations of discontinuity, failure, and suspensiveness dogmatize irresolution, rather than producing it through the undecidability of certain (comic) statements. Beckett, unlike some contemporary writers, does not exchange an impossible definition of the real with a lucid tautology that can only seem to bypass reality. Rather, his insistence on (the importance of) missaying seems to reflect a truly Nietzschian nihilism, inasmuch as it deals with the impossibility of defining, without transforming this impossibility into a positive negation or a totalitarian theme. Beckett's comic strategies are essentially communicative strategies which question communication; they have been and are endowed with "an ideal of the highest degree of powerfulness of the spirit, the over-richest life—partly destructive, partly ironic."[69]

Notes

1. "Sait-on ce que c'est qu'écrire? [. . .] C'est, ce jeu insensé d'écrire, s'arroger, en vertue d'un doute [. . .] quelque devoir de tout recréer, avec des reminiscences, pour avérer qu'on est bien là où l'on doit être (parce que, permettez moi d'exprimer cette appréhension, demeure une incertitude)." Stéphane Mallarmé, *Oeuvres complètes* (Paris: Bibliothèque de la Pléiade, Éditions Gallimard, 1945) p. 481. Translation mine.

2. I would like to point out that it is not possible to provide a clear, indisputable definition of the comic, as it is an "umbrella term" that "gathers together a disturbing ensemble of diverse and not completely homogeneous phenomena, such as humor, comedy, grotesque, parody, satire, wit, and so on." Umberto Eco, "The Frames of Comic 'Freedom'" in *Carnival!*, Thomas A. Sebeok, ed. (Berlin-New York-Amsterdam: Mouton, 1984) pp. 1–9. Quotation p. 1. A similar observation can be found in Benedetto Croce's "L'umorismo" in *Problemi di estetica e contributi alla storia dell'estetica italiana* (Bari: Laterza, 1903). Croce writes: "Le definizioni dell'umorismo e di simili altri concetti debbono di necessità essere vaghe e fluttuanti perché, piuttosto che concetti rigorosi sono raggruppamenti di rappresentazioni che ubbidiscono a scopi pratici." (p. 286).

3. As shown in the Introduction to this book, many critics have investigated and discussed different aspects of Beckett's comic. Among them, I would remember in particular here the contributions of Porter H. Abbott, *The Fiction of Samuel Beckett: Form and Effect* (Berkeley: University of California Press, 1973); John Chalker, "The Satiric Shape of *Watt* " in *Beckett the Shape Changer: A Symposium*, Katherine Worth, ed. (Boston, Routledge & Kegan Paul, 1975) pp. 19–37; Ruby Cohn, *Samuel Beckett: The Comic Gamut* (New Brunswick, N.J.: Rutgers University Press, 1962); Raymond Federman, *Journey to Chaos: Samuel Beckett's Early Fiction* (Berkeley: University of California Press, 1965) and "Samuel Beckett: The Liar's Paradox " in *Samuel Beckett: The Art of Rhetoric*, E. Morot-Sir, H. Harper, D. McMillan III, eds. (Chapel Hill: North Carolina Studies in the Romance Languages and Literatures, 1976) pp. 119–41; Hugh Kenner, *Samuel Beckett: A Critical Study* (New York: Grove Press, 1961); Edith Kern, "Ironic Structure in Beckett's Fiction " in *L'Esprit Créateur* 11 (Fall 1971) 3–13, and "Samuel Beckett et les poches de Lemuel Gulliver," Paul Rozenberg, trans., *Revue des Lettres Modernes: Samuel Beckett; Configuration Critique* 8, 100 (1966) 69–81.

4. Umberto Eco, "The Frames of Comic 'Freedom'," p. 8.

5. Teun A. Van Dijk uses the term "frame" to indicate a type of information that is predetermined by context. His definition, which suits my purpose, derives from both cognitive psychology and artificial intelligence. See his *Text and Context. Explorations in the Semantics and Pragmatics of Discourse* (London: Longman, 1977).

6. Umberto Eco, "The Frames of Comic 'Freedom'," p. 8.

7. See Peter Steiner, *Russian Formalism. A Metapoetics* (Ithaca, N.Y. and London: Cornell University Press, 1984) p. 118:

In the last stage of his theoretical career, Tynjanov attempted to link the infraliterary textual elements to the extraliterary level as well. He introduced the notion of the "constructive function" of an element that consists of two simultaneous relations: infrarelations proper, which he called the "syn-function" or the relations of an element to the other elements of a given [work-]system; and the intraliterary and extraliterary relations, which he termed the "auto-function" or the relations of an element "to the similar elements of other work-systems and even of other series."

8. According to Algirdas J. Greimas's definition, "sememes" are figures of meaning, which can be accepted as compatible, or rejected as incompatible, by a particular context in which they are related. See his *Sémantique structurale* (Paris: Larousse, 1966). In particular, he discusses (comic) incongruity as follows: "Le contexte [. . .] fonctionne comme un système de compatibilité et d'incompatibilité entre les figures sémiques qu'il accepte ou non de réunir, la compatibilité résidant dans le fait que deux noyaux sémiques peuvent se combiner avec un même sème contextuel," p. 52. In his more recent work, *Du Sens* (Paris: Larousse, 1970), Greimas no longer refers to sememes but only to "isotopy," as the overlapping of different semantic categories, which could be exploited for the creation of comic effects.

9. "Le jeu de mot(s) [. . .] porte sur les mots eux-mêmes, sur la forme, sur le signifiant alors que le *bon mot* ou *mot d'esprit* porte sur les pensées, sur les idées, sur le signifié." Pierre Guiraud, *Les jeux de mots* (Paris: Presses Universitaires de France, 1976) p. 101.

10. In her remarkable essay "L'histoire drôle" which first appeared in *Communications* 8 (1966), Violette Morin focuses her attention on a "disjunctive element" which allows the bifurcation of a story from a serious to a comic plane. According to the nature of the *disjoncteur* she goes on to distinguish between semantic and referential disjunctions: "Nous avons distingué les récits à disjonction sémantique, lorsque le disjoncteur est un signe, des récits à disjonction référentielle, lorsque le disjoncteur est un élément auquel se réfèrent les signes, un Référentiel." Reprinted in *L'analyse structurale du récit* (Paris: Éditions du Seuil, 1981) pp. 108–125, quotation p. 109.

11. Jean Cohen, "Comique et poétique," *Poétique* 61 (February 1985) 49–61.

12. Umberto Eco, "Introduzione a R. Queneau" in *Esercizi di stile* (Torino: Einaudi, 1983) pp. xiii–xviii.

13. "Le plus souvent les signes s'effacent devant les éléments référentiels du récit: geste, action, sentiment, dont les diverses significations ou la polysémie, alimentent la disjonction." Violette Morin, "L'histoire drôle," p. 109. Translation mine.

14. Building on Mikhail M. Bakhtin's definition of *heteroglossia* (and "heteroglot") in "Discourse in the Novel," Cesare Segre has created the term *interdiscorsivo* ("inter-glot") to indicate the relationships a given text bears with all of the texts a given culture records and orders, according to ideology, registers, and levels. Segre's term does not imply any direct source or link with a different text, nor does it involve any shift from one sign system to another, as in Julia Kristeva's *Semiotiké: Recherches pour une sémanalyse* (Paris: Seuil, 1969). For a detailed discussion of Bakhtin's term see *The Dialogic Imagination,* M. Holquist, ed. (Austin: University of Texas Press, 1981). For a discussion of Segre's term see

his "Intertestuale—interdiscorsivo. Appunti per una fenomenologia delle fonti" in A.A.V.V., *La parola ritrovata* (Palermo: Sellerio, 1982) pp. 15–28.

15. "Ce n'est pas en effet la simple contradiction logique de l'énoncé qui est comique, mais la contradiction axiologique." Jean Cohen, "Comique et poétique," pp. 56–57.

16. Raymond Federman, "Samuel Beckett: The Liar's Paradox." Quotation pp. 120–21.

17. Geoffrey Hartman, "Preface " in *Deconstruction and Criticism* (New York: Seabury Press, 1979) p. viii.

18. Samuel Beckett, *ill seen ill said* (London: John Calder, 1982) p. 40.

19. Ronald Sukenick, "Thirteen Digressions," *Partisan Review* 43, 1 (1976) 98–99.

20. Jacques Derrida, *Positions*, translated and annotated by Alan Bass (Chicago: University of Chicago Press, 1981) p. 14.

21. For a discussion of Surrealistic and Dadaistic "ready-made" see Giovanni Manetti, "Ready-made: Semantica e pragmatica dell'umorismo dadaista e surrealista," *VS* 25 (1980) 65–84. See also André Breton, *Anthologie de l'humour noir* (Paris: J. J. Pauvert, 1939).

22. Umberto Eco, "The Frames of Comic 'Freedom'," p. 6.

23. For a definition of "background entailment," and for the various uses of the term "entailment" in linguistics, see Neil Smith and Deirdre Wilson, *Modern Linguistics: The Results of Chomsky's Revolution* (Bloomington and London: Indiana University Press, 1979). In particular I am referring to Chapter 7, "Semantics and Meaning," pp. 148–71.

24. *Ibid.*, p. 149.

25. Samuel Beckett, *More Pricks than Kicks* (New York: Grove Press, 1970) p. 11.

26. Mikhail M. Bakhtin, *The Dialogic Imagination,* pp. 50, 52.

27. Samuel Beckett, *More Pricks than Kicks,* p. 10. Emphasis mine.

28. Roland Barthes, *Writing Degree Zero,* Annette Lavers and Colin Smith, trans., preface by Susan Sontag (New York: Hill and Wang, 1968) *passim.* Quotation p. 30.

29. *Ibid.*, pp. 36–37.

30. Samuel Beckett, *Murphy* (London: Picador-Pan Books, 1973, first published 1938) p. 41.

31. Samuel Beckett, "First Love" in *Collected Shorter Prose 1945–1980* (London: John Calder, 1984) p. 12.

32. Samuel Beckett, "First Love," pp. 15–16. Emphasis mine.

33. Samuel Beckett, "Enough" in *Collected Shorter Prose,* pp. 141–42.

34. For a critical presentation of novels as mythologies, see Roland Barthes, *Writing Degree Zero;* see in particular "Writing and the Novel." For a discussion of Beckett's early denunciations of novels as mythologies, see Carla Locatelli, *La disdetta della parola. L'ermeneutica del silenzio nella prosa inglese di Samuel Beckett* (Bologna: Patron, 1984).

35. Samuel Beckett, "From an Abandoned Work" in *Collected Shorter Prose,* p. 129.

36. Paul de Man, *The Resistance to Theory* (Minneapolis: University of Minnesota Press, 1986) p. 10.

37. Samuel Beckett, "From an Abandoned Work," p. 130. Emphasis mine.

38. *Ibid.*, p. 135.

39. Samuel Beckett, "Ping" in *Collected Shorter Prose*, p. 149.
40. For the definition of the French terms *mention* and *emploi* see Dan Sperber and Deirdre Wilson, "Les ironies comme mentions," *Poétique* 36 (November 1978) 399–412.
41. Jacques Derrida, *Positions*, p. 14.
42. Samuel Beckett, "Ping," p. 150.
43. Jacques Derrida, *Positions*, p. 12.
44. Jacques Derrida, *Writing and Difference*, translated with an Introduction by Alan Bass (London: Routledge & Kegan Paul, 1978) p. 11.
45. Samuel Beckett, "Ping," p. 151. Scansion added.
46. I am using Derrida's quotation for my own purpose, my emphasis falling on temporality rather than on the elucidation of the value of the *a* in *différance*. See Jacques Derrida, *Margins of Philosophy*, Alan Bass, trans. (Chicago: University of Chicago Press, 1982) pp. 3–27. Quotation p. 3.
47. Samuel Beckett, *ill seen ill said* (London: John Calder, 1982) p. 59.
48. *Ibid.*, p. 40.
49. Samuel Beckett, "He is Barehead" in *For to End Yet Again and Other Fizzles* (London: John Calder, 1976), p. 27. Reprinted as "Fizzle 1" in *Fizzles* (New York: Grove Press, 1976) p. 10. Emphasis mine.
50. Johann Wolfgang von Goethe, *Werke*, Band IV (Hamburg: Christian Wegener, 1967).
51. "C'est par sa répétition que la phrase acquiert pour l'auditeur sa transparence ironique. La répétition des phrases est en fait l'un des rares 'signaux' (au sens de la théorie de l'information) dont dispose le mode de la parole ironique; *mais* il faut tout de suite dire que *l'ironie littéraire renonce la plupart du temps à tels signaux*." Beda Alleman, "De l'ironie en tant que principe littéraire," *Poétique* 36 (November 1978) 385–98. Quotation p. 390. Emphasis given here, and translation, mine.
52. Barbara Johnson, *The Critical Difference* (Baltimore: Johns Hopkins University Press, 1980) p. x.
53. Samuel Beckett, *Worstward Ho* (London: John Calder, 1983) p. 7.
54. *Ibid.*, p. 31. Emphasis mine.
55. *Ibid.*, p. 7.
56. *Ibid.*, pp. 42, 11, 9.
57. *Ibid.*, p. 42.
58. *Ibid.*, pp. 46–47.
59. *Ibid.*, p. 39.
60. *Ibid.*, p. 47.
61. *Ibid.*, pp. 38–39.
62. Samuel Beckett, *The Beckett Trilogy: Molloy, Malone Dies, The Unnamable* (London: Picador-Pan Books, 1979, first published 1959) p. 33. Emphasis mine.
63. Hugh Kenner, *Samuel Beckett: A Critical Study* (Berkeley: University of California Press, 1968) p. 167.
64. *Ibid.*, p. 177.
65. *Ibid.*, p. 189.

66. Ruby Cohn, "Warming up for My Last Soliloquy" in *Samuel Beckett: The Art of Rhetoric,* pp. 105–18. Quotation p. 110.

67. Raymond Federman, "Samuel Beckett: the Liar's Paradox," pp. 126–27.

68. *Ibid.,* p. 133.

69. Friedrich Nietzsche, *The Will to Power,* Walter Kaufmann, ed. (New York: Vintage Books, 1963) p. 14.

3. Beckett's Theater Since the 1970s

The Theatrical Double

The purpose of this investigation, centering on Beckett's theatrical works written and performed after 1970, is to find ideological and aesthetic links with his prose production of the same period. I believe that, particularly in the past twenty years, Beckett's "work in progress" has developed from the center of the linguistic-communicative problem. Hence his theatrical work should be read as a demystifying discourse oriented toward the typology of culture,[1] not only Irish and French but modern Western culture in the broadest sense.

Since I believe that the theme and structure of communication are central to the understanding of Beckett, I will develop the discussion of Beckett's theater in a hermeneutical frame which is greatly concerned with the communicative problem and similar to the one used in my readings of his prose works. Obviously, some redefinition of the frame becomes necessary for discussing the specificity of drama. In fact, I intend to focus on the ideological implications of the plays as a unified body of work, and on the philosophical relevance of dramatic communication. Rather than provide exegetical readings of all the plays, I will identify a pattern of recurrent themes that unify them conceptually and semiotically. The philosophical and hermeneutical relevance of dramatic communication will be investigated in relation to twentieth-century thought, in order to focus Beckett's innovations in this field.

Beckett's work has become emblematic of the epistemic knots that characterize the philosophy of our century because it acknowledges the primary role of language in the structuring of cultural models and the indispensable role of communication in the advent of culture. It is easy to place Beckett's works at the center of the gnoseological questions (that is, at the center of questions regarding the content of knowledge) at least up to the 1960s, and at the center of epistemological and hermeneutical issues (that is, at the center of issues regarding types and modes of knowing) in the following years. His poetics share the concerns about conditions of knowledge and modes of interpretation that underlie contemporary philosophical thought. We could say that Beckett deals with both the question of what can be known and the mode in which knowledge develops, while exploiting aesthetic communication as the primary field and instrument of his investigation.

One of Antonin Artaud's significant statements about drama suggests the intrinsic oscillation within every recent work by Beckett, regardless of its structure as prose or poetry, as drama, film or radio theater. In a letter to Jean Paulhan of 26 January 1936, Artaud wrote: "I think I have a suitable title for my book. It will be *The Theatre and its Double,* for if theatre doubles life, life doubles true theatre."[2] In a way, the full cycle of Artaud's "double" evokes Kierkegaard's critique of Hegel's dialectic through the notion of repetition.[3] In fact repetition, or "the double," should not be understood as a mere mirror image but as a complex temporal and gnoseological category. As such the double seems to reappear in Beckett in order to open a new possibility for the articulation of life. It is not a simple dramatic device used to imitate action, and thus it does not lead to a transcendental gnosis and to the usual closure of naming. On the contrary, it works towards an original representation of phenomenalism. In this sense we could say that Beckett's recent drama faces the same radical problem as that confronted by his prose: the problem of reference. Following Paul de Man's formulation, I would say that Beckett's work exploits the problem of the referential function of language in relation to ideology, that is in relation to "the confusion of linguistic with natural reality."[4] The insurmountable difficulty one encounters in the reproduction of life derives from the fact that the materiality and logic of the signifier allow for a development of signifieds which is different from the development of phenomena, or, in other words, any reproduction of life has to confront the struggle between figure and concept. As a consequence, language, and especially conventional literary language, is charged with referential ambiguity. However, as we shall see, the dramatic "double" in Beckett becomes a significant means for the reproduction of life, since it implies the erosion of literariness, a deconstruction of figurality, and the structuring of a full hermeneutical cycle including the vision of "real" time.

It is well known that dramatic language is closer to "things" than narrative language because of the quality of its temporal articulation. Beckett's theater exploits this proximity and doubles life in such a way that the temporal dimension of what actually happens can be shown as it happens. The temporal dimension of events, which is normally hidden in reproductions in order to achieve a "true-to-life" representation, is expressed in Beckett's works as part of the definition of the event itself. This is his great innovation. Beckett's dramatic double actually shows time as the common dimension shared by life and drama, and shows it in spite of the fact that every ordinary definition of reality conceals it, within symbolic designations of temporality that seem, but are not, time referents. Beckett's double is very unlike Artaud's loathed repetition because Beckett's theater, which doubles life with no concessions to realistic mimesis, expresses the temporal dimension intrinsic to whatever occurs, and the object "time" is designated without recourse to any referential function expressing temporality.[5] Through the theatrical double we are made to "see" time without receiving any definition of it: the figurality of language is no longer hidden within a referential fallacy. Beckett's theatrical double enacts Nietzsche's revelation: "facts is precisely what there is not, only interpretations. We cannot establish any fact 'in itself'."[6] In other words, as we shall see, Beckett's theater deconstructs the performative figurality of language through the temporal literality of a theatrical performance. This means that "facts" (which are already always the result of an interpretation of "original events") are shown as (theatrical) "acts," because the interpretive articulation of original events is repeated, doubled, in a theatrical prescription. The double figurality in a theatrical act, that is, the double figurality of the prescription in the script, reproduces the original interpretation that defines events, and by mirroring the original naming of phenomena shows the radical impossibility of reproducing reality as it is together with the impossibility of avoiding the effects of such interpretation.

One of the recurrent features of Beckett's double is the *mise en abîme* of the play within the play. The use of this defamiliarizing device doubles the impossibility of reproducing life, not only literally, because it repeats the theatrical "act" (or, more precisely, those minimal components of reality that have already become part of fiction: the "framed" voice, the light, words, etc.), but also because it makes the public aware of the impossibility of reproducing the "same" reality. The irretrievable continuity of life is expressed through the discontinuities of "how the story was told" on stage. The play within the play, often a repetition of the scene, comes to express the transient and yet real immediacy of life rather than life as a concept; thus, as Artaud suggested, life doubles the theater. This doubling occurs because the theatrical prescription of an "act" doubles a "fact," and thus repeats (and can show) the original transformation that determined "facts" from "scattered events," from "life." Life doubles the theater because it becomes visible as indivisible life, before the determinations of the show.

Furthermore, it is worth noticing that in Beckett the play within the play is not structured through "a scene within a scene," but rather through a "scene and an extra-scene,"[7] or through a scene and another scene which is simultaneously related to it, so that the spectators (or implied readers) have to be, and are, directly, actually involved in the tracing of these links. They come to share the ambiguity of an actor's role because, after having accepted and even chosen their suspension of disbelief, they are forced to question it, because they can no longer "figure out" reality. Their distance from fiction becomes very problematic because by consenting to fiction, with a simulation of understanding, they discover how weak is their understanding of a simulation: just like actors they are both accomplices and victims of a play.

The tragic lack of knowledge that traditionally opened the way to catastrophe in Greek drama becomes a dramatic lack of knowledge regarding the boundaries of reality, particularly in plays such as *Ohio Impromptu* (1981, over three hundred years after Molière's *Impromptu de Versailles*, 1663), *Catastrophe* (1982), and *What Where* (1983). The only way in which the public can understand Beckett's plays has to include the knowledge of the effects of fiction on the shaping of their understanding, not only of the play but extensively of reality as well. When immediate evidence takes the place of the concept at the end of a process of conceptual understanding, the member of the audience sees that he or she is coming out of the fiction he or she had chosen, and out of an unseen representation: the play of his or her awareness. The spectators realize that they had been programmed to wait in order to understand, that they have to include the present in their understanding, just as much as the actors are programmed to use that time on stage. Seeing their seeing is part of the global representation. The structural elements of Beckett's plays are so lucidly disconnected that, if the spectators or readers are to understand the ongoing global theatrical communication with and among the actors, they have to see the lack of boundaries of this theater, or rather they have to acknowledge the conventional, interpretive nature of boundaries, against the light of the inescapability of the temporal dimension (normally repressed in representation). They must swing back and forth between the scene and the extra-scene, between fiction (in relation to which they feel "external" and superior, as consenting "real" spectators) and reality (in relation to which they are "internal," but where they lose all kinds of superiority).

In Beckett's plays the absence of a mediation between the scene and the extra-scene reveals that the fiction of reality is, after all, also the reality of fiction, a fiction in which real people participate. Spectators and readers can alter conceptual and chronological links conceptually, but it is only by acknowledging and suspending the conventionality of their understanding and the figurality of their position that they can experience and recognize the way in which life doubles the theater. The theater doubles life until the spectator sees the "act" as a literal repetition of a "fact," and the "actor" as a repetition of "himself" or "herself." But life doubles the theater when the spectator finally comes to see himself or herself "played" by the play, and acting the role of the spectator in relation to the immediate. In Beckett this hermeneutical cycle (of the theater and its double) cannot be broken, and this is what prevents his "negative knowledge about the reliability of linguistic utterance"[8] from becoming a positive or negative dogma. If there is a catharsis in Beckett's theater, it is only in the deep sense of a liberation ensuing from finding the conceptual "voiding" and the problematic subversion of fiction, against the closed, dogmatic certainties of both idealism and nihilism. In fact, only *simul*taneous *simul*ations can unveil the repressed vision of the tropological movements that, according to Nietzsche, articulate the truth, the truth being "A moving army of metaphors, metonymies and anthropomorphisms."[9]

Since in Beckett's plays we encounter the actor-spectator double together with the theater-life double, we can really say that literature as simulation becomes a literal, visible site of power and resistance, and that this conflict regards the problematic subversion of truth by rhetoric.

Subtraction Within the Reproductive Impossibility

According to Paul de Man, whenever an "autonomous potential of language can be revealed by analysis, we are dealing with literariness and, in fact, with literature as the place where this negative knowledge about the reliability of linguistic utterance is made available."[10] In Beckett, the "play within the play" is literally a *mise en abîme,* in the sense that his works deconstruct their own literariness, so as to come to designate life as immediate evidence.

Beckett's plays grow within the challenge of the reproductive impossibility; more precisely, the fact that life cannot be re-produced leads him towards a representation of life that displays this impossibility. Again, Beckett proceeds by subtraction: he subtracts the conventional literary quality of literature from literature, just as he tends towards a representation of life deprived of the meaning "life." This means that he is always showing precisely the conceptual frame of language, which undermines the possibility of representing the immediacy of life as it is. Therefore, only when what seems the immediate is unrepresented can it reappear as authentically free from the bounds of conceptualization. Beckett's willed mis-representations are actually un-representations because they are irreducibly dynamic and subtractive. They result from a syntagmatic, combinatory movement that proceeds through drastic reduction, rather than ensuing from the accumulation of paradigmatic alternatives which assert specific representations. The reduction of the seemingly "same" represented scene constitutes the dramatic movement through which the immediate comes to be represented as different from all the conceptual generalizations that create the similarity of events occurring at different times. This flight from conceptualization is synthesized by one of the charaters in *Footfalls* (1976), who says: "the motion alone is not enough, I must hear the feet, however faint they fall."[11] After all, "footfalls" are an actual reproduction of movement: an iconography of "steps" less its abstraction.

This tension towards "the real," which marks all of Beckett's recent works, must certainly reinforce his mistrust of critics who perceive symbols where they are not intended, and develop their readings along the lines of an arbitrary, enforced semanticism, as an antidote to the "voiding" of the literary word that they should instead witness in his works. In fact, the dialectical movement of the text with respect to reality, its radical openness, can be perceived only if the interpretation of textual elements is never final. Furthermore, in his recent works Beckett seems to denounce not only the overtones of what he calls "symbols" but conceptual thinking itself. In this sense Beckett's theater really works with the impotence of representation (against the "apotheosis of the word"), because he plays the actual return of "acontextual" signs against the false movement of mimesis (which is always a conceptual recognition of reality). He represents representations until the figurative quality of language can really be seen, and the issue of truth separated from the needs of mimetic reproduction. His recent works tend towards silence, not because silence constitutes some sort of sublime, ineffable perfection, nor because it is a pure negation, but because it is only through subtraction of the uttered expression from the uttered expression, of the word from the word, that language may go beyond itself and point to the site of thought before the formulation of concepts. The purpose of Beckett's subtractions leads him to a silence described as "nothing left to tell"; the scope of his unwording is not confined to the self-reflection of the literary artifact, and is well described by the character R (Reader), in *Ohio Impromptu* (1981):

Thoughts, no, not thoughts. / Profounds of mind. Buried in who knows what profounds of mind. Of mindlessness. Whither no light can reach. No sound. So sat on as though turned to stone. The sad tale a last time told. /(*Pause.*)/
Nothing is left to tell.[12]

The tragic scene here is again, as in all of Beckett's plays, centered on the problematics of knowledge, and on the tragedy of language. Since only what is "sayable" can be known or become visible, "profounds of mindlessness" are invoked, as the site of silence, the site where the power of the concept can be silenced at last.

Beckett's Recurrent Themes: Aesthetic Reproduction, Identification, and Temporality

At the core of all of Beckett's works there are three essential themes: (1) the problem of the aesthetic reproduction of reality, whose hermeneutical implications have been discussed in relation to his entire production, (2) the dilemma of (self-)identification, and (3) the issue of temporality. These themes are developed so intricately and simultaneously that they could be seen as the epistemic coordinates of Beckett's universe. Although they are connected, I will have to discuss them separately, so as to be able to be informative about different plays. Furthermore, each theme will be related to specific dramatic works or group of works written in the 1970s or 1980s. However, before developing a critical presentation of Beckett's plays after 1970, I would like to comment on their chronological arrangement and to underline the often recurring, interesting discrepancy between the date of their first performance and the date of their publication. Beckett's production for the theater in this period includes:

1. *Not I,* first performed at the Forum Theater of the Lincoln Center, New York, in September 1972. Published by Faber and Faber, London, 1973.
2. *That Time,* first performed at the Royal Court Theatre, London, on May 20, 1976. Published in the same year by Grove Press, New York.
3. *Footfalls,* first performed at the Royal Court Theatre, London, on May 20, 1976. Published in the same year by Grove Press, New York.
4. *A Piece of Monologue,* first performed in New York in 1980 by the actor

David Warrilow, for whom it was written. Published by Faber and Faber, London, 1982.

5. *Rockaby,* first performed in Buffalo, New York, in 1981. Published by Faber and Faber, London, 1982.

6. *Ohio Impromptu,* first performed at Ohio State University in 1981. Published by Faber and Faber, London, 1982.

7. *Catastrophe,* written in French and dedicated to Vaclav Havel, the Czech writer befriended by Beckett during many imprisonments in the 1970s and 1980s, and who became president of Czechoslovakia a few days after Beckett's death. First performed at the Avignon Festival in 1982. Published by Editions de Minuit, Paris, 1982. First published in English by Faber and Faber, London, 1984.

8. *What Where,* first performed in New York, at the Harold Clurman Theater, on June 15, 1983. Published by Faber and Faber, London, 1984.[13]

The recurrent discrepancy between the date of the first performance and the date of publication seems to imply not only Beckett's awareness of the structural and semiotic difference between codification and function of the relation of the "form of the expression" with the "form of content,"[14] in theatrical and prose works, but also the fact that he conceives his theatrical works for actual performance. In this respect Alec Reid's words are very significant:

> Beckett's plays must be considered not for their message but for their impact, not for their philosophy but for the feeling they evoke.[15]

The refusal of conceptualization and abstraction and the dread of "false movement" are still central to Beckett's plays in the 1980s; indeed his recent works display an extreme precision in the formulation of stage directions and a passionate concern for the composition of the signs of the theater (variations of lights, duration, gesture, motion, etc.). The materiality of signifiers can be endowed with special semantic value in the theater, since it is one of the most expressive means to denote the immediate. I will quote Reid again to underscore the existential importance of performance in the conception of Beckett's plays:

> Beckett has deliberately designed his plays to be performed by actors for an audience sitting in a theatre or beside a radio. He means them to be experienced immediately, as the sounds come at us across the footlights or out of the loudspeaker; they are not intended to be read from the silent, immobile

page [. . .] So Beckett will describe the initial run-through of a text with actors as a "realization" of the play; and when it is performed publicly, he will say that it has been "created."[16]

For Beckett, then, the "creation" of a play implies the actual public performance, and the publication of the script should therefore be regarded as irrelevant to the completion of the play itself. Gilles Deleuze's insightful comments on repetition come to mind to reinforce the idea of the centrality of this point in the interpretation of Beckett's plays:

> When we say that movement, on the contrary, is repetition, and that our true theater is right there, we are not talking about the effort of the actor who 'repeats' inasmuch as we are talking about the piece not yet known.[17]

The novelty of repetition consists in its being the structure of awareness of the immediate, the evidence of a feeling as it is felt. The knowledge of the spectator is a seeing that doubles what is shown, a seeing of the immediate structured as repetition: a theater in relation to consciousness, and a double in relation to phenomena. Just as in modern existential philosophy, the theatralization of experience is conceived as a primary form of knowledge, challenging conceptualization.

Repetition Against the False Movement of the Text

The problem of the aesthetic reproduction of reality, which is central to Beckett's concern, manifests itself through the recurrent epistemic coordinates of visibility and communicability, which are crucial, as we have seen, in *ill seen ill said* (1982) and *Worstward Ho* (1983).

In Beckett's works for the theater the difference between presence and speech, between chronology and duration is expressed and designated as repetition, a linguistic, often performative repetition that connotes the problematic aspects of visibility as well as the conventionality of reproduction. In fact, the repetition of nearly identical portions of the text in many of Beckett's works, which are otherwise remarkably compressed and economical, indicates that the text is part of reality and no longer a closed structural mechanism. It is important to note that minimal variations occur mostly at the level of rhythm and prosody, rather than at a semantic and lexical level: *That Time* (1976), *A Piece of Monologue* (1980), and *Rockaby* (1981) are typical in this respect. This means that no paradigmatic expansion of the motifs of these texts accounts for a significant expansion of their meaning, but rather that new elements, drawn directly from reality, are shown as concurring in the constitution of the hermeneutical code of the plays. In fact, the code is one of the most relevant meanings of the text, as it opens onto the present of the performance.

In Beckett's works the materiality of signifiers is loaded with semantic value because signifiers are shown to be partaking of both reality and the verbal code. The plays expand because they open onto reality, not because they enrich the numerical variety of their representations. In fact, the spectators basically hear what they already know, but they hear it again, so that, through the aesthetic double, they come to know immediacy as repetition and they see a temporal difference within apparently identical elements. Beckett's use of repetition shows that any text is strictly based on temporality, and that only its repetitions prevent it from being seen as "pure literature," either a poetical refrain or a mimetic narration.

In *Footfalls,* for example, the echoes of a "single chime" become progressively fainter while repeating themselves, according to precise stage directions that require first a "Faint single chime. Pause as echoes die." followed by a "Chime a little fainter. Pause for echoes." and then by a "Chime a little fainter still. Pause for echoes."; until finally the prescription requires a "Chime even a little fainter still. Pause for echoes."[18] This slight acoustic modification has the power to express the impossibility of a perfect coincidence between identity and presence. In fact, in line with the general theme of the play, the name suffices for the evocation of self, for an abstract definition of identity, but this conscious subject fits an image of an atemporal being which betrays that very self, while portraying it. The protagonist of *Footfalls* (1976) is said to remember and "revolve it all in her poor mind," but she cannot "revolve it all" in reality. Indeed the problem of the aesthetic reproduction of reality can be formulated in M(ay)'s words: "How could you have responded if you were not there?"[19] The issue of presence is central to the legitimacy of a successful reproduction of reality, and a good aesthetic reproduction cannot ignore the relevance and inescapability of the temporal flux.

In *A Piece of Monologue* (1980), which could be defined as a play of penultimates against the lie of an absolute, ultimate reproduction, Beckett makes his refusal of atemporal and purely conceptual statements explicit. He does so through repeated reformulations of his own starting formulas. At the opening of the play the protagonist, Speaker, makes a declaration reminiscent of the opening of *Fizzle IV,* "I gave up before birth"[20]:

"Birth was the death of him. Again. Words are few. Dying too. Birth was the death of him."[21]

However, not until the protagonist's iconoclastic rejection of images is evoked do we come to a perfectly intelligible reproduction of his life, a reproduction which, unlike pictures, is intrinsically dynamic and true to the mobility of life. This process is synthesized as follows:

> Backs away to edge of light and stands facing blank wall. Covered with pictures once. Pictures of . . . he all but said loved ones. Unframed. Unglazed. Pinned to wall with drawing pins. All shapes and sizes. Down one after another. Gone. Torn to shreds and scattered. Strewn all over the floor. Not at one sweep. No sudden fit of . . . no word. Ripped from the wall and torn to shreds one by one. Over the years. Years of nights. Nothing on the wall now but the pins. Not all. Some out with the wrench. Some still pinning a shred. So stands there facing blank wall. Dying on. No more no less. No. Less. Less to die. Ever less.[22]

This short passage could be subdivided into three parts: the first indicating the "triumph" of pictures of "all shapes and sizes," so true to life as to appear/be "unframed" and "unglazed." These attributes are obviously ironical to the extent that they work literally in relation to the picture as object, but they also indicate the deceitful nature of mimetic identification: some reproductions, like these, are so unframed and unelaborate as to seem authentic and real. The second part of the passage is pervaded by an iconoclastic rage whereby images are "torn to shreds and scattered." Yet this drastic negation produces a knowledge, a negative knowledge, not only in the sense that it allows a rejection of the previous iconographic ingenuities, but also because it points to the existence of un-iconic realities, realities that cannot be illustrated but which substantiate human experience. Life and its intrinsic transience should then be reproduced as a diachronic subtraction, a metamorphosis of images from images, or of definitions from definitions (as in the progressively redefining iconography of "pictures torn to shreds and scattered . . . Not at one sweep . . . one by one . . . over the years," and until "nothing on the wall but the pins" becomes the vision of "pins still pinning a shred"). Life, which was defined by the historical yet abstract opening formula "Birth was the death of him," is redefined again and again, through a rhetorical repetition minus the rhetoric. In this way, the apparent contradiction that the formula had entailed becomes a plausible description of human experience: "Dying on. No more no less. No. Less. Less to die.

Ever less." Life is, after all, a "dying on, less to die," given the fragility inherent in human experience and given the inescapability of one's own ineluctable, ever-approaching death.

Were it not for the visible coincidence of speaker and speech, which has an enormous relevance in relation to the issue of presence, and which can actually be enacted only in the theater, we can see that the borders between Beckett's prose works and his works for the theater become progressively thinner in the course of the years.

In *A Piece of Monologue* (1980), as well as in a number of other plays,[23] a character enacts the telling of his story (also not "his," to the extent that he has changed), while in many prose works the story of somebody telling a story produces again a temporal coincidence which doubles "real time" (see, for example, *For to End Yet Again and Other Fizzles,* 1976, and "Still" in particular). Beckett's striking innovations are due to the fact that in both his dramatic and narrative works a new mimesis of actions substitutes the old representation of events: temporality is brought into visibility, and the reproduction of reality includes the duration of things.

Of all the works written after 1970, *Not I* (1972), *That Time* (1976), *Footfalls* (1976), and *A Piece of Monologue* (1980) exploit the mechanism of repetition in a totally new way, since the mimesis of actions no longer regards specific events, but expresses events as the result of repetition. In other words, Beckett's theater reveals the fact that there already is a sign where there seems to be a pure phenomenon, because the very concept of phenomenon implies a recognition, a recollection of defining traits. Furthermore, a theatrical quality is intrinsic in knowledge. The process of recognition, an existential awareness normally unseen and thought of as simple and direct knowledge, comes to light as "the content" of Beckett's theatrical double. To the extent that his performance is structured as repetition, it also shows it, where it was unseen before. The expression of the immediate through repetition and as repetition condemns habit as the "great deadener," as Beckett called it in his essay on Proust, and constitutes the original revelation of his recent plays. This is why I think that what Gilles Deleuze has written about Kierkegaard, Nietzsche, and Péguy can be applied to Beckett as well: "they oppose repetition to all the forms of generalization,"[24] and

What they reproach Hegel about, is his confinement to a false movement, to the abstract logical movement, that is, to a 'mediation.' [. . .] So, it is not enough for them to propose a new representation of movement; representation is already mediation. On the contrary, a movement should be produced within the work, capable of moving the spirit out of all representations; movement itself should be made a work, with no interpositions, direct signs should take the palace of mediated representations[25]

Already in *En attendant Godot* (1952) the first act is "like" the second, and that happens again in *Not I* (1972) and in the amazing false reduplication of *Footfalls* (1976). Sometimes the first act is "self-reflected" in the second (see *Ohio Impromptu,* 1981 and *Catastrophe,* 1982), or the "monologues" are characterized by the return of identical syntagms (*Rockaby,* 1981 and *What Where,* 1983). These pseudo-identical signs become the only "foundation" of the unity of a subject (*A Piece of Monologue,* 1980), even when the subject is structured by a multiplicity of voices (*That Time,* 1976).

At any rate, the return of identical linguistic elements implies the return of the repressed, the showing of a difference (repressed within language) between the becoming and the meaning of the becoming, between the "pure" happening and the event, which is always the result of a linguistic determination. The aesthetic "compulsion to repeat" of Beckett's plays is literally the enacting of the repression by duplication, and a way of bringing forward, under one's eyes, the exteriority of language in relation to phenomena. Words theatralize phenomena because of their abstraction, but repetition is a movement that struggles against conceptualization and mimetic representation. In Beckett the theatrical double doubles life to the extent that it refuses to illustrate it. What is actually shown is the role of signifiers in the definition of experience and in the structuring of meaning. In both his prose works and his works for the theater Beckett devoids words of their contextual value, so as to reveal on one hand the power of the signifier, and on the other hand the maximum of referentiality: a reference that cannot be designated but can be expressed by repetition and subtraction, and coincides with immediate evidence.

A brief quotation from *A Piece of Monologue* (1980) can synthesize the twofold nature of the semantic movement relating language and life in Beckett's works:

Thirty thousand nights of ghosts beyond. Beyond that black beyond. Ghost light. Ghost nights. Ghost rooms. Ghost graves. Ghost . . . he all but said ghost loved ones. Waiting on the rip word. Stands there staring beyond at that black veil lips quivering to half-heard words. Treating of other matters. Trying to treat of other matters. Till half hears there are no other matters. Never were other matters. Never two matters. Never but the one matter. The dead and gone. The dying and going. From the word go. The word begone. Such as the light going now.[26]

The first part of the passage indicates how the "will to mean" in meaning conceptualizes experience, past experience in this case, making it immaterial: "he all but said ghost loved ones." Furthermore, the full conceptual paradigm of recollections, of "nights," "the black," "lights," "rooms," and "the grave" indicates through a lexical progression the ineluctability of death, facing which a "rip word" is invoked. However, before the advent of the "rip word," that is, before being rejected, the conceptualized word develops even further, producing an even wider generalization: "Stands there [. . .] treating of other matters." This concatenation of signs, unrelated to an existential context but seemingly referring directly to one's own life, produces a false generalization regarding the possibility of "Treating of other matters." However, when repetition occurs, it proves to be the "rip word," a "word" indicating a rupture of conceptual discourse vis-à-vis actual experience. "Treating of other matters" becomes "Trying to treat of other matters," and the play of signifiers comes to dramatize experience instead of representing it as a generalization. Just like the character of the play, the spectator hears and sees that "there are no other matters. Never were other matters. Never two matters." Therefore, the immaterial ghostly recollections become the actual "dying and going. From the word to go." Repetition shows that there is no possibility for a full revocation, but there is an ongoing elaboration of what, through the signifier and still unknown, moves simultaneously Psyche and Physis, the spirit and the earth: "the *word* begone. *Such as* the *light* going now."

Indeed, the success of Beckett's aesthetic reproductions lies in the fact that they are "f/acts," because mimesis is structured as a process rather than being the result of an abstraction. Beckett's theatrical "acts" show the original interpretation that determines "facts" (from the flux of the becoming), rather than confirm that primary interpretation with a mimetic reproduction of those facts. They question the interpretation of "what" happens, and by deconstructing facts they point to an indivisible, invisible "real" life.

(Self-)Identification as Communicative Strategy

Another theme that seems crucial to the understanding of Beckett's works is the one of (self-)identification. The originality of Beckett's treatment of this typically modern subject derives from the fact that all of his works show us that (self-)identification is always strictly dependent on a dialogical practice. Self is established only as the object of a dialogical (self-)awareness.

This communicative practice is particularly evident in works such as *Company* (1980), which is based entirely on the exploration of strategies of self-communication, and in *ill seen ill said* (1981), where the issues of memory and visibility structure an intrinsically dialogical "story." These same issues are articulated in plays, such as *Not I* (1972), *A Piece of Monologue* (1980), and *Rockaby* (1981). In all of them, the establishment of (one's own) identity is again shown to be dependent on a strategic communication between the self and other, or between the self and the self-as-other. Communication is mostly enacted in a way that involves the characters of the play (directly, or as protagonists of the story they tell), but at times, communication involves the public as well.

In *Footfalls* (1976), for example, the identity of characters can be partly retrieved only as the solution of a temporal cryptogram, as the composition of a puzzle that eventually identifies, or at least correctly separates, mothers and daughters. The elusive nature of the verbal exchange in the play requires an inferential reading, so as to achieve an interpretation of what is said, which could resolve its otherwise insoluble, blatant contradictions. At one point in the play the spectator hears from V ("Woman's Voice," one of the protagonists), that "the child's given name" is "May," but later, when May is speaking, apparently telling the same story, a story with the same strange details and a very similar development, she declares that "the daughter's given name, as the reader will remember" is "Amy."[27] "May" is certainly not "Amy" conceptually and in principle, but no one will ever know if "May" is "Amy" for May who, through the anagram, expresses a different position of her self in relation to herself (thus creating the ironical analogy of the different positions of the letters of her name). Actually, May is and is not Amy: both statements will prove right in the light of the problematic nature of the self that emerges as the dialogue develops, and in the light of the complex unity of a text about a subject. In order for a unity to be found, the hermeneutical code of the play has to become part of its thematic structure. In fact, a subject is more than the sum of its "selves," and his or her unity can be grasped only when the spectator perceives the movement, not the addition, of the many, different representations of those selves.

The appearance of the hermeneutical code as a constitutive element of

Beckett's plays cannot be regarded as a self-reflection of the aesthetic artifact. On the contrary, it is a means through which un-iconic referential meanings can be articulated. His metalanguage is not circumscribed by the play, nor does it circumscribe the play: it opens directly onto reality. The thematic level includes the hermeneutical code of the play as one of its constitutive elements, as the only element on which the global unity of the play can eventually be established. In *Footfalls,* as in many of Beckett's works, the hermeneutical code has to become part of the meaning of the play in order for the public to understand what the characters are talking about in their dialogues. In this sense we can say that there is no traditional unity in *Footfalls,* because apparently incompatible but identical stories are narrated in it. And yet, if the spectator does not want to subscribe to the perception of an intrinsic incongruity in the play, he or she must stop expecting a linear and progressive thematic development of the story. If a unity can be established it is because the play is endowed with the co-herence of repetition, a coherence that allows an inferential reading of its elements, which become "full" referents only in the present of the enuncia-tion.

In *Footfalls,* an inferential, coherent interpretation of the play suggests that the characters relate to one another *as* and *from* different positions of their selves, and that the representation of an existentially polymorphic self coincides with the final thematic unity of the play. Obviously, the coherence of such an interpretation necessarily transforms the conceptual, abstract unity of a traditional mimetic representation (of one story about one self) into the revelation of the generative and progressive unity of the represen-tation, a representation of the different stories related to a subject. One representation occurs as two or more stories are told, but the unity of the play is not in the unification of the stories, even if they involve the "same" person.

The openness of representation points to the fact that the conceptual unification of self cannot be mistaken for the unity of the subject. In *Footfalls,* the conceptual unity of the conscious self is deconstructed, as repetition comes to express the intrinsic difference within a subject, against the conceptual unity of the conscious self. This "restoration of difference" is achieved by means of an extremely sophisticated dramatic strategy, includ-ing an open typology of characters, which establishes that the characters in the play must be two ("May" and "Woman's Voice"), while leaving unan-swered their referential identity and the subsequent referential quality of their relationship. At any rate, it is only in relation to the enunciation that reference can occur. At the opening of the play May is alone on stage, visible as a person; the other character is there only as a voice, enacting a dialogue with her. It will become progressively problematic, and never finally clear, whether the other *dramatis persona* is May's Voice (remembering her mother, and later a Mrs. Winter and an Amy), or whether the other character is, at least at some point, really May's Mother's Voice. The opening verbal exchange, which suggests the reproduction of a relationship between mother and daughter, will not let the spectator decide as to the actual referential ground of these characters. Is the voice inside May? Is the verbal exchange a true dialogue, or is it an interior monologue? These questions that seem preliminary to the understanding of the play reveal the play's ultimate meaning, that is: they indicate the fact that the play strives to represent difference while deconstructing the image of conceptual identity. It seems to me that Beckett's typology of characters and the structuring of their relations succeeds in accomplishing a "restoration of difference." According to Gilles Deleuze,

> To restore difference within thought is to untie the first knot, which consists in representing difference disguised under the identity of the concept and the thinking subject.[28]

Beckett "unties the knots" of monolithic mimesis and produces a differential representation of self and of reality.

When the Woman's Voice ("V") starts speaking alone, after "a long black pause," she asserts: "I walk here now. /*Pause.*/ Rather I come and stand."[29] She then continues, telling the story of "a child" whose name is May, and who "called her mother," one night. The spectators, who are trying to decide whether the "Woman's Voice" is May's or May's mother's, are still deprived of the final piece of information that will let them decide. If they assume that "V" is the mother's voice because of an analogy with the previously enacted dialogue which seemed to denote the presence of the mother (as voice answering May, the daughter), they are going to be surprised, because the voice tells the story of a girl who "called her mother," instead of talking about a girl who "called her." The morpho-syntactic ambiguity of "her" (which could be a personal pronoun or a possessive adjective) is paralleled by the ambiguity of the enunciation (who exactly is the subject of the enunciation?). The determination of reference is impossible, and reference is transformed into a hermeneutical hypothesis. The presumed mother does not say "she called me," and yet what the voice says seems to be the story of May's childhood, an intimate story that a mother could tell, even while representing herself as "mother," for the sake of objective impersonation. However, it is also possible to interpret the voice as May's, and imagine a May who is *speaking to* herself first (while using the first person pronoun, "I") and then *describes* herself (while using the "she" or her own name in a story about herself). Finally, it is also possible to imagine that the story about "a girl calling her mother" does not refer to May nor to her mother, and is simply the story of some unidentifiable mother-daughter relationship. However, a preference for the interpretation of the voice as May's seems acceptable in the light of the fact that when May speaks again on stage, her first words "Sequel. [. . .] Sequel"[30] seem to guarantee a narrative continuity, and perhaps promise a key to a final understanding of what has been a very confused verbal exchange and a very fragmentary, inconsequential story. However, no easy solution can be found, particularly since the characters enacted or evoked in the play become four (May, V, Mrs. Winter, and Amy), in spite of the fact that an apparent repetition of the same story occurs, now through the words actually spoken by May. The spectator is left to realize that memory can only produce bad repetitions, repetitions that are not linked to any existential or truly referential level.

At this point, he or she sees that the only reference posited in the text can be represented by the subject of the enunciation, but that this subjectivity emerges together with the sense of the inevitable division of the subject, whose identity is always separated from the conceptualized self that can be narrated. The final protagonist of *Footfalls* is a divided self mapped out by different discursive practices. Beckett's theater about experience becomes the movement of experience itself.

In Beckett's works, and particularly in these plays and in his recent antilyrical novels (novels that do not celebrate a subject, for the very reason that the subject itself is problematic in them), a "healthy" communication will eventually entail the establishment of a subject, whereas an "ill saying" keeps deferring it. All of these works reveal the intrinsic conflict faced by the subject, who needs to distinguish himself/herself but can rely only on a common language, a language that does not distinguish differences within identities while expressing visibility. In other words, the subject is caught in the dilemma of acquiring the visibility of language and the impossibility of expressing his or her extra-linguistic existence.

In his conception of identity Beckett never comes to share Hegel's notion of an "absolute spirit," devoid of alterity and contradiction, but

Hegel's notion of the "objective spirit" comes close to Beckett's idea of language and linguistic visibility inasmuch as the "objective spirit" represents the supra-individualistic and pervasive power of social and anthropological institutions, a power that does not depend on the freedom of any one subject.[31] In Beckett's works, including those of the 1970s and 1980s, the existential dialectics of consciousness and self-consciousness are portrayed as a conflict of contexts and of cotextual signs. Communication is charged with highly dramatic connotations because of the undecidability of reference, and because terms co-occurring in the same statement resemble near-synonyms but actually prove to be different and even untranslatable because of the diversity of their contexts. Thus the conflict of subject and concept is irresolvable because of the ultimate untranslatability of one into the other. This irreducible conflict is not new to Beckett; for example, we can look at *Not I* (1972) as a further variation on the theme of *Film* (1965), since it develops the same need to define a subject from the point of view of an observer. However, the final revelation of identity reached at the end of *Film* is not achieved in *Not I,* in which the dislocation of the subject remains as the result of a communicative tragedy. In *Film,* according to Beckett's directions: "It will not be clear until the end of film that pursuing perceiver is not extraneous but self."[32] After all, a revelation of identity is finally achieved. On the contrary, in *Not I* no unity of subject can be assessed, as the protagonist does not recover from "vehement refusal to relinquish third person."[33] The subject fails, till the end of the play, to perceive self as "I." This incapacity can easily be ascribed to a communicative failure, to an unbalanced relationship between "Mouth" and "Auditor," and extensively, also to a lack of balance in the relationship between a silent public and logorrhoeic actors. The issue of communicability is posed by the heterogeneous nature of the participants in the communication: "Mouth" is a character and also the metonymy of a character, while "Auditor" could be both a character (listening to "Mouth" as "other"), or another metonymy, perhaps even of the same subject, intent to listen to himself (the "ear" listening to the "mouth" speaking). However, the contextual irreducible ambiguity of the signs involved does not let the public come to a decision as to the unity or separate identity of the two (?) "characters," so that the spectator is literally caught into the articulation of a "Not I." He or she is faced by the presence of someone who cannot be ultimately defined, since the relationships between the characters can be conceptualized in an open number of ways, not leading to a final certainty.

Specifically, the iconic codes that represent a "mouth" and a "human being" also legitimize the allusions to a metonymy which relates them into a unity: the mouth is a "detail" of the auditor. Furthermore, the different position of Mouth and Auditor in relation to the stage, could represent the different positions of a unified subject, in relation to consciousness or self-consciousness. On the other hand, the verbal and rhetorical codes of the play present them as two characters, with equal power in terms of their identity as "characters" of a play. In other words Mouth is *qua* character similar to Auditor, but from an iconic point of view Mouth is only a part of Auditor, and so it remains for the whole play, under the spectators' eyes, in spite of counter-conceptualizations that respond to verbal codes and dramatic conventions.

The irresolvable entropy[34] of the play is reinforced by the disposition of space: Mouth is certainly "on stage" but where is Auditor? Outside or inside the theatrical space? Does "downstage" mean in an "extra-scene" or in another scene of the same theatrical space? These questions, again, remain unanswered, even though the spectators would probably tend to perceive the space of the actors as one, external to their space. However, the space of "reality" where the spectators situate themselves should include the theatrical space, which would then make it no longer external, and would make Auditor a different sort of character, a character representing the audience in general. In this way the spectators themselves have an experience of a fragmented self similar to them, of a "not I" which derives from the fracture of perception and thought which they themselves are experiencing, a "not I" deriving from a discrepancy in their awareness between the *meaning* of what they see, and *what* they literally see. Besides, a "not I" is found with the awareness of the interpretative quality that presides over any definition of phenomena, an awareness of a meaning that precedes any reading of the uninterpreted world, a meaning that presides over "in-tell-legibility." In this way the "not I" is not simply thematized or described, but is a meaning that occurs in the intelligent spectator, thanks to the repetition of the play. The "not I" is the experience of one's own meaning in relation to the power of language, the experience of a reality effect, not of a conceptual opposition. A staggering tragic irony catches the spectators in the trap of condemning in Mouth the same limitations they bear: they suffer because of Mouth's inability to draw objective borders while they themselves oscillate in and out of the theatrical space, divided selves incapable of either rejecting or of accepting an assimilation with Auditor, incapable of establishing contextual borders. In any case, it is important to note that a "not I" always results from the structural or functional shortcomings of the communicative system: logorrhoea points to a scattered subject, incapable of identification. Silence, on the other hand, indicates a closed subject, incapable of relating to anything other than itself and suffering from the objective alienation engendered by such a relational incapacity. In fact, silence can constitute the other only as an object, whereas an attempt at communication would somehow indicate the acknowledgement of the other as person. Silence produces a "not I" object, something totally other, just as much as logorrhea reveals a "not I" subject, incapable of receiving a reply in a true dialogical exchange. In both cases the subject cannot be constituted as "I" because the presuppositions for a "healthy" communication are lacking: an "I" cannot be structured because there is no dialectical other, so that speech is always monological rather than dialogical. Structurally, the great monologue eroded by pauses constituting *Not I* comes to a tragic climax when Mouth acknowledges herself but goes on refusing self-perception, incapable of appropriating her own words about herself. No existential linking of past and present, and the atemporality of conceptualization put Mouth in the trap of a continuous deferral of self-awareness. See the tragic conceptual continuity of the following passage:

> when suddenly she realized . . . words were–. . . what? . . who? . .no! . . she! . . / *Pause and movement 2* / . . . realized . . . words were coming . . . imagine! . . words were coming . . . a voice she did not recognize . . . at first . . . so long since it had sounded . . . then finally had to admit . . . could be none other . . . than her own . . . [. . .] till she began trying to . . . delude herself . . . it was not hers at all . . . not her voice at all . . .[35]

The problem of self-identification is structured through remarks that deeply involve the relationship of semantics and cognition: the logical links that organize discourse can produce a semantic development which is totally removed from existential connections. This gap can occur precisely because language is "not felt at all," as the following quotation suggests:

> gradually she felt . . . her lips moving . . . imagine! . . her lips moving! . . . as of course till then she had not . . . and not alone the lips . . . the cheeks . . . the jaws . . . the whole face . . . all those–. . . what? . . the tongue? . . yes . . . the tongue in the mouth . . . all those contortions without which . . . no speech possible . . . and yet in the ordinary way . . . not felt at all . . . so intent one is . . . on what one is saying . . . the whole being . . . hanging on its words . . .[36]

The tragic thematization of consciousness in relation to language points to the existence of "all those contortions without which no speech is possible." We must notice that they are not simply physical but conceptual, and they condition perception. The "contortions" described by Mouth simultaneously constitute and obliterate speech and consciousness. Insisting on speech as she does binds her to the limits of a metalanguage, rather than opening her consciousness to a sense of self. Consciousness should be "intermittent" in order to lead to self-consciousness and to the constitution of an I. But Mouth is trapped by the objectifying continuity of consciousness, either as consciousness of an investment in meaning ("so intent one is on *what* one is saying") or as consciousness of the actual production of speech ("and not alone the lips . . . the cheeks . . . the jaws . . . the whole face"), or also as consciousness of the structure of speech itself ("the whole being hanging on its words"). The absolute need to fill consciousness with an object prevents Mouth from acknowledging herself as the site of all those operations: for her the mind is an object and the body has to be a "she." The tragic irony about her metalanguage consists in the fact that it never leads her to the perception of a subject of the enunciation in tune with the spoken message. The impossibility of perceiving her own subjectivity even while speaking depends on the fact that she can only see that she is speaking *about her*self, ignoring the fact that *she is* speaking. Furthermore, the lack of self-awareness makes her intentionality of saying disappear into "what she is saying," so that coincidence of meaning and will to mean is dramatically portrayed as the impossibility of stopping the verbal flux:

> no idea what she's saying . . . imagine! . . no idea what she's saying! . . and can't stop . . . no stopping it.[37]

For Mouth, the "vehement refusal to relinquish third person" is one with the tragic incapacity of "losing herself" which, however, is a precondition to "finding herself."[38] Narration could produce self-identification as a result of the appropriation of one's self, seen as narrator of one's own story. However, for Mouth her story becomes a systematic negation of self-reference, because no opening onto the enunciation ever occurs, so that her own story is made of mere words: it is a deceiving pseudo-autobiography. The personal pronoun she uses never enters into a speech act, producing performative effects. It remains a purely abstract designation of a position, a syntactic preference that is devoid of any referential meaning. The pronoun is no more than a pure textual anaphora and produces no trace of self.

Alec Reid has described Krapp's words as "immaterial," and has spoken about "words that have no context" in the case of *Play* (1962). That is absolutely correct, but we cannot forget that the tragic knowledge of Beckett's drama derives from the fact that those "immaterial" words always tend towards reference; they are tragic because they are precise *and* immaterial. The impossibility of establishing reference or retrieving it constitutes the essence of Beckett's epistemic tragedies. His works display, in the words of Derrida, an "anxiety about language which can only be an anxiety of language, within language itself."[39] Anxiety ensues precisely from the fact that, even without context, Beckett's words always relate to reality and phenomena.

The Problem of Temporality

The great innovation concerning temporality in Beckett's recent works is not so much the inclusion of the "writing time" of the story with the "story time "[40] as it is the exploitation of temporal incongruities in order to point to the way in which narration, or dramatic use of time, structures meaning.

Allusion to the writing time is a common feature of many modern artifacts which represent the recounting time as part of the represented time. In Beckett, however, the effects of this coexistence are exploited in such a way that what emerges from his works is not primarily the artificial nature of narration but the impossibility of reducing existence to some sort of unity. In the words of Nietzsche, "the overall character of existence may not be interpreted by means of the concept of 'aim,' the concept of 'unity,' or the concept of 'truth'."[41] And yet, "Once we have devaluated these three categories, the demonstration that they cannot be applied to the universe is no longer any reason for devaluating the universe."[42] The manipulation of temporality seems the crucial key to understanding Beckett's "nihilism" as extremely ironical and not dogmatically negative. It is also crucial for the understanding of his concept of mimesis: in fact his representations do not portray the universe according to the categories of aim, unity and truth, but they do not devaluate the universe either. Beckett attacks mimetic illustrations of time because they conceal the irreducibly a-categorial, polymorphic character of existence; yet, time is an essential feature of his aesthetic representations. In fact, I believe that he aims at representing things as determined by their intrinsic duration, and human beings as determined by their own, specific mortality.

In my previous reading of *Footfalls* I tried to show the limits of naming in relation to the definition of identity. I maintained that the shortcomings of naming in the play can only be posited in relation to reference and, further-more, that the problematic nature of reference in Beckett's works is largely dependent on the fact that he tries to illustrate its intrinsic temporality. Thus, the distinguishing feature of Beckett's "objects" is their chronologi-cal duration; there is no such thing as a "still life" in his portraiture of reality. According to him, reference is dynamic and should not be other-wise, precisely because it does not represent the thing "in itself," as a concept, but represents it as a result of visibility. In fact, in *Footfalls,* for example, the dramatic impossibility of answering questions such as "whose is the voice speaking to May? " or "is May the same as Amy?" derives also from the fact that there is no chronological order in the exposition of events. The incapacity of providing specific answers comes to be felt as tragic because the whole vision of the universe is thus shown to be depen-dent on a degree of convention that establishes that life can be understood only when it is arranged. After all, the Greek word "κοσμος" means "order," and the Latin word "universum" insists on the necessity of one direction for such ordering.[43] Beckett shows us that together with spatial ordering we need temporal ordering because, to borrow Philip Larkin's words, "days are where we live."[44] The narratives we understand are chron-ologically arranged according to conventions that seem natural to us only because they provide interpretations of life through representations of time. If events are presented to us in a non-systematic or unusual way, we need time, and we have to take time, to arrange them into a system that makes them intelligible. This "reader's time," a time of understanding which is external to the text conceived as an object, has an important role in Beckett's works, because it is shown as necessary for the constitution of the text as communication, because it animates reference. The spectator's time is normally hidden, because the time of understanding of linear, mimetic narratives coincides with the time of the representation of events, or obeys the habitual laws of chronological ordering. However, in Beckett this spectator's time can be expressed, once the coincidence of the time of performance (or of reading) with the time of understanding is abolished. When the meaning of the units of the text does not develop according to a common sequential chronology, the reader's time, that is, the hermeneu-tical time, becomes evident.

If, as in *Footfalls,* referential units are problematic and their exegesis requires more time than their perception, the spectator has an interpretative option: either ignore referentiality and decide in favor of a symbolic coherence, or try to interpret referentiality on a different basis, including temporality. The latter option seems Beckett's hermeneutical challenge, particularly in his works for the theater, where the semantic stability of linguistic notations can only be decided in relation to the issue of the theatrical immediate, that is, of the evidence ("mental") of what is actually there ("physical"). This means that referentiality cannot be ignored in a hermeneutics of Beckett's theater, even if reference relates to a diachronic object which, as referent, becomes the object of different, subsequent projects of meaning. It may seem hard to recognize reference because it is constituted by the temporal nature of interpretation, but this reference as process is really a recurrent feature of Beckett's works, and no exegesis of textual meanings can be fulfilled without it.

For some critics, one way of avoiding the sequential nature of the various, perhaps rival projects of interpretation of referential elements in the text is constituted by a total bypassing of reference. Symbolic, allegorical or ideological readings are endowed with a coherence that can be totally external to the textual elements, even though it is obviously internal to various disciplines to which critical methodologies refer (psychology, philosophy, aesthetics, etc.). However, these hermeneutical options would result in a mere tautological imposition of an external meaning onto the text, and the reading of the text becomes an imposition of a meaning devoid of its duration.

For example, one could say that *Footfalls* is incoherent precisely because it is a play about the absurd. Yet this would be a hermeneutical circumvention of the text, as well as of the readers of such an interpretation. In fact, the understanding of a play (and of a text in general) is not simply a formal relationship between a part and a whole: it is a diachronic process involving the interpretation of the actual elements on which the text is based. A lot of these elements are referential, even when the determination of reference is problematic, and they have to be interpreted in relation to reality. Only by maintaining reference as an interpretive option, can what is up to a point an invisible reality become a "visible" one, through textual, diachronic hypothesis. This unveiling of the hidden reality of the process of perception, this epiphany of the process leading to visibility, is essential in Beckett's representations. His plays deconstruct visibility and show how the "seen" is always already the result of a process of perceptive repetition.

As I have said, *Footfalls* compels the spectator to reformulate several anticipations of meaning; in time these become semantic hypotheses, rather than plausible expectations. In the process of interpretation these hypotheses work as referents; in this sense temporality affects, and is shown to affect, textual meanings and the nature of reference itself: reference becomes diachronic rather than conceptual. In Beckett's theatrical works reference to the immediate is produced through incongruous referents that come to show time as the foundation of the event of understanding, and subsequently, they come to show the temporal nature of objects. Furthermore, in the light of the present of the understanding, symbolic temporality shows its conventional nature, but also how deeply it affects the nature of perception, which is always already an interpretation. The evidence of the present, as the time of the interpretation of what is before our eyes, can extend Larkin's question "where can we live but days?"[45] into further, parallel questions such as "can we live without interpreting?" and "how can we interpret, but in time?"

Beckett's theatrical double produces the perception of a time of interpretation that does not coincide with the time of representation. The *evidence* of what is seen does not overlap with *what* is physically present before our eyes. Thus, a theatrical double that involves the immediate as time of the interpretation of what is seen shows the conventional nature of the temporal ordering in representations, as well as the temporal quality of knowing. In other words, the theatrical double shows the visibility of what we see. In this sense, the movement of understanding does not abolish reference, but firmly relates to it and shows its temporal and noncategorical determination. Beckett's theatrical double shows us that things do remain on stage while their linguistic constitution defines them diachronically. If, as Heidegger maintained in *Being and Time,* understanding is a "categorial fundamental determination of the being-there of humans,"[46] the showing of such an understanding connotes the theater as the main road to the understanding of understanding as being structurally temporal, not only because the process of knowing can be self-reflected in representation, but because the sequence of masks produces the unmasking of symbolic temporality. The theater becomes the mirror of the theatrical quality of experience: it enacts the impermanence of determinations, through the display of different masks (facts reproduced as theatrical acts), and at the same time it shows the impossibility of their repetition (because theatrical acts immediately become facts).

The importance of reference can be shown by the typology of characters in *Footfalls,* because no "formal" clue can help in the explanation of the referential complexity of the text. In fact, even when the sophisticated spectator recognizes and enjoys ludic disseminations and paronomastic inversions within the protagonist's name, still, he or she cannot determine her identity. The fact that "May" later on becomes "Amy" does not provide any clue for recognizing her (as the same or as a different "daughter"), in spite of the sameness of the letters spelling her name. Furthermore, the reader who can appreciate the familiar Beckettian inversions of "M" into "W" and the truncated inversion of "M" into "V" can only conjecture about the possibility that May is related to Mrs. Winter as "M" is related to "W," or that the "Woman's Voice" is a part of "May" as much as "V" is a part of "M." Amy could mirror herself in a part of herself, her own voice "V" being a metonymical acoustic image of her entire being. The reader will never find a final, objective answer to these questions, yet this prolonged series of metonymies succeeds in showing identity as duration. These literary hyper-determinations[47] underline the fictitious nature of literary artifacts, but above all they lead interpretation beyond the literal boundaries of the letter of the text, showing its perpetual diachronic differing from itself. Formal hints such as parallelisms and analogies compel the reader to reformulate a series of successive hypotheses about the unity of the text, but it is impossible not to take reality and existence into account as grounds of reference and time of interpretation. Formal analogues do not bind the structure of meaning onto an abstract conceptual level, and in spite of apparent clues of interpretation they provide no explanation of the referential obscurities which remain the real problem of the play. Formal structures push interpretation towards the abstract levels of conceptual allusions, only to find that the terms of the allusions remain void, often lacking formal counterparts that confirm the meaning of the allusion itself. This means that ultimately these formalized elements are only meant to show the tension between literality and reference within the text, until reference is seen as a dynamic element, and the real, in turn, is seen as the place of the process of interpretation.

The referentiality of textual units emerges even when reference cannot be defined, either because formalized elements prove too unsystematic, incapable of articulating complete formal messages, or because they prove incapable of providing clues that go beyond the self-reflexivity of the text. Against a metalanguage, circumscribed and circumscribing the literality of the text, referential interpretation is shown as the only way to articulate an existential sequence of meaning, ultimately a real "textual movement," that is, the movement of the text which actually comes to coincide with the movement of interpretation. Reference proves to be the root from which the movement of understanding had begun. Beckett's theater shows the necessity of including the immediacy of the present of the interpretation in those textual obscurities that can thus point to the non-unity of the real. If the polymorphic nature of reality has to be represented, representation certainly has to include the actualization of its being understood, thus showing the limits of all purely conceptual interpretations. The present has to become the site of the dramatic powerlessness to unify reality through formal interpretation. Beckett's theater is a temporal icon of the non-unity of the real: the time of the events shown is always interacting with the present of representation. His extremely lucid manipulation of temporality prevents his obscurities from becoming mere incongruities: time constitutes them as referential units rather than conceptual contradictions.

Significantly, in *Footfalls* we are told that for a definition of footfalls, "the motion alone is not enough, I must hear the feet, however faint they fall."[48] Thus, an explicit contrast is established between the conceptual nature of movement and the actuality of its perception. The theater can represent the difference between "steps" and "footfalls" through the use of signs whose varying degree of referentiality and modes of reference express different degrees of presence within conventional signs. In this sense, reference can block a virtually unlimited proliferation of hermeneutical possibilities. The subjects of enunciation become the only real protagonists of Beckett's plays because they are undisputably the only actual referents of the play. Only reference, as a form of presence in the sign, can regulate the richly unlimited, yet sometimes alienating possibilities of linguistic games. After all, *Footfalls* ends with a thematization of the problem of presence: "How could you have responded if you were not there?"[49] asks one of the protagonists of the story told, and a repeated question, similar in its structure, and still positing the problem of presence, puts a seal on both the first and third part of the play:

> . . . /*Pause*/ Will you never have done? /*Pause*/ Will you never have done . . . revolving it all? /*Pause*/ It? /*Pause*/ It all. /*Pause*/ In your poor mind. /*Pause*/ It all. /*Pause*/ It all.[50]

The possibility of "revolving it all" pertains only to the abstract: there is no such reversibility in the "real" world, and an end to the possibility of unlimited reversal can only be found in relation to reality. The issue of reversibility and symmetry also applies to the interpretation of the text itself: if one wants to avoid informational entropy one must stop ignoring referentiality, however difficult it may be to specify referents in a play that systematically confounds narration and discourse, dialogue and mono-logue. Reference regulates the process of anticipation of meaning, even if realistic effects are not the primary scope of the text and even when refer-ence itself is not specifically determined. We must remember that reference in Beckett is not an analogue of traditional mimesis: on the contrary, it is a form of diachronic reproduction of reality which establishes "the thing" as the result of a process. Beckett's referents reproduce things as intrinsically temporal. Their incompleteness as referents, their lack of context, repro-duces both the duration of things and the diachronic process of their definition. Interpretive readings have to be formulated and reformulated again and again, as hypotheses which constitute the real movement of the text, a movement so real as to involve the present.

Beckett's use of dramatic temporality runs opposite to the use of mi-metic temporality; if traditional drama, and narration in particular, tend to hide the conditions of the enunciation, Beckett keeps showing that chro-nology can become informative only in relation to the enunciation. Refer-ential information can be conveyed only in direct relation to the enunciative situation. At times there is a blatant contradiction among the chronological indications given by the same text, and incongruence comes to indicate the presence of the subjects of the enunciation, as a possible source of clarifica-tion. Interesting discrepancies between linguistic and existential time de-nounce the fictional nature of information, especially when the conditions of enunciation are hidden. In this respect, Artaud's belief that the theater doubles life underlines the fact that the theater doubles the existential, un-iconic time of life, with linguistic ("symbolic") representations of time itself. Furthermore, the theater doubles life because it reproduces that repressed primary scene in which life presents itself as the presence of what is there, a presence that is one with the "what" as it is seen. Significantly, in the letter to Jean Paulhan that I have already quoted, Artaud wrote: "It is on the stage that the union of thought, gesture and act is reconstituted."[51] On the other hand, "life doubles true theater" because of the primordial quality of repetition as a theatrical sign of the immediate, a sign that organizes perception of what is immediately recognizable as life. Life doubles true theater in the sense that it exceeds the moment of its original representa-tion: the epiphanic moment of representation (of reality as it is) can be connoted as preceding semiotic conceptualization but only when semiotic conceptualization has already occurred. So, as it goes on, life continually copies (doubles) the linguistic event in which the present presents itself, while being the repetition of the primary "theatrical" appearance of phenomena. Obviously one cannot expect the emergence of pure presence from the systematic texture of textual signs; in fact, as Jacques Derrida has repeatedly explained, "Presence, in order to be presence and self-presence, has always already begun to represent itself, has always already been penetrated."[52] However, it is important to acknowledge the fact that Beckett keeps challenging the borders of textuality, and keeps showing how a text opens onto the presence of its enunciation.

In *That Time* (1976), for example, the use of a vocal polyphony, one voice as a "threefold source"[53] expressing the unity of a subject, shows the difference between good and bad repetition. A bad repetition is habit, or the presumed return of sameness; a good repetition brings forward the cogent theatrical quality of any experience when oriented towards knowledge. A good repetition entails the vision of the double, an epistemic vision of experience as knowledge.[54] Together with the impossibility of pure repetition, that is, together with the impossibility of a return of sameness, *That Time* shows how a subject is always constituted in time, and how, in the words of Michel Foucault, "time is always more dissolved than thought."[55] The "dissolution" of time challenges the principle of non-contradiction. Significantly, Beckett's introductory note to the play requires the enacting of the character through "moments of one and the same voice,"[56] thus undermining the metaphysical unity of the "one and the same" with the scattered diachrony of "moments." The law of non-contradiction can only be formulated as a result of a temporal suspension; the issue of self-sameness can only be applied to a conceptual definition of self, a definition that deprives subjectivity of its intrinsic diachronic structure and of its internal difference (of self, existing while differing from itself).

The title of the play, *That Time,* provides a clue to the crucial problem developed in it, in much the same way as in *Not I* (1972), *Footfalls* (1976), and *What Where* (1983). The exegesis of *That Time* must confront the problem of temporal figuration: time is shown at the root of representation and diachrony becomes the indispensable factor of a correct representation. The great many referential uncertainties of the play (the recurrent "whosoever," "whoever," "whenever," etc.) point to the fact that the structure of reference is a matter of temporality, and that time is necessarily implicit in every referential designation. The play goes even further, and thematizes the fact that past events keep changing because of the passing of time, and because of the successive enunciations of the same event. Representations are necessarily bound to differ because of the diachronic structure of the enunciation. However, time is not only the "devouring time" of human life, but it is also the condition of self-awareness, the indispensable medium of successive, incessant self-representations. The strongest cohesion among the different tones of the speaking voice in *That Time* is to be found in the awareness of the temporal flux expressed in each message. Yet, at the same time, the hardest and most problematic reference to be established is precisely the temporal reference. In fact, the uncertainty at the core of the definition of reference shows that even the affirmation "that time" is always an implicit question about "what time," and that it has no sense outside its enunciation. Even when statements are made by the same voice and presumably refer to the same event, the representations of this event are diachronically different. So statements become questionable in relation to the act of the enunciation. In the play the voice differs not only because of its different pitch at different moments, but because tones emphasize different aspects of temporality. It seems to me that "A" is preoccupied with continuity, "B" with temporal distinctions (exemplified by the symbolic dichotomy of "after" and "before"), and "C" with the awareness of one's own mortality. Polyphony helps represent mortality as different from death, being a constant experience of life. Mortality is experienced while living as the impossibility of recapturing one's own lived moments. It is not a metaphysical experience of the end, but the common experience of ending. One's own mortality is experienced as irreversibility, and it transforms the abstract conception of death into the disturbing awareness of the impossible definition of death's boundaries. In the words of "C" we find a representation of one's own realization of one's incapacity of being what one was, together with the impossibility of indicating death's precise beginning:

> Never the same after that never quite the same but that was nothing new if it wasn't this it was the common occurrence something you could never be the same after crawling about year after year sunk in your lifelong mess muttering to yourself who else you'll never be the same after this you were never the same after that.[57]

The awareness of the polyphonic protagonist of *That Time* is almost the opposite of the non-awareness of a "not I," and its complexity derives from the fact that the present manages to open the stage of time, and to reveal itself as the time of the staging of the self. However, the sense of tragedy cannot be avoided because, in the words of Derrida: "*the present offers itself* as such, appears, presents itself, opens the stage of time or the time of the stage *only by harboring its own intestine difference,* and only in the interior fold of its original repetition in representation."[58] A climax is reached at the end of the play, when the spiraling doubt expressed a few moments earlier—"was that the time or was that another time another place another time"[59]—finds an answer in the vertigo of impending death and in the evidence of "the common occurrence" of one's own mortality:

> was that it something like that come and gone come and gone no one come and gone in no time gone in no time[60]

Along the lines of a "theatrum philosophicum," representation becomes a further investigation of the nature of reference, and the importance of temporality is emphasized by positing the issue of reference in strict relation to the enunciative situation.

Beckett's latest play, *What Where* (1983), represents the failure and, quite literally, the torture one encounters while attempting to represent reality, even when including the enunciation in the representation. In fact, the sequence of proliferating "what" and "where" is virtually endless and self-perpetuating, as enunciations are bound to become messages, endlessly. Each image contains in itself the conditions of its production; these can be considered as possible elements of the representation itself. When the conditions of representation are questioned, one can see that they can be represented, but only at the cost of transforming the enunciative act into the fact of a story. A significant fragment of dialogue from *What Where* can illustrate this point:

> BIM: *What* must he confess?
> BAM: That he said it to him.
> BIM: Is that all?
> BAM: *And what.*
> V.: Good.
> BIM: Is that all?
> BAM: Yes.
> BIM: Then stop?
> BAM: Yes.[61]

As one can see, the question is structured as a double question since it regards both the content of the message and the occurrence of its enunciation: Bam seems eager to know whether an enunciation occurred, and what the message was. Later on a similar, double question recurs, in a dialogue between Bam and Bem:

> BAM: Take him away and give him the works until he confesses.
> BEM: What must he confess?
> BAM: That he said where to him.
> BEM: Is that all?
> BAM: And where.[62]

These recurrent questions significantly emphasize enunciations, in the sense that reference is shown to be dependent on the act of enunciation as the precondition to a representation of reality. Besides, the dramatic situation mirrors the act of enunciation because the whole play is structured as a questioning about questioning, as a series of interrogations about interrogations. The spectator is made to realize that, however hidden, the enunciation is actually the only means of realization of a representation. Furthermore, the conditions of the enunciation are to be found in the present, a time which can be either hidden or symbolically expressed. The present is, in the words of the play, a "time without words, at first," or else it is a "*now,* a time with words." The present can be designated or not, but unlike the "what where," which can be identified merely as the objects of different enunciations, the present is the condition, but not necessarily the object, of the enunciation. "Without journey. Time passes," says "V" (Voice of Bam) at the end of the play; it reminds us that time passes whether or not there are words to indicate it, whether or not objects and space seem to change. At the opening of the play we hear:

> We are the last five.
> In the present as were we still.
> It is spring.
> Time passes.
> First without words.
> I switch on.[63]

It is a situation of "general dark," when it is even possible to conceive of "the present as were we still," that is, when it is possible to believe that the self can be still or immortal, almost as if the "what where" elements of reality did not change because of time. Most representations produce the illusion that time does not pass, yet Beckett keeps reminding us that "time passes." This is the only recurrent, invariable statement throughout the whole play, either when time is represented or not represented in it (and designated respectively as "time with" or "time without" words). At different times in the play we hear that we are in spring, summer, autumn or winter; we can even imagine time as a sequence, because of this representation, but we cannot escape time's inexorable flux. However, the passing of time cannot be properly described, because it is also the condition of description. Time does not belong to the realities of the "what where"; it is categorical, even when hidden or disguised by symbolical representations. Time is always the condition of the designation and in this sense it cannot designate itself.

At the end of the play, as we shall see, the protagonist urges: "make sense who may." Indeed the expression of time that has occurred in the play demands a new way of making sense. In this light "V," who has been constructing the world as he pleased ("starting again" whenever he was not happy with what he wanted to see), is making a revolutionary request. His awareness leads him to renounce determining meaning because he becomes imbued with the awareness of time that passes. His mind opens onto the possibility of having no control on the appearance of "sense." The vision of time as categorical reveals how every conceptual construction of meaning transforms knowledge into a predetermination, and reality into a stage.

The role of the "downstage" in relation to the "playing area" is very significant also in this play, because it maps out the limited powers of "V" as a creator of reality. After all, he is always contained by a wider space and is determined by the "what where" that time transforms. In the final, total darkness he concludes his act with a "better failure" because he finally ends his staging of reality, having seen the limits of his decisions to "switch on" or "switch off," decisions that do not reach the ultimate boundaries of the chronological real. He says:

Without Journey.
Time passes.
That is all.
Make sense who may.
I switch off.[64]

We must notice that his final "I switch off" is radically different from the previous ones, not only because it literally indicates that we are at the end of the play and that there will be no sequence to "V" 's staging of reality, but also because his renunciation grows out of a declared impotence: "Make sense who may." The creator "V" finds the limits of his creation when he sees time as the unforeseen but more powerful agon in the determination of reality. The romantic belief in truth and beauty, "all / Ye know on earth, and all ye need to know"[65] has become a modern revelation: "Time passes. That is all." A new "negative capability" is needed, as a capacity of surrender and acceptance, perhaps as the capability of a "Gelassenheit."[66]

Conclusions: Repetition as the Denial of Tautology

Many critics, most recently Martin Esslin, have pointed to the fact that "Beckett's theater has always been primarily a theater of images,"[67] and that

> Beckett has reached the point zero of language, the compression of the maximum of experience into the most telling and graphic metaphor which could then be incarnated, made visible and audible, in the most concise and concrete form of a living, moving image.[68]

Even though it is not literally possible to "reach the point zero of language" in a play, I think that these suggestions are very valuable because they indicate the tension towards drastic reduction, a tension which is typical of Beckett's works. Furthermore, in the light of a distinction between verbal language and a strictly iconic, visual language I think that Beckett's preference for "graphic metaphors" points to the specificity of his theatrical works, to the quality of his many "acts without words." A different quality of language distinguishes his prose from his plays, even when a remarkable thematic similarity proves the continuity of all his recent works. The theater shows how visual images inevitably become verbal metaphors in the eyes of the beholder, and the prose works show how every illustration is an abstraction.

Furthermore, I think that Esslin's "maximum of experience, compressed in the most concise form" should be interpreted in relation to what I have called his "poetics of impotence." The "maximum" of Beckett's works is constituted by the unveiling of the essential conditions of experience, rather than by the illustration of a variety of experiences. His investigation of those conditions, carried out through drastic and progressive reductions of themes and linguistic structures, produces a sort of epistemological maximum. Beckett's subtractions open before our modern eyes those issues that traditional philosophy has called "categorical issues." He has surprised us by showing that the maximum is achieved through simplification: he has formulated the most complex image of reality by unwording the words we use to construct it.

Visibility, which is both iconic and linguistic, is a main issue at the core of Beckett's representations, and his greatest innovation is in the fact that he shows us that visibility cannot be conceived outside of time. The theater, because of the simultaneity of the codes it employs (unlike narration, which is based on the linearity of verbal language) can posit the issue of visibility in relation to the immediate. Beckett's theater exploits the theatrical double in showing how the determinations of visibility are a matter of tropological movements that diachronically link figures and concepts. The visual codes of drama, mixing with verbal codes (which are used most of the time directly on stage, and always in the present of the interpretation), produce the representation of non-tautological relationships between subject and predicate. Particularly in the theater, the interplay of "seen" and "said" develops the awareness of the figurative quality of language as the interpretive quality implied in all definitions. Beckett's theater reveals the tropological, diachronic movements that produce the effect of reality, effects because the links between figure and concept are not atemporal, but constitute the *process* through which reality is constructed. His plays display what Foucault calls "the genitality of thought," in a critique of common sense that makes him assert:

> The morally good-will of thinking within the lines of a common sense basically had the function of protecting thought from its singular "genitality."[69]

In Beckett, thought is no longer "protected" from its internal differences; on the contrary, his recent plays transform conceptual connections into mere hypotheses of interpretation. Spectators have to formulate hypotheses throughout the whole play without finding any stable confirmation to them, because the context of every figure cannot be determined. By eroding the effectiveness of the links between figures and concepts, by diminishing the hidden power that determines the interpretation of reality, he reveals the enormous effects of figurality and, most important, he brings forth the unseen struggle of difference within the visible.

Beckett's theater deconstructs the performative figurality of language through the literality of a theatrical performance. He doubles the performance of figurality by using theatrical signs, signs that show the fact that what is shown can be shown only because it has already been said and seen.

Notes

1. For a discussion of cultural typologies from a semiotic point of view see Jurij M. Lotman and Boris A. Uspenskij, "O semioticeskom mechanizme kul'tury," *Trudy po znakovym sistemam* III (Tartu: Tartu University, *Studies in Sign Systems* Vol. 3, 1971); Italian translation: *Tipologia della cultura,* R. Faccani and M. Marzaduri, eds. (Milan: Bompiani, 1975), and "Problems in the Typology of Culture" in *Soviet Semiotics: An Anthology,* Daniel P. Lucid, ed. (Baltimore and London: Johns Hopkins University Press, 1977). See also Cesare Segre, *Semiotica e cultura* (Padova: Liviana, 1977) and *Semiotica filologica: testo e modelli culturali* (Torino: Einaudi, 1979).

2. Antonin Artaud, quoted in Jacques Derrida, *Writing and Difference,* translated with an Introduction by Alan Bass (London: Routledge & Kegan Paul, 1978) p. 333.

3. For a discussion of repetition as a basic category of Kierkegaard's thought see *Gjentagelsen* (1843) and *Frygt of Baeven* (1843), translated as *Repetition* with *Fear and Trembling,* Howard V. Hong and Edna H. Hong, eds. and trans., in *Kierkegaard's Writings* VI (Princeton, N.J.: Princeton University Press, 1983). See also *Begrebet Angest* (1844), translated as *The Concept of Anxiety,* Howard and Edna Hong, eds.; translated by R. Thomte in collaboration with A. B. Anderson, in *Kierkegaard's Writings* VIII (Princeton, N.J.: Princeton University Press, 1980). Kierkegaard's existentialist critique of Hegel's dialectics certainly deserves a much lengthier discussion and more textual evidence than I can supply here. However, a few quotations from the *Concluding Unscientific Postscript,* Walter Lowrie, trans. (Princeton, N.J.: Princeton University Press, 1941), excerpted as "Concluding Unscientific Postscript" in *Deconstruction in Context,* Mark C. Taylor, ed. (Chicago and London: University of Chicago Press, 1986) pp. 170, 175, 184 should help to emphasize his critique of conceptual abstraction. Kierkegaard maintains that if being is understood according to Hegel, "as the abstract reflection of, or the abstract prototype for, what being is as concrete empirical being," then

   there is nothing to prevent us from abstractly determining the truth as abstractly finished and complete. [. . .] But if being is understood in this manner, the formula becomes a tautology. Thought and being mean one and the same thing, and the correspondence spoken of is merely an abstract self-identity. [. . .] In this manner we give expression to the fact that truth is not something simple, but is in a wholly abstract sense a reduplication, a reduplication which is nevertheless instantly revoked. Abstract thought may continue as long as it likes to rewrite this thought in varying phraseology, it will never get any farther.

   Furthermore, Kierkegaard's imperative "to hold fast what it means to be a human being" brings him to reformulate the Hegelian idea of dialectics:

   It is not possible for an existing individual, least of all *as* an existing individual, to hold fast absolutely a suspension of the dialectical moment, namely, existence. This would require another medium than existence, which is the dialectical moment. If an existing individual can become conscious of such a suspension, it can be only as a possibility.

4. Paul de Man discusses at length the referential function of language in relation to natural cognition. In *The Resistance to Theory* (Minneapolis: University of Minnesota Press, 1986) p. 11, he writes:

In a genuine semiology as well as in other linguistically oriented theories, the referential function of language is not being denied—far from it; what is in question is its authority as a model for natural or phenomenal cognition. Literature is fiction not because it somehow refuses to acknowledge "reality," but because it is not *a priori* certain that language functions according to principles which are those, or which are *like* those, of the phenomenal world. [. . .] What we call ideology is precisely the confusion of linguistic with natural reality, of reference with phenomenalism."

Similar epistemological problems are raised in the works of various contemporary theorists. Julia Kristeva opposes "matter" and "sense"; see *Polylogue* (Paris: Seuil, 1977), partly translated in *Desire in Language,* Leon S. Roudiez ed., T. Gora, A. Jardine and L. S. Roudiez, trans. (New York: Columbia University Press, 1980) and *Révolution du langage poétique* (Paris: Seuil, 1974), English translation: *Revolution in Poetic Language,* Margaret Waller, trans., L. S. Roudiez, Introd. (New York: Columbia University Press, 1984). Jacques Derrida formulates and works with a sort of opposition between "différance" and "presence." See in particular *De la Grammatologie* (Paris: Éditions de Minuit, 1967), English translation: *Of Grammatology,* Gayatri Chakravorty Spivak, trans. (Baltimore and London: Johns Hopkins University Press, 1976) and *La Dissémination* (Paris: Seuil, 1972), English translation: *Dissémination,* Barbara Johnson, trans. (Chicago: University of Chicago Press, 1981).

5. In order to clarify the significant difference between "designation" and "expression" from a semiotic point of view, I would like to recall Marcello Pagnini's presentation of Lazar Osipovic Rèznikov's definition: "The sign designates the object—he says—and expresses the signified." *The Pragmatics of Literature,* Nancy Jones-Henry, trans. (Bloomington and Indianapolis: Indiana University Press, 1987), p. 107. For the problem of reference, see also Chapter 4.

6. Friedrich Nietzsche, *The Will to Power* (New York: Random House, 1968). The quotation is given in *Deconstruction in Context,* p. 198.

7. For a discussion of the problems of the "play within the play," of the theatrical device of *mise en abîme,* and of the relations between scenes, and "scene and extra-scene" see Cesare Segre, *Teatro e romanzo* (Torino: Einaudi, 1984), and in particular Chapter 4. See also R. J. Nelson, *Play within a Play: The Dramatist's Conception of his Art: Shakespeare to Anouilh* (New Haven, Conn.: Yale University Press, 1958).

8. Paul de Man, *The Resistance to Theory,* p. 10.

9. The quotation in English, from Nietzsche's essay "On Truth and Lie in an Extramoral Sense," is given by Paul de Man in "Rhetoric of Tropes (Nietzsche)" in *Allegories of Reading* (New Haven, Conn. and London: Yale University Press, 1979) p. 110. The original German reads as follows: "Was ist also Wahrheit? Ein bewegliches Heer von Metaphern, Metonymien, Antropomorphismen . . ." Friedrich Nietzsche, "Über Wahrheit und Lüge im ausser-moralischen Sinn" in *Werke,* Karl Schlechta, ed. (Munich: Carl Hauser, 1966), III, p. 314.

10. Paul de Man, *The Resistance to Theory,* p. 10.

11. Samuel Beckett, "Footfalls" in *Collected Shorter Plays* (London and Boston: Faber and Faber, 1984) p. 241. All subsequent references to Beckett's plays are to this edition.

12. Samuel Beckett, "Ohio Impromptu" in *Collected Shorter Plays*, p. 288.
13. I would like to specify that I am discussing only Beckett's works for the theater, without any reference to his radio or TV plays of the same period. This is because the dialectics of "visibility/readability," which are critically approached here in relation to his prose and theater works, are very different in radio and TV works. Specifically, the sign composition of these works is different from the materiality of signs in drama. This diversity opens considerable theoretical problems regarding the stability of verbal notations in relation to the virtuality of the performance of texts, but a discussion of them would lead me out of the present field of investigation. For a presentation of Beckett's radio plays, see Robert Whilcher, " 'Out of the Dark': Beckett's Texts for Radio" in *Beckett's Later Fiction and Drama*, James Acheson and Kateryna Arthur, eds. (Houndmill and London: Macmillan, 1987) pp. 1–17.
14. For a discussion of "form of content" and "form of expression" see Maria Corti, *An Introduction to Literary Semiotics*, Margherita Bogat and Allen Mandelbaum, trans. (Bloomington and London: Indiana University Press, 1978). See in particular Chapter 5 and the Conclusion.
15. Alec Reid, *All I Can Manage, More than I Could: An Approach to the Plays of Samuel Beckett* (Dublin: The Dolmen Press, 1968) p. 12.
16. *Ibid.*, p. 19.
17. "Quand on dit que le mouvement, au contraire, c'est la répétition, et que c'est là notre vrai théâtre, on ne parle pas de l'effort de l'acteur qui 'répète' dans la mesure où la pièce n'est pas encore sue." Gilles Deleuze, *Différence et répétition* (Paris: Presses Universitaires de France, 1968), p. 19. Translation of this text is always mine.
18. Samuel Beckett, "Footfalls," pp. 239, 240, 242, 243.
19. *Ibid.*, p. 243.
20. Samuel Beckett, "I gave up before birth" in *For to End Yet Again and Other Fizzles* (London: John Calder, 1976) pp. 43–46.
21. Samuel Beckett, "A Piece of Monologue" in *Collected Shorter Plays*, p. 265.
22. *Ibid.*, p. 266.
23. The relationship between enactment and narration is central to Charles R. Lyons's stimulating reading of "Beckett's Fundamental Theater: The Plays from *Not I* to *What Where*" in *Beckett's Later Fiction and Drama*, pp. 80–97.
24. "ils opposent la répétition à toutes les formes de la généralité," Gilles Deleuze, *Différence et répétition*, p. 13.
25. "Ce qu'ils reprochent à Hegel, c'est d'en rester au faux mouvement, au mouvement logique abstrait, c'est-à-dire à la 'médiation.' [. . .] Il ne leur suffit donc pas de proposer une nouvelle représentation du mouvement; la représentation est déjà médiation. Il s'agit au contraire de produire dans l'oeuvre un mouvement capable d'émouvoir l'esprit hors de toute représentation; il s'agit de faire du mouvement lui-même une oeuvre, sans interposition; de substituer des signes directs à des réprésentations médiates." *Ibid.*, p. 16.
26. Samuel Beckett, "A Piece of Monologue," p. 269.
27. Samuel Beckett, "Footfalls," p. 241.
28. "Restaurer la différence dans la pensée, c'est défaire ce premier noeud qui

consiste à représenter la différence sous l'identité du concept et du sujet pensant." Gilles Deleuze, *Différence et répétition*, p. 342.

29. Samuel Beckett, "Footfalls," p. 241.

30. *Ibid.*, p. 242.

31. I am indebted to Hans-Georg Gadamer for this interpretation of Hegel's "absolute" and "objective spirit." See in particular his "I fondamenti filosofici del XX secolo" in *Filosofia '86*, Gianni Vattimo, ed. (Roma and Bari: Laterza, 1987). For a discussion of consciousness in Hegelian terms see Joseph L. Navickas, *Consciousness and Reality: Hegel's Philosophy of Subjectivity* (The Hague: Martinus Nijhoff, 1976).

32. Samuel Beckett, *Film* (New York: Grove Press, 1969), p. 11.

33. Samuel Beckett, "Not I" in *Collected Shorter Plays,* p. 215.

34. Although the term "entropy" was originally used in thermodynamics in relation to the transmission of heat, it was later employed by information theorists to indicate a measure of disorganization of a closed information system, that is, to indicate "noise" or chaos. See Umberto Eco, ed., "Introduzione" in *Estetica e teoria dell'informazione* (Milano: Bompiani, 1972) pp. 7–27. In Thomas Pynchon's short story "Entropy" (*Kenyon Review* 22,2 [Spring 1960]), the entropic state becomes a form of terminal sameness. Entropy is described by one of the characters as follows: "Ambiguity. Redundance. Irrelevance, even. Leakage. All this is noise. Noise screws up your signal, makes for disorganization in the circuit." (p. 285). The literary relevance of entropy seems remarkable in relation to Beckett's works, particularly as they always seem to approach the ultimate limit of rupture of discourse, before the disappearance of discourse itself.

35. Samuel Beckett, "Not I," p. 219.

36. *Ibid.*

37. *Ibid.*, p. 220.

38. I am alluding to one of Jesus' sayings, often repeated in the Gospels. See Matthew 10:39 and 16:25; Luke 9:24 and 17:33; Mark 8:34–35 and John 12: 25.

39. Jacques Derrida, "Force and Signification" in *Writing and Difference,* p. 3.

40. For a concise and clear definition of "story time" (as "narrated or represented time") and of "writing time" (as "recounting time") see Oswald Ducrot and Tzvetan Todorov, *Encyclopedic Dictionary of the Sciences of Language,* Catherine Porter, trans. (Baltimore and London: Johns Hopkins University Press, 1979) pp. 319–20. Exemplifications of "internal" and "external" times can also be found here.

41. Friedrich Nietzsche, *The Will to Power,* p. 193.

42. *Ibid.*, p. 194.

43. See entries in *The Oxford English Dictionary* (Oxford: Clarendon Press, 1933). Specifically: "cosmos"—Gr. κοσμος = order, ornament, world or universe. So called by Pythagoras or his disciples, for its perfect order and arrangement. "Universe"—Latin *Universus,* fr. "unus" + "versus"; "vertere" = to turn. The whole of created or existing things regarded collectively; all things (including the earth, the heavens, and all the phenomena of space) considered as constitut-

ing a systematic whole, especially as created or existing by Divine power, the whole world or creation; the cosmos.

44. Philip Larkin, "Days" in *The Whitsun Weddings* (London: Faber and Faber, 1964) p. 27, l.2.

45. *Ibid.,* l.6.

46. This interpretation of Heidegger's thought is provided by Hans-Georg Gadamer in *Text und Interpretation,* Philippe Forget, ed. (Munchen: Fink, 1984) pp. 24–55. Quotation p. 25. Translation mine.

47. The expression "literary hyperdetermination" is borrowed from Aldo Tagliaferri's work *Beckett e l'iperdeterminazione letteraria* (Milano: Feltrinelli, 1979). In English translation see his "Beckett and Joyce" in *Samuel Beckett: Modern Critical Views,* Harold Bloom, ed. (New York: Chelsea House, 1985) pp. 247–61. For a discussion of "The Elusive Ego: Beckett's M's," see Frederick J. Hoffman's article in *Samuel Beckett Now,* Melvin J. Friedman, ed. (Chicago: Chicago University Press, 1970) pp. 31–58.

48. Samuel Beckett, "Footfalls," p. 241.

49. *Ibid.,* p. 243.

50. The first part of the play ends with a dialogue which will be repeated, almost identically, as narration at the very end of the play. The significant variation seems the transformation of dialogue into monologue, of drama into dramatic narration. The role of repetition and temporality is indisputably important in the structuring of meaning. Compare *ibid.,* p. 240, with p. 243.

51. Antonin Artaud, quoted in Jacques Derrida, *Writing and Difference,* p. 333.

52. Jacques Derrida, "The Theater of Cruelty" in *Writing and Difference,* p. 249.

53. Samuel Beckett, "That Time" in *Collected Shorter Plays,* p. 227.

54. See in particular Kierkegaard's discussion of his return to Berlin and to the Königstädter Theater, and his ironical recounting of his methodical life at home, as an imitator of the emperor Domitian, in *Repetition,* pp. 168–69, 179.

55. Foucault's original statement reads as follows: "(il tempo è sempre più sciolto del pensiero)". It can be found in the Introduction ("Theatrum Philosophicum") to the Italian edition of Gilles Deleuze's *Differenza e ripetizione* (Bologna: Il Mulino, 1971) p. XXII. Translation mine. The original appeared as "Theatrum Philosophicum" in *Critique* 282 (1970) 885–908.

56. Samuel Beckett, "That Time," p. 227.

57. *Ibid.,* p. 230.

58. Jacques Derrida, "The Theater of Cruelty," p. 248. Emphasis mine.

59. Samuel Beckett, "That Time," p. 234.

60. *Ibid.,* p. 235.

61. Samuel Beckett, "What Where" in *Collected Shorter Plays,* pp. 313–14. Emphasis mine.

62. *Ibid.,* p. 315.

63. *Ibid.,* p. 310.

64. *Ibid.,* p. 316.

65. John Keats, "Ode on a Grecian Urn" ll. 49–50. In *The Poems of John Keats,* Jack Stillinger, ed. (Cambridge, Mass.: Harvard University Press, 1978). For a

definition of "negative capability" see *The Letters of John Keats,* Hyder Edward Rollins, ed. (Cambridge, Mass.: Harvard University Press, 1958).

66. For a discussion of a modern conception of temporality in relation to being, see Martin Heidegger, *Gelassenheit* (Pfullingen: Verlag Gunter Neske, 1959), and its implications of surrender, resignation, and impassiveness.

67. Martin Esslin, "Towards the Zero of Language" in *Beckett's Later Fiction and Drama,* pp. 35–49. Quotation p. 35.

68. *Ibid.,* p. 46.

69. "La volontà moralmente buona di pensare nel senso comune aveva in fondo la funzione di proteggere il pensiero dalla sua singolare 'genitalità'." Michel Foucault, "Theatrum Philosophicum," p. XI.

Part Two

4. Beyond the Mirror and Below the Concept: The "I" as *Company*

Immediacy of Consciousness and Linguistic Inescapability

The primary problem that Beckett raises in *Company* (1980) concerns the need to situate the subject by letting "it" speak, that is, by means of a definition which avoids naming.[1] By this process, *the absence of definition* imitates the discrepancies, the fragmentation, and the incongruities that occur in sign-systems, both during the actual process of the definition of an identity and, more specifically, of an "I."

In his *An Outline of Psychoanalysis* (1940), Freud stated that "Psychoanalysis makes a basic assumption," (actually a "double-barrelled one," according to James Strachey, translator of Freud's German text).[2] This "assumption" regards the two things "concerning what we call our psyche or mental life: first, its bodily organ and scene of action, the brain (or nervous system), and secondly, our *acts of consciousness,* which are *immediate data* and cannot be more fully explained by any kind of description."[3] Thus Freud rejects the notion of a Cartesian *cogito* and the metaphysical implications that go with it.

Beckett's *Company* takes the refusal of the *cogito* even further, through questioning its assumed "self-evidence" as well as Freud's notion of its "immediacy" (Freud's "immediate data"). The whole issue of "verifiability," which is introduced from the beginning and permeates Beckett's text, thematizes this concern: "Only a small part of what is said can be verified."[4] The ideological distance from the *cogito* seems wider in Beckett, even if the task of both the Freudian and the Beckettian texts seems to be the understanding of the process of consciousness, to be conveyed respectively as description and as reproduction of it. In *Company,* the reproduction is carried out as a verbal drama, a pronominal action, a mimesis of the process of perception-consciousness. Unlike Freud in the 1940s, Beckett relies primarily on language, and consciously takes it as his starting point. Furthermore, in order to avoid traditional descriptions, which only *seem* to explain "acts of consciousness" but are bound to fail (as Freud had pointed out), Beckett allows a "processive" use of language to take the place of a definition, so that the assertive quality of description can be challenged and its intrinsic logocentrism can be questioned. Thus, language appears as the background, in the sense of ground and horizon, of the visibility of the "acts of consciousness," showing why indeed "immediate data" (which are linguistically substantiated) "cannot be more fully explained."

Company talks about a present state in a way that indicates it as a present stated, and the constant self-reflective quality of narration foregrounds the fallacy of an "immediate" knowledge, self-evident and perhaps even conceived as universal. In *Proust* (written in 1931), Beckett himself warned us against the "caricature furnished by direct perception" and stated that "permanent reality, if any, can only be apprehended as a retrospective hypothesis."[5]

In a way *Company* starts where Malone stopped. Malone's writing program indicated an awareness of the temporal discrepancies involved in writing of self, but Malone (or the "earlier Beckett") did not dare deal with them so radically and so systematically as *Company* does:

> When I have completed my inventory, [Malone says] if my death is not ready for me then, I shall write my memoirs. That's funny, I've made a joke.[6]

His project is a joke because of the constant and inescapable overlapping of consciousness and subjectivity, of "parts of the subject" (inventory) and actions identifying him (memoirs), and also because of the impossibility of maintaining self-sameness within the temporal flow. In *Proust* Beckett had already stated that even "the most ideal tautology presupposes a relation and the affirmation of equality involves only an approximate identification, and by asserting unity denies unity."[7] Malone's if-clause is a "joke," that is, a piece of nonsense, because no inventory nor any memoirs have any relation to the presence of the subject, nor any verifiable objectivity, apart from the objectivity conferred on it by the outcome of a decision. At most, an inventory is the trace of a will in the absence of the subject (who has completed it) and of the "things" listed in it.

Furthermore, given the fact that the relationship between subject of the enunciation and subject of the uttered utterance could be different in "memoir" or in "inventory," Malone cannot possibly be perceived as being exactly the same in both, unless we metaphysically attribute a sameness to a conceptualized subject within such instances. But, of course, that attribution would obliterate the difference between inventory and memoir. So, un-like Malone in *Malone Dies,* the subject in *Company* is "company," precisely because he manifests itself as a subject that never totally coincides with himself. This non-coincidence was skillfully described by Søren Kierke-gaard while talking about the "magic of the theater"; he pointed to the fact that

> In such a self-vision of the imagination, the individual is not an actual shape, but a shadow, or, more correctly, the actual shape is invisibly present and therefore is not satisfied to cast one shadow, but the individual has a variety of shadows, all of which resemble him and which momentarily have equal status as being himself.[8]

Obviously, this subject, like the one in *Company,* cannot posit either the verifiable objectivity of its "whole," nor the verifiable "truth" of its pres-ence. Beckett states quite clearly that a mere rhetorical device is responsible for the belief in the truth of the self, when the presence of remembering is translated into the objectivity of memoirs, forging the image of one's self:

> Only a small part of what is said can be verified. As for example when he hears, You are on your back in the dark. Then he must acknowledge the truth of what is said. But by far the greater part of what is said cannot be verified. As for example when he hears, You first saw the light on such and such a day. Sometimes the two are combined as for example, You first saw the light on such and such a day and now you are on your back in the dark. A device perhaps from the incontrovertibility of the one to win credence for the other.[9]

In other words, the immediacy of presence "wins credence" for a "you" that does not exist, but shows an "I" that does not actually coincide with the image of self produced by a conscious self. So in *Company* the "I" tena-ciously remains plural, against the traps of conceptual unifications. In fact the deferral from self, which ultimately constitutes itself linguistically as the "I," is a necessary deferral, as it reveals the "I" only through the articulations of different acts of consciousness. These acts can structure the "I" as the result of a verbal interplay of referents related to immediate perception and memory. Thus, in *Company,* what is perceived as the referential immediacy of the "I" is conveyed by a skillful narrative choice which suspends the naming of it. In this way, the narrative reflects a conception of the subject that is essentially "plural" and not immediate, while narration also conveys the notion that this phenomenological "plurality" would be obliterated in the figure of a singular pronoun.

In turn, the decision to express these phenomenological implications denies the possibility of conferring a monolithic quality to the theme of the narrative, since the linguistic referent of the "I" has to be deconstructed *as* it is given. The endlessly changing formulations which occur within the narrative show a constant movement within the linguistic referent: the subject-pronoun is caught and established by its relation to other pronouns. Thus the "I" is established as the outcome of the dialogue of several selves. The fact that the subject-pronoun is continually given and suspended shows that the person cannot enter language appropriately, but also that "it" resists assimilation with the "I." In fact, the very appropriation of language hides the actual fragmentary nature of the subject of/in a discourse. As Roland Barthes has noted:

> Linguistically, [. . .] *I* is nothing other than the instance saying *I:* language knows a 'subject,' not a 'person,' and this subject, empty outside the very enunciation which defines it, suffices to make language 'hold together,' suffices, that is to say, to exhaust it.[10]

Thematic and Modal Fragmentation: "The Play of the I"

We could say that fragmentation in *Company* is a pertinent feature, and indeed a relevant one, of the "play of the I," which is both the theme and the communicative mode of the text. The "I" is the result of a voice which constitutes the subject as metonymical and as subject to temporality. It is metonymical insofar as it is one instance within the pronominal system, and it is temporal inasmuch as the subject of the enunciation is diachronically realized as the connection of the different metonymical instances provided by the various subjects of each utterance. I could say that the subject manifests itself only as the result of a diachronic "entailment"[11] among different levels of semiosis which alternate the foregrounding of subject of narration and subject of discourse. This necessarily contrapuntal structure reveals that the presumed unity of the immediate "I" can be achieved only after the alternation of pronouns and voice, and that any idea of the "I" as unity is an abstract image of simultaneity, achievable only after the decision to operate on visibility and perspectives, in the name of unification.

I feel that the scope of narration in *Company* makes it very hard to forget the plurality of semiotic levels that are unified in the image of an immediate

"I." In order to produce this awareness, Beckett endows the elements of narration with improbability, or with a disquieting unfamiliarity. For instance, memory and present experience (which are generally kept separate in narratives, even when the order of plot-elements is altered in relation to the story)[12] are not clearly distinguished here. No matter which narrative solution is adopted, whether the order of the story is kept or altered, the conceptual implications that legitimize the distinction of past and present are never posited by narration itself, nor confirmed by it. In *Company* images of the past and of the present do not comply with a traditional portraiture of time: traditionally, once the reader is accustomed to a formal difference, which indicates the alternation of past and present, he or she will hence perceive them as being different, because he or she has learned to distinguish them on the basis of the use and recurrence of different elements (such as pronouns, for instance). On the contrary, in *Company* the reader has to deal with a text where no such textual "law" is enacted. I am referring in particular to the exemplary "Fragment 46" and "Fragment 47":

> Roll as he might his eyes. Height from the ground?

> Arm's length. Force? Low. A mother's stooping over cradle from behind. She moves aside to let the father look. In his turn he murmurs to the newborn. Flat tone unchanged. No trace of love.[13]

These fragments constitute a sequence, which we can read as an answer following a previous question ("Height from the ground? Arm's length"), and which are followed by a declarative sentence: "You are on your back at the foot of an aspen," which seem to constitute the description of a present position. Yet, "Fragment 47" conveys the idea of childhood, and implies a memory from the past which the reader can decode as a mere narrative "confusion" of temporal planes. Rather than perceive a "temporal confusion," I interpret that (willed) temporal combination as a sign of the fact that presence allows no break and that, in spite of "conscious" evidence, the discontinuity of consciousness will never be commensurate with the continuity of presence.

Continuity and disruption lie at the core of the theme and at the core of the narrative strategy in *Company:* the subject is "company" because, after all, it is "more" than each single self. On the other hand, the subject can perceive itself only thanks to this very discontinuity, and through the multiplicity of different, successive, specific images.

Furthermore, the establishment of a link between representation of self and self as point of view indicates the impossibility of drawing a definite distinction between narrative and drama. Inasmuch as narration develops the critique of the "I" not through a referential designation, but as a temporal realization, the narration of the "I" cannot be separated from its performance. The text shows and tells; it narrates and performs. Its fragmented illustration of time, and its use of temporality, confer an unprecedented original mimetic quality to the narrative.[14]

In this light I see the important role of reformulation, which is a typical trait of Beckett's style, as totally separate from concerns for the aesthetic imperative of clarity, or the didactic imperative of clarification. Rather, I see reformulation as representative of the disruption of a presupposed unity, of time, character, and plot, entailing no subsequent monolithic certainty. The theme of verifiability, which Beckett introduces from the very beginning, helps to underline the erratic nature of immediate data, which can eventually be confirmed only through reformulations, but whose immediacy is simultaneously denied by the very reformulations that denote them. Hence, immediate data are connoted as being totally inadequate in relation to a sound foundation of knowledge and of self.

Some important questions, such as the relevance of conscious subjectivity and the legitimacy of subjugating signs to one logic (the logic of *a* subject?), are raised in relation to the constitution of the "I" and the role of language is emphasized, inasmuch as it substantiates the subject as meaning.

Beyond an Ideal Notion of Self: Experiences of Meaning in the Constitution of the "I"

It seems to me that *Company* is structured and animated by a systematic refusal to reproduce the usual meaning of "I," a meaning that implies a unity which is actually never there. The focus of Beckett's investigation falls on how language works in the definition of an "I," without ignoring the complexities of his or her "will-to-mean," which is often hidden in the meaning of self. The portraiture of the "I" in *Company* tries to move beyond the accepted but simplistic dualism that opposes self and world, the subjectivity of perception and the "objectivity" of things. Furthermore, we must remember that this is a presupposition on which the very concept of "imitation" can traditionally, but only improperly, rest.

If we look at Husserl's *Logical Investigations* on "The Phenomenological and Ideal Content of the Experiences of Meaning," we can find a number of suggestions helpful to the understanding of Beckett's notion of the complex meaning of the "I." The presence of the "I" is always separated from language, and yet the perception of the "I" seems to share the "act-character of meaning,"[15] that is, it derives from a production of meaning, from a "work in progress," rather than from an atemporal concept. Husserl's discussion of meaning helps in defining the limits of the conscious self in relation to the "wider" I. If, as he maintains, in the *act* of meaning we are not conscious of mean*ing* as an object, when one is meaning one's own self, he or she is not conscious of the act-character of meaning it, not conscious of himself or herself as subjects of that act; thus he or she is ignoring part of his or her "I." Specifically, *Company* seems to enact the philosophical presuppositions of one of Husserl's statements:

> The manifold singulars for the ideal unity Meaning are naturally the corresponding act-moments of meaning, the meaning-intentions.[16]

In *Company,* these act-moments of meaning are given as manifold singulars of a mimetic process that never tries to imitate a concept. Beckett's iconoclasm against linguistic signs is not really indicative of a neopositivistic ideology working in the text. On the contrary, it expresses an interest in a phenomenological use of language, so that any a priori subjectivism becomes untenable. In fact *Company* produces a movement of signs rather than a sophisticated definition, a naming that would once again articulate an ideal, unified "I." Thus the positing of the subject is carried out in the narrative through a sort of phenomenological paradigm which, by playing upon a series of differences (similar to act-moments of meaning), reveals the dynamism that brings about the effect of the "I" (similar to the ideal unity Meaning).

The absence of a unified, ideal "I," which would be provided by an easily identifiable thematic referent, leads in *Company* to the negation of a single dominant narrative point of view. This is how mimesis becomes critical rather than reflective: instead of positing the issue of adequacy of self-representation, the very subject of representation is questioned. Inasmuch as it is shown to be both an object and a subject, at different moments of the narrative, a radical demystification of the possibility of linguistic self-expression in narrative can thus take place. Paradoxically, that process occurs thanks to the obviously mystifying devices of literature.

The "*epoché*" of the character, which occurs in *Company* as a showing of his limited nature as a mere subject *in* the text (as subject of the uttered utterance), is functional in revealing his non-coincidence with the subject *of* the text. In other words, the reduction of the character to its textual boundaries puts into focus the existence of the unspeakable subject of the text (a subject of the enunciation). Thus, also, the triadic nature of the narrative model, involving author, character, and reader, finds a way to appear, instead of being censured, hidden in the compact flatness produced by literary conventions and by traditional mimesis.

Diegesis into Mimesis: The Moving Boundaries of Self-Representation

In the light of the epistemic presuppositions which I have foregrounded, the narrative task of the transcription of reality compels a movement beyond the looking glass of traditional mimesis, that is, beyond conceptualized and fragmented images of the self. The aesthetic reproduction of a subject compels a form of transfer by which imitation becomes dramatic, open, dialogical. Specifically, narration has to become more than self-reflective; it has to abolish a clear, tenable boundary between the diegesis of the story told and the mimesis of story-telling. This means that the self telling the story (of himself) has to be included in that story. The mirror held up to nature becomes a *procedure* of identification, rather than the reflection of an a priori concept. In fact, the very opening of *Company* both illustrates and enacts a communicative situation:

> A voice comes to one in the dark. Imagine.[17]

The injunction to imagine enhances the description by specifying the content of the message uttered by the voice. However, it also exceeds the borders of the diegetic text by being directly oriented towards the reader, inviting him or her to imagine, that is, to read. It is an invitation to see the expanding boundaries of the text, moved by the constructive, imaginative act of reading. Thus *Company* is not conceivable as detached from "performance": the text cannot be reduced to a mere diegetic discourse, because the reader's imaginative experience has been prompted as the performance of the text. Reading shows itself, reflected in the looking glass of this unusual presentation of the character's identification. As a consequence, every textual message will be connoted as partial, in relation to the wider system of the ongoing communication. In other words, the pseudo-referents of the character's experience and imagination are only fragments of a vaster semantic universe in which they can be uttered, and in such a way that the enunciation will not disappear into the message but will become part of the global meaning constituted in the act of reading.

Company is more than self-reflective because it does not merely self-reflect its narrative conventions; by deconstructing the traditional dichotomy of mimesis and diegesis the text opens itself onto the presence of reading. Its semantic closure keeps opening onto the present of reading, and the semantic stability of textual units is undermined by their becoming semantic hypotheses (in the course of reading). As Barbara Johnson has written of "rigorous unreliability":

> the privilege traditionally granted to showing over telling is reversed: "telling" becomes a more sophisticated form of "showing," in which what is "shown" is the breakdown of the show/tell distinction.[18]

The expositional techniques which are normally different in narratives and in theatrical texts are here used together. This textual strategy shows the impossibility of maintaining textual borders solely determined by the word-sequence. The *Lebenswelt* of *Company* is literally an act of communication, which develops into the positing of an "I." The opening statement: "A voice comes to one in the dark," constitutes "The World of the Living Present" of the fictional world, but also the living present of the beginning of a communication with the reader. This "surrounding world" constitutes the unquestionable supplement through which the questioning of presuppositions can take place.

Noesis (which Aristotle defined as intuitive knowledge) is connoted in *Company* as present communication, and is thus opposed to any form of intellectual knowledge or concept. The voice is given as the unquestioned starting point of a narrative, which will develop as a critical speculation, eventually leading to a mimetic portraiture of self as the object of self-observation. The expositional technique in *Company* seems to enact the phenomenological "abstention from ordinary presuppositions" (the Husserlian *epoché*) in relation to the definition of the subject, which is in fact told through a number of predicators that undermine its presupposed unity. I do not see Husserl's "ego" or any transcendental connotation in the final word of *Company* describing a subject "Alone." However, a performance of the reduction on the "I" occurs throughout the entire work, and functions as a critique of the linguistic nature of the "I."

Company, rather than being a search for an unshakable foundation of knowledge, questions and deconstructs the monolithic definition of the subject as "I." In this respect, it enhances epistemological issues that are quite different from those of transcendental philosophy and even transcendental phenomenology. In fact, the task of describing the workings of consciousness, which provides some sort of thematic unity in the narrative, leads to a questioning of language because of its definitory power. I believe that to a large extent the role of the theme in *Company* is that of providing a ground where epistemological issues regarding language can be developed. The legitimacy of this reading seems confirmed by the generality and impersonality of the "protagonist" whose specificity is never achieved, in spite of the many "episodes" regarding his past. These "recollections," whose importance cannot be ignored, especially in relation to the apparently expository structure of the text, concur in destabilizing the internal coherence of "The fable of one with you in the dark."[19] As I have previously noted, they provide a temporal differentiation, but with almost no narrative indication of such difference between past and present. Hence the figurations of temporality can be shown as the result of a choice. At the same time, it becomes clear that different figurations of self do concur in the telling of "The fable of one fabling of one with you in the dark."[20] As I have said, only through the movement of his selves, can the "I" be seen. *Company* shows this *différance,* and talks about it in such a way that the fragmentariness hidden in the linguistic compactness of the "I" can in fact appear.

Reformulations and Doubling: The Coordinates of Self-Visibility

The process of doubling is essential in indicating the cleavage, but not the split, of subject/object in *Company.* First, the voice which seems to indicate a non-identity of listener and speaker does in fact produce their correlation, and makes the tenability of the split highly suspect. Then, the past which seems so different from the present does in fact produce a temporal shift that works as a concordant system of definition of the same subject. As a result, the difference between presentation and representation is posited and erased by the peculiar mimetic quality of this text. It is also worth recalling the doubling of tone in the speaking voice, as pointed out by Eric P. Levy:

> The voice in the mirror addresses M in an *earnest* tone. For example the
> phrase 'You have never forgotten' is attached to many of the recitations to

invest them with urgency and validity. In contrast, the voice outside the mirror speaks in the opposite tone of *sarcasm,* implying that all is false, all lies.[21]

Finally, the very title "Company" is endowed with a brilliant ambivalence, since it regards a self described as "Alone," but it also denotes it through a "company" of different pronouns. The narrative shows that it is only through relations that the self can experience itself, and the pronominal shifts and the interplay of voice and hearer signify (in the double sense of "to mean" and "to structure") this relation. *Company* makes it clear that any formulation of self has to be relational, and so speaker and listener, as much as "you" and "he," provide the screen on which the "company of self" can be projected and seen. Personal pronouns as characters become the coordinates of self-visibility.

In this sense, not only would a "relation of sameness with himself"[22] be incapable of confirming identity, as Eric Levy has suggested, but it simply could not structure it. In fact, *Company* reveals a "consciousness [which] is on the one hand the negation of all the fictions, on the other, is their only source."[23] Besides, as I have said, "fictions" are necessary for the positing of consciousness itself, because even though no certainty can be achieved in relation to truth, memories and perceptions work together in mapping out the different positions of what comes to appear as a subject. In this respect we can see the relevance of self-citation, a peculiar form of doubling, which works as the structuring principle of self-awareness, and not as an investment in monologic logocentrism. This literally means that the foundation of an "I" is shown in *Company* as depending on a number of citations which, being repeated, can be recognized and are then appropriated as self-citations.

I would like to point out that the voice, and no written word, conveys the immediacy of such an experience. Even if the reading is obviously dependent on the written word, the pseudo-reference of the narrated experience emphasizes the oral quality ("A voice") of the communication involved in appropriating the self. This seems a brilliant way to reproduce the suspense and openness of consciousness, whose workings cannot be predicted, nor organized and arranged by the closed formal teleology of the written word. When an "I" is achieved, the perfection of the written word de facto denies an adequate image of the living subject. In fact, it can only convey a *perfect*ed, posthumous, image; an image where the duplicity of a self that is simultaneously playing and is played by language has to disappear. So, even if the issue of presence remains open, even if it cannot be captured in discourse, self-citation works as the presentation and not the re-presentation of a composite subject.

The fact that the "I" is achieved through a suspended designation of a subject through partial selves underlines a significant difference between a "self of speech" and a more markedly "symbolical self," such as the one of the written word. An orally designated self is regulated by the laws of a mimetic temporality; it is characterized by flaws and hesitations, by a certain degree of incoherence, and a plurality of articulations. The image of this subject shares the structure of a non-linear development, and does not imply the supremacy of a finalizing consciousness. Here again, Husserl's opposition between *Gegenwärtigung* (the primary memory) and *Vergegen-wärtigung* (the secondary memory) helps to emphasize the difference between a repetition and a bad repetition, between a formulation of self and a crystallized re-formulation in which the subject is actually betrayed.

The protagonist in *Company* is not a closed, traditional character and is not a pure consciousness. He is not even a pure voice, but appears as the unresolved movement of a voice that knows the inanity of words to verify one's own experience of the world, or to entail the truth of this experience. In this respect it is important to remember a passage from the next to the last "fragment" of the text:

> Till finally you hear how words are coming to an end. With every inane word a little nearer to the last. And how the fable too.[24]

Words in *Company* are connoted as being very similar to Husserl's mental acts: their "intentionality" makes them fallible in principle, but they are also inescapable. This is the reason why the "I" produced as the "final" character in *Company* cannot be named, and even has to be designated by something other than "I," and as a "supplément": "*And* you as you always were. / Alone."[25] The "I" cannot be named but can be perceived, thanks to the perseverance of the images of its relations and to the fact that, in the long run, the doubt about the self becomes a self-doubt which cannot be doubted as it occurs. In his essay, "Adventures of the First Person," Robert Champigny asserts that in *The Unnamable* "the variety of attempted identifications, their ludicrous aspect, their repeated failures, serve to point out the impossibility of a reduction"[26] of the subject. This non-reduction is superbly achieved in *Company,* where the positing of the "I" is given only as the result of a series of *occurrences* of its various identifications. This drama-tized narration (absent in *The Unnamable*) shows that subjectivity cannot possibly be reduced to any one of the selves which, however, play a constitutive role in configuring the "I."

The images provided by "he," "you," "one," "voice," etc., produce what I would call a paradoxical ontology, an "ontology of dialogue" among figures. Reference to "Company" seems to imply that, only so long as the "I" is thought of and portrayed as *différance,* can it adequately con-*figure* itself. However, as soon as a definition hides the image of its "figural" quality, that is, as soon as it predicates the self as "I," the "I" is reduced to an object, rather than respectively (as at different times in the reading) a category, a relational way of being, a hypothesis, a *différance.*

Thus, this reading of *Company* may explain why the voice cannot stop, and perhaps why the entire Beckett canon does not stop. Given that the subject is not one, but is essentially relational, narrative images of it have to be produced by a way of writing that comes as close as possible to the openness of speech. As I have previously said, this narrative strategy would allow the reproduction of hesitations, fragmentariness, and suspension, and would deny the supremacy of conceptual awareness (opposing subject and object), and of a narrative authority, in relation to the logic of *one* subject.

An Oral Difference, Against Logocentric Closure

In order to express the "polymorphic" structure of the "I" and the polyphony of his or her discourse, it is necessary for a narrative to reproduce the oral quality of discourse and thus represent the "I" as *différance.* The inclusion of the voice in the reproduction of the "I" implies that the representation has to be, or has to indicate, that it is virtually interminable, and that it could go on indefinitely, as an interplay of different elements (the "voice," "one," and other pronouns). Thus, I am saying that the creation of *différance* in the text can indicate the movement sustaining the modern category of self-identification, by being virtually interminable and somehow irreducible.

The "voice" is with "one" from the very beginning (*Company,* p. 7), but this "one" will be able to become "Alone" only when, after having been posited in a series of instances, its textual specifications are eroded, in the perception of a higher, more encompassing, semantic level: "self-identification" for the character, identification of an "I" for the reader. In other words, the "one" (as character) and the "voice" produce the "I" as the result of a synthetic abstraction which is shown, rather than repressed in the narrative. When this synthesis is achieved, the verbal flow can be interrupted: "And how better in the end labour lost and silence " (p. 89). In fact, the linguistic compactness of an "I" thus constituted has been deconstructed; the "I" can be named because we remember that it has been temporally composed, through the dialogue of its named parts. It can be named, but it will actually be quoted because it is no longer assumed as an entity. If, at the end of *Company* we read: "How better *in the end* is silence," it is only because the deconstruction of the "I" has been achieved, so that it is no longer necessary to continue the enumeration of selves, nor is it important to continue the unraveling of different and specific oppositions that have temporally constituted it. The epistemological denouement at the end of *Company* focuses on a radical opposition that cannot be deconstructed any further: the final silence, in fact, shows the past naming as necessary and the page as inescapable, as they constitute and map out the system of transformation on which the "I" is built.

Yet, having indicated the instability of concepts by the very process that constitutes them, writing has thus lost some of its totalitarian, logocentric power. This astounding revelation about logocentrism leads the reader to suspect all that is given as the "immediate," not because of a belief in the fact that a transcendental truth can be achieved (perhaps through a phenomenological reduction), but because the immediate has shown itself, in the case of the use of the "I," as the result of a conceptualization: the immediate was a concept.

Subjective Immediacy and the Illusion of Presence

Whatever comes through language is "already gone," even when it seems "there," or seems to be endowed with the timeless immortality that could have founded writing. I am obviously using the term "writing" in relation to Roland Barthes's observations in *Writing Degree Zero,* which I believe helps to clarify some aspects of *Company:*

> All modes of writing have in common the fact of being 'closed' and thus different from spoken language. Writing is in no way an instrument for communication, it is not an open route through which there passes only the intention to speak. A whole disorder flows through speech and gives it this self-devouring momentum which keeps it in a perpetually suspended state. Conversely, *writing is a hardened language* which is self-contained and is in no

way meant to deliver to its own duration a mobile series of approximations. It is on the contrary meant to impose, thanks to the shadow cast by its system of signs, the image of a speech which had a structure even before it came into existence.[27]

These observations allow me to address the objective difficulty of transposing *Company* on stage,[28] since I believe that the problem resides primarily in the coexistence of mimetic and diegetic elements in the novel, or in the ambivalence of its "writing mode" which becomes as close to being "oral" as possible, but of course is not "really" oral. A good rendering of *Company* for the stage should be based on a mirror reproduction of the alternation of diegesis and mimesis produced in the text, but that is hardly conceivable, outside a theoretical hypothesis. In fact, Eileen Fisher, talking about the "intended experience of *Company*," asserts "That experience is decidedly silent, readerly, and solitary."[29] I totally agree with her statement that "Beckett's choice of a readerly 'form', makes the best aesthetic sense,"[30] not only because de facto there is no other Beckettian choice, but because she substantiates her assertion with the elucidation of an important difference between the Mabou Mines adaptation of *Company* and two recent Beckett plays:

> Spectator complicity dramatically completes a production of *Not I* and *A piece of monologue,* but in *Company* it creates an extraneous dynamic which perverts the communication circuit at hand.[31]

A spectator's "complicity" constitutes a radically different formulation of the question of subjectivity, especially when compared to the articulations of a reader's "complicity." The performative objectification of the polarity "voice/hearer" pragmatically resolves certain questions on the nature of boundaries. The narrative text can deal with the instability of boundaries, whereas the dramatic text endorses them with a firmness deriving from the interpretive choices that necessarily precede the performance. Obviously, the most radical problem is whether to involve one or two actors. Unless the part is played by a ventriloquist, there is no way of representing the simultaneous coexistence of and distinction between "voice" and "hearer." The problem of their relationship (which indeed characterizes the narrative), would not remain equally problematic.

Company deals with the positing of boundaries between self and other, and between concept and perception, whereas its "adaptation" into drama only erodes a boundary that has already been posited. Its thematic insistence on a

> Devised deviser devising it all for company[32]

is a witty development of a radical epistemological issue. The certainty of an identification is suspended through a lexical choice which emphasizes the artifact undermining the quest. On the other hand, it truly reveals the role of syntax in any definition of a subject (Devis*ed*, devis*er*, devis*ing*). The figurations of self and other are shown as a matter of syntactic value in the narrative. They are put under scrutiny within a narrative frame that develops as a questioning of definitions, using a full variety of linguistic representations of subjects.

The polyphonic nature of this form of narration erodes from within the possibility of finding in *Company* the compact nature of a dramatic monologue. In drama, one speaker, a speaker and a voice, or a number of speakers would necessarily be speaking, or, at least, would be indicated as linguistically active. Here, on the contrary, the doubt as to the number of actual speakers of the "monologue" is kept open, and what appears is the fact that a systemic coherence (of predicators) can be mistaken for a unity in the referent (the person). Interlocution is shown to be the necessary movement of subjectivity because the "I" is the result of dialogical practices enacted by the conscious self with an unconscious self, a self as other. Yet, the acknowledgment of the morpho-syntactic nature of the interlocutors involved in these dialogues, and the awareness of the conventional value of pronouns erodes the presumed compact referentiality of the resulting "I."

The Networks of Self-Identification: Visions of Otherness

At times, the mixing of systems of designation converging on the same referent produces anti-reality effects that undermine the referential unity and the clarity of the message. See, for example, "Fragment 8":

> If the voice is not speaking to him it must be speaking to another. So with what reason remains he reasons. To another of that other. Or of him. Or of another still. To another of that other or of him or of another still. To one on his back in the dark in any case. Of one on his back in the dark whether the same or another. So with what reason remains he reasons and reasons ill. For were the voice speaking not to him but to another then it must be of that other it is speaking and not of him or of another still. Since it speaks in the second person.[33]

This masterpiece of reasoning, quite ironical and based on the rhetoric of a *via negativa*, does in fact contain a piece of knowledge regarding the use of referential systems. This typically Beckettian exercise in subtraction provides the evidence that if the voice were speaking to another of the same another (and not of "another still") it would speak in the second person ("were the voice speaking [. . .] to another/then it must be of that [*same*] other it is speaking [. . .] *since* it speaks in the second person"). The fact that the use of the second person implies an overlapping of hearer and subject of the message, is confirmed by a subsequent statement, whose complexity needs discussion:

Were it not of him to whom it is speaking speaking but of another it would not speak in the second person but in the third.[34]

A new piece of information derives from this statement, regarding the fact that the voice *is* speaking to him. Therefore we can infer that it is also *of* him that it is speaking, since it is speaking in the second person (were the voice speaking to him of another, it would speak in the third person). This laborious disclosure of a referent (*a* subject to whom and of whom the voice is speaking) is achieved only after the disclosure of a system of referentiality, on which the specific reference is shown to be totally dependent. In other words, the visibility of self depends on the systematic nature of discourse. This narration suspends the direct reference to an "objective I," and tells us precisely that the "I" apprehends himself only by moving through a network of systemic relations. Yet this movement is hidden in the linguistic referent, which comes across as a "thing in itself," rather than as the meaning of a relation. In other words, language hides the fact that the referent is constituted by a relational value.

So, strictly speaking, the "I" *is* "Company" (even if it can be "Alone"), because the condition of self-visibility is determined only by a relation with otherness. That is, the "I" becomes visible as one when consciousness can master the systemic nature of the different alternatives of designation which constitute it in time as value, rather than constituting it as a literal paradigmatic alternative. The "I" in itself would be an "empty word" without the pronominal system, and the person that says "I" would never know himself or herself only through an experience of self-sameness and literality.

Furthermore, Beckett exploits a vast number of paradigmatic alternatives of designation in showing that there is no final, no total way of naming the subject, but that concurring systems produce the effect of the "I." The danger of "reasoning ill" lies in the acceptance of the literality of each designation (in the belief of its autonomy from the system) or in the preference for one system of designation, because of the naive assumption that it is more truthfully expressive of the self.

The condition of self-visibility requires the vision of "otherness," and this "otherness" is indicated in *Company* in more than one way.

First, it is thematized: the voice is said to be speaking to him "speaking but of another." This specification literally means that when the *self* speaks to *him*self, it cannot coincide with the self who is speaking. The "use of the second person" indicates how this coincidence is only partial; it is the "referential sameness" of a "speaker" addressing himself as a "you."

Secondly, the narrative reproduces the "plural" structure of the "I," thanks to a complex communicative model, which involves an addresser and an addressee who are found to be the same person only after they have been described. In fact, the referential coincidence of subject and addressee is given as the result of an "abduction " that involves and links at least two designative systems describing the subjects of the communicative model. One system is pronominal (involving "him" and "whom"); and one is metalinguistic, in the sense that it describes the linguistic system, referring to "the second person" and "the third." We can discover that the speaker is speaking to the same person precisely by linking the two heterogeneous systems.

Speaking: The Founding Mirror of Self-Identification

I have shown that the network of self-identification is more complex than the network of subject-visibility. In fact, in order to achieve subject-visibility, the use of the pronominal system is sufficient, but in order to achieve self-identification, the subject has to go through the looking-glass of the pronominal system, and has to relate to it metalinguistically.[35] In other words, in order to be able to recognize himself as "I," the speaker has to see himself also as "first person," a configuration derived from a perception of a "you" as "second person." This perception occurs through the use of the second person; it is the actual "speaking" that allows the supplement of visibility that produces identification.

As we have seen, the use of the second person in the narrative indicates a coincidence of subject and addressee ("Were it not of him to whom it is speaking [. . .] it would not speak in the second person"), but this perception of one character is developed even further (towards the establishment of an "I") by enlarging the frame of the message, including the illustration of its enunciation.

The description of the link between message and enunciation (indicated in the narrative by the sentence: "*use* of the second person"), shows that the perception of this connection is the necessary condition for any identification. Significantly enough, in the same sentence, a special emphasis goes to "speaking": "Were it not [. . .] speaking/speaking but of." From this statement we have to infer, first of all, that speaking takes place only as "speaking of," and secondly, that the speaking of the "I" is always a "speaking but of another," since the presence of the "I" cannot be captured. Its "multiple structure" can only be alluded to, or hinted at, by an awareness of the *use* of persons in a message that thus opens onto its enunciation. This dialectical movement transforms the visibility of the subject of the message into a visibility of "otherness," through the negation of the referentiality of what (necessarily) is being said ("speaking but of").

The correlation of the subjects involved in the use of persons and subject(s) of the enunciation maps out the different positions of the self (selves) in relation to the "I." That is, it indicates the different ways in which the self is "other," without being "another." The sentence: "Were it not of him to whom it is speaking but of another it would not speak in the second person" shows that the "another" is "essentially other" only because there is no coincidence, between the speaker and the addressee (the "it" and the "to whom"). Yet, the "other" is necessarily within the "I," since it speaks to him addressing him as "you," while being the "other" about whom it speaks.

From Basic Figures to Narrative Articulations: The Temporality of Self-Identification

As we have seen, the epistemological quest that pervades *Company* extends from the basic figures at the root of language to the strategies of their conjunctions and disjunctions. Such dynamic relatedness can appear when suspension is created within the narrative: this happens through the aesthetic originality of the epistemological questions asked in *Company,* which consists in the use of a narrative structure similar to a riddle and involving the subject(s) to be defined. The questions "who is speaking?" and "to whom?" are posited in such a way that they become metanarrative, and yet they remain the main theme of the work. They regard the protagonist of

Company, but this protagonist can be apprehended only through a metanarrative reading of the code that structures it.

This perspective allows the "showing" of an "I" which is simultaneously both the object and the subject of the definition. In other words, the use of persons performs the definition that defines them. Let us see how the anticipation of the solution concerning the narrative riddle is formulated in "Fragment 23," where the reader can understand that those who take part in the described intra-psychic communication, are simultaneously spoken and speaking by/through what they say:

> If *he were* to utter after all? However feebly. What an addition to company that would be! *You are* on your back in the dark and one day you will utter again. One day! In the end. In the end you will utter again. Yes *I remember. That was I.* That was I then.[36]

The anaphoric texture of this passage becomes indicative of the fundamental importance of signifiers and temporality in the development of self-awareness. It also indicates how an essentially verbal condition determines the self-visibility of the subject. The recurrence of quasi-identical signifiers illustrates how the process of self-identification develops, determining the "I" as a subject that can be expressed only obliquely: temporally and anaphorically. The slightly changing signifiers of the recurring statements show that a *direct,* final referentiality cannot occur. It is interesting to note that as soon as an image of self is shaped and given ("That was I"), this self is also deprived of totality and of the possibility of unification ("That was I *then*"). The *sub*ject is literally "under" the figures of speech which map out its relational nature. Yet, the difference between the "I then" and the "I" seems to reinvest language with the capacity of speaking of the I without totally betraying its fleeting actuality. The issue of presence is opened when the trace of a subject of enunciation manages to appear through the fore-grounding of a difference (between an "I then" and an "I").

The "I" is shown as deriving from the actual utterance of sentences in which he is "masked" by pronouns, but revealed by the use of persons. Through the utterance, the linguistic code shows in such a way that the figurality of the "I" can be seen. A metalinguistic reading of pronouns shows that, after all, all the "others" are also images. Paul de Man has forcefully made this point in an essay on autobiography:

> the spectacular moment is not primarily a situation or an event that can be located in a history, but [that] it is the manifestation, on the level of the

referent, of a linguistic structure. The specular moment that is part of all understanding reveals the tropological structure that underlies all cognitions, including the knowledge of self.[37]

Even though it is not on the autobiographical level of referentiality that the subject is figured out in *Company,* yet "the manifestation of a linguistic structure" is essential for the reader in order to acknowledge how the constitution of the subject as "I" takes place.

Towards a New Epistemology: Exploring The Literariness of Self

Speech acts at the level of experience and at the level of consciousness necessarily become tropes in a narrative, but the knowledge of their figurative quality enhances the (self-)knowledge, as knowledge of the figures of (self-)identification.

In *Company* the reader encounters many thematic formulations of the fact that, in order to see that it is "company," the subject must display a certain mental activity. I believe that, from an epistemological point of view, this mental activity consists in the animation of figures, as opposed to their conceptualization. In fact, the text repeatedly states that this activity "need not be of a high order":

> In order to be company he must display a certain mental activity. But it need not be of a high order. Indeed it might be argued the lower the better. Up to a point. The lower the order of mental activity the better the company. Up to a point.[38]

I believe this passage indicates that a purely metalinguistic use of figures would not provide any sort of self-identification. This is because of the closure provided by a conceptual "mental activity" involving a "high" level of abstraction. However, self-identification becomes possible when the use of tropes and figures positing the self (as "he," "you," "one," "speaking voice," etc.) remains within the limits of a "lower" mental activity, that is, "up to the point" of not identifying with the literality of each one.

In this sense, *Company* develops Beckett's view of language inasmuch as it transforms the epistemological nominalism of works like *The Unnamable* and *How it is* into the problematic practice of a ceaseless use of language. In an article on Beckett and Fritz Mauthner, Linda Ben-Zvi pointed out that:

While Mauthner displays no humour in his self-proclaimed battle against the limits of language, Beckett recognizes the irony inherent in waging a war with weapons supplied by the force you wish to vanquish.[39]

I agree with this statement, and would even emphasize the value of the battle that seems to emerge from the late Beckettian works. It is the value of a phenomenological reducing, that does not transcend into the metaphysics of a reduction. Linguistic practice and literary practice survive as a constant questioning of epistemological boundaries, knowing that these boundaries are shaped by the very questioning that actually occurs.

Beckett's latest works show that, even though the access to reality is not ensured, the questioning of the means of knowledge can acquire a new direction and a new value, as actual exploration of these limits. A new insight derives from what Linda Ben-Zvi describes as "the impossibility of verification and the impossibility of proving this impossibility."[40] An ethical imperative is provided precisely by this undecidability, which becomes a new theoretical perspective and an actual starting point. Even if there is no way of transferring reality into words, there is also no way of denying the epistemological value of an investigation of the quality and mode of the limits of language in relation to reality, questioning language as the means of construction of reality itself. Even if presence is forever excluded from language, yet the working of consciousness is manifested by different (in time and structure) figural choices. Tropes, then, corrode the absoluteness of the imperative which denies the possibility of knowing anything, because they imply the recognition of a *différance* within language itself. This is why, I think, the issue of verifiability is posited in *Company,* from the very beginning, within the scope of rhetoric:

> Only a small part of what is said can be verified. As for example when he hears, You are on your back in the dark. Then he must acknowledge the truth of what is said. By far the greater part of what is said cannot be verified. As for example when he hears, You first saw the light on such and such a day. Sometimes the two are combined as for example, You first saw the light on such and such a day and now you are on your back in the dark. A device perhaps from the incontrovertibility of the one to win credence for the other. That is then the proposition. To one on his back in the dark a voice tells of a past.[41]

There are at least two central sentences concerned with an epistemological issue in this passage. One regards the unverifiable nature of most statements or parts of statements ("By far the greater part of what is said cannot be verified."); the other, endowed with a metalinguistic nature, calls to the reader's attention the verbal nature of any statement ("That is then the proposition."). Thus the narrative invites the reader to see that there is no innocence nor immediacy in reformulations, which is like saying that "sameness" can never be kept, in spite of the presumed sameness of referents. Furthermore, the enhancement of knowledge is often just a form of "translation," carried out through devices subjugated by a different logic, and directed by a different teleology (a "device perhaps from the incontrovertibility of one [statement] to win credence for the other"). In order for any self-knowledge to be achieved, it is necessary to go through a self-reflective formulation, which, on one side, does not rely on an a priori ontological objectivity, but, on the other, strives beyond the closure of a metalinguistic description. We can see an example of this type of knowledge in the last two sentences of the above passage, which should never be interpreted separately. Only by being together do they produce the image of a modern episteme: "That is then the proposition. To one on his back in the dark a voice tells of a past." Not only is the linguistic nature of description shown by a metanarrative statement ("that is then the proposition"), but description is substantially modified by it, as it becomes impossible for the reader to ignore the visibility of language in relation to the referent, and hence the linguistic structure of reality.

The Invisible Self: Between Utterance and Enunciation

A deconstructive epistemology can begin only by taking into account the linguistico-temporal nature of a formulation, instead of escaping into pure metalanguage, in the name of some formal truth yet to be achieved. One of the ways in which the refusal of abstraction can be expressed in narratives is the showing of the frame of the enunciation. In *Company* Beckett illustrates the different positions of the subject of a message in relation to the message itself. In "Fragment 51" and in "Fragment 52" the unwilled "formulations" of perceptions are played off against the formulations of a conscious will:

> What if not sound could set his mind in motion? Sight? The temptation is strong to decree there is nothing to see. But too late for the moment.[42]

> So while in the same breath deploring a fancy so reason-ridden and observing how revocable its flights he could not but answer finally he could not. Could not conceivably create while crawling in the same create dark as his creature.[43]

The inescapability of perception-representation formulated in the first fragment is followed by the declaration of the necessity of achieving a statement that, by including the enunciation into the message, could posit the subject as both "creature" and "creator," "the one who sees" and "the one who decrees there is nothing to see." The unnamable subject which actually underlies all utterances is thus foregrounded, according to the epistemic choice of not separating the process of concept production from the concept itself. Both "Fragments" allude to the subject of the enunciation and show us that it always has an active power on the utterance, even when the utterance itself seems to revoke that power. Here we are reminded of the fact that one cannot create "as his creature" what substantiates oneself, which is like saying that it is not possible in narrative to create a statement in which the subject of the enunciation is perfectly co-extensive with, and inclusive of, the subject of the utterance (and vice-versa). Their heterogeneity is described by Lacan as "the organism and its reality," the *Innenwelt* and the *Umwelt* whose relation is established in "the mirror stage" of identification.[44] Thus, the statement "Could not conceivably create while crawling in the same create dark as his creature," seems to me a reminder of the power of the invisible subject of the enunciation, a subject simultaneously hidden and revealed by the messages in which it is systematically "alienated " because it can surface only as "creature" rather than as "creator-creature."

Furthermore, the awareness of the relationship of enunciation and statement casts a new light on the major theme of *Company,* which actually regards the "exchanging of words" (the voice coming to one in the dark), and also foregrounds the fact that *Company is* a verbal exchange, a "speech act" performing "company" with a reader. In this light, the perception of the pseudo-homogeneity of the participants in the linguistic exchange comes to question also the pervasiveness of the indicative system of narration. The riddle concerning the nature of the interlocutors, formulated at the thematic level within the narrative (as "who is speaking?" and "to whom?"), is paralleled by the somewhat critical development of communication with the reader (who is . . . , or who are . . . the characters?). The reader needs to presume the existence of a speaking subject (or subjects?), but the very process through which he or she can identify it as an "I" (speaking to himself about himself) discloses to him or to her the irreducible complexity of the interlocutors involved in the verbal exchange. Furthermore, the epiphany of the "I" can be achieved only if the reader overcomes the resistance to abandon the designative system which must be adopted in order to formulate any hypothesis concerning the character(s). We must remember that, once a designative system has been adopted, it is very hard to defamiliarize its referents, even though it is only the passing from one designation to another that can account for the perception of one subject, narrated as "a composite of perceiver and perceived."[45]

Through a systematic fragmentation, a narrative suspension, and the simultaneous use of different referential systems, discourse in *Company* manages to challenge the objective limits of reference, as well as the immediacy of the "I." As I have said, the "I" acknowledged by the reader as (a result of) "company," and at the end of *Company,* derives from a defamiliarization of the pronominal paradigm, because the semantic "content" of each pronoun is shown as a mere position, in relation to the others. The defamiliarization of the "he" and of the "you" erodes the literality of these pronouns, the literality of the *imago,* and leads the reader to question who the subject(s) involved "really" are. The answer is provided in showing that many different pronouns work as functional constituents of the "I," rather than by confirming "it" as the object of a simple, direct reference. The substitutive exchanges that constitute the "I" become the designation of a subject conceived in a modern manner, a subject that cannot be expressed, perhaps even with the illusion of retaining his or her presence. It is the very coexistence of at least two systems of referentiality that becomes the instrument through which reference can achieve a certain degree of clarity and precision, once the reader perceives their convergence on the "same" composite subject. For example, the following passage ("Fragment 3") provides an essential clue to this understanding of "company":

> Use of the second person marks the voice. That of the third that cankerous other. Could he speak to and of whom the voice speaks there would be a first. But he cannot. He shall not. You cannot. You shall not.[46]

As one can see, "persons" are designated here through two simultaneous systems of reference: one is the habitual pronominal and lexical apparatus (using the "he" and "you," the "other," "to/of whom" and "the voice"), and the other does not use, but merely describes, the elements of the first system ("the second person," "the third," "a first"). This duplicity, of use and description of the same system of reference (the pronominal system), produces the general ambiguity of reference which characterizes Beckett's literary discourse, as it suspends a direct reference to the object (the "I"), and only provides a figure of it (as "a first" person). On the other hand, the use of the two systems clarifies the fact that the passage talks about an "I," because the two systems converge in pointing that out: "there would be a first" person, if "he could speak to and of whom the voice in the second person speaks."

The complex typology of this (pseudo-)referential discourse works inferentially, and thus shows the inadequacy of naming the "I" while hiding its essentially relational nature, which, however, tries to appear in the narrative. In this narrative, the meaning of the "I" is achievable through morphosyntactic and metanarrative *movements,* so that the reader sees that no lexical unit could adequately capture its complex nature. No single mask of the "I" can provide an adequate indication of its wholeness ("Could he speak . . . But he cannot. He shall not. You cannot. You shall not"), but the *movement* of the masks can show an, until then invisible, "I."

We must remember that simulations of self cannot be avoided, since the very definition of the "I" occurs through the language that alienates it from presence. But a blockage in the flow of images would be much worse, because it would transform the refusal of using them into the failure of not being able, ever, to indicate the fact that they are precisely images.

A Suspended Referentiality: The Tropology of the Subject and the Effects of Readability

Beckett's refusal to name the "I" can thus be read as an attempt to "wear out" logocentrism, insofar as differences in "being" can appear in the narrative, thanks to a suspended referentiality. Inevitably, that suspension will lead to a vision of the inescapable "tropology of the subject." As de Man noted: "it demonstrates in a striking way the impossibility of closure and of totalization (that is the impossibility of coming into being) of all textual systems made up of tropological substitutions."[47]

Beckett's mimesis critically mirrors the pervasive network of "masks," figures, and analogies through which language works, so that the reader comes to see that they (in)form the reality of the world. His narrative strategy, so obstinately paradigmatic, fragmentary and obscure, posits here the question of the legitimacy of translatability of persons into referents. This translatability occurs in language all the time, mostly through pronominal and tropological exchanges. However, in Beckett these exchanges do not and cannot mirror an uncracked, unified, "I," endowed with referential self-sameness; at best they show a configuration of positions, never extraneous to language. This configuration becomes readable as a sequence or a coherence, and produces the "effect of an I."

The "I" shown by a Beckettian mimesis turns out to be the result of an interpretation; it does appear, but as an effect of readability, not of a conceptual, abstract referentiality. In this profound sense, I think that in *Company* we can find the culmination of the process of disjunction of body from self which in Beckett's previous narratives was equally radical but was always formulated within the frame of literary referentiality. For example, it is easy to read the emblematic portrait of *The Unnamable* (1953) as a warning against the illegitimate identification of person and physicality. In a similar way, the ironical ending of *From an Abandoned Work* (1957) constitutes a real challenge for the imagination, as it rests on the image of "my body doing its best without me." More recently, "the vehement refusal to relinquish third person" that Mouth exhibited in *Not I* presents a figure that "fails to acknowledge a unified self."[48] Whether we interpret this refusal as a choice or as failure, the significance of a non-unified self goes beyond the achievements of a successful character and foregrounds the impossibility of unification outside a concept. In *Company* mimesis is critical, epistemologically oriented, rather than bound to the prescriptions of genre. The use of fragmentation and repetition prevents the accomplishment of a metaphysical concept (a "unified I" or a "transcendental ego," for example). Here, the apprehension of mutually determined predicators of subjectivity (e.g., syntactic values) that produce the effect of a referential definition deconstructs the fallacious apprehension of the "I" as a cohesive sameness, which unduly abolishes the intestine difference within the "I."

It is important to note that this mode of narrative makes equally clear the fact that the self administers but cannot master the full meaning of the subject, which is to say that consciousness can only capture the self as an object, ignoring the simultaneous double of its subject-object relation (as subject of the enunciation, in the act of relating to itself as the subject of the utterance). In his essay on the mirror stage Lacan has shown how the subject is an effect of the symbolic, but also how the mastered image of self inevitably forecloses the authenticity of the subject. If "the mirror-image would seem to be the threshold of the visible world,"[49] I believe that in *Company* the enactment of language provides a similar, pervasive horizon. A mimetic, non-diegetic use of language mirrors the use of "persons" (the use of pronouns, and the role of designative systems), through the words of the subject of the narrative that is constituted by it.

Thus the un-iconic image of the "I" provided by this narrative "portrays" the subject of the narrative as the result of legibility, as an "I" deriving from the related images of "others." Also, according to Lacan, the "I" is "objectified in the dialectics of identification with the other, and before language restores to it, in the universal, its function as subject."[50] What Lacan calls the final "orthopedic form of a totality"[51] coincides in *Company* with the reader's perception of an "I" at the end of the narrative, an "I," however, that masterfully refers to a subject performing his definition.

In *Company,* furthermore, the inevitable alienation of the subject from his or her own discourse remains open, suspended forever by the actual silence following the final "Alone." A subject that is caused by language can, perhaps, be "restored" by silence, as silence can be a subtraction, a subtraction of the signifiers that have played the role of his "alienated" constitution. When silence follows the use and role of signifiers, when silence comes after the "mediatization" that according to Lacan has forever banned the subject from itself while constituting it, it literally suspends that alienation, even if, obviously, it engenders oblivion, and the invisibility of the "I."

Notes

1. Samuel Beckett, *Company* (London: John Calder, 1980). All subsequent references are to this text. In the case of short quotations page numbers will be given directly in the body of the text.
2. Sigmund Freud, *An Outline of Psychoanalysis,* James Strachey, trans. (New York: Norton Library, 1963) p. 13.
3. *Ibid.,* p. 13. Emphasis mine.
4. Samuel Beckett, *Company,* p. 7.
5. "Voluntary memory [. . .] provides an image as far removed from the real as the myth of our imagination or the caricature furnished by direct perception [. . .] permanent reality, if any, can only be apprehended as a retrospective hypothesis." Samuel Beckett, *Proust* (New York: Grove Press, 1957) p. 4.
6. Samuel Beckett, "Malone Dies" in *"The Beckett Trilogy: Molloy, Malone Dies, The Unnamable"* (London: Picador-Pan Books, 1979, first published 1959) p. 169.
7. Samuel Beckett, *Proust,* p. 52.
8. Søren Kierkegaard, *Repetition* with *Fear and Trembling,* Howard V. Hong and Edna H. Hong, eds. and trans., in *Kierkegaard's Writings* VI (Princeton, N.J.: Princeton University Press, 1983) p. 154. See Chapter Three, n. 3.
9. Samuel Beckett, *Company,* pp. 7–8.
10. Roland Barthes, "The Death of the Author" in *Image—Music—Text,* Stephen Heath, trans. (New York: Hill and Wang, 1977) p. 145.
11. For a discussion of the technical term "entailment" see Neil Smith and Deirdre

Wilson, *Modern Linguistics: The Results of Chomsky's Revolution* (Bloomington and London: Indiana University Press, 1979). In particular see pp. 148–71.

12. A pioneering definition of "plot" and "story" was provided by E. M. Forster in his Cambridge lectures of 1927, published as *Aspects of the Novel* (New York: Harcourt, Brace & World Inc., 1927). Today a vast bibliography is available for the critical discussion of literary narratives. I note here the important issue of *Communications* 8 (1966) which was devoted entirely to the analysis of narratives. See in particular Roland Barthes, "Introduction à l'analyse structurale des récits" (later translated and included in *Image—Music—Text* as "Introduction to the Structural Analysis of Narratives," pp. 79–124); and Tzvetan Todorov, "Les catégories du récit littéraire" (translated as "Analysis of the Literary Text" and included in his *Introduction to Poetics* [Minneapolis: University of Minnesota Press, 1981] pp. 13–58).

13. Samuel Beckett, *Company,* pp. 65–66.

14. For a discussion of temporality in narratives and drama see Angela Locatelli, *Introduzione semiologica al teatro shakespeariano* (Milano: Cooperativa Libraria I.U.L.M., 1976) and Keir Elam, *The Semiotics of Theatre and Drama* (London: Methuen, 1980).

15. Edmund Husserl, *Logical Investigations,* J. N. Findlay, trans. (London: Routledge & Kegan Paul, 1970). See in particular Volume II of the German Edition, Chapter 4, "The Phenomenological and Ideal Content of the Experiences of Meaning," pp. 327–36. Quotation p. 329.

16. *Ibid.,* p. 330.

17. Samuel Beckett, *Company,* p. 7.

18. Barbara Johnson, "Rigorous Unreliability," *Critical Inquiry* 11, 2 (Dec. 1984) 278–85. Quotation p. 280. Now in *A World of Difference* (Baltimore: John Hopkins University Press, 1986) p. 18.

19. Samuel Beckett, *Company,* pp. 88–89.

20. *Ibid.,* p. 89.

21. Eric P. Levy, "'Company': The Mirror of Beckettian Mimesis," *Journal of Beckett Studies* 8 (Autumn 1982) 95–104. Quotation p. 99.

22. *Ibid.,* p. 100.

23. Hans Joachim Schulz, *This Hell of Stories: A Hegelian Approach to the Novels of Samuel Beckett* (The Hague and Paris: Mouton, 1973) p. 17.

24. Samuel Beckett, *Company,* p. 88.

25. *Ibid.,* p. 89. Emphasis mine.

26. Robert Champigny, "Adventures of the First Person" in *Samuel Beckett Now,* Melvin J. Friedman, ed. (Chicago and London: University of Chicago Press, 1975) pp. 119–28. Quotation p. 128.

27. Roland Barthes, "Political Modes of Writing" in *Writing Degree Zero,* Annette Lavers and Colin Smith, trans. (New York: Hill and Wang, 1968) p. 19. Emphasis mine.

28. According to Virginia Cooke (see *Beckett on File* [London: Methuen, 1985]), *Company* was written in English between 1977 and 1979, and was then translated into French as *Compagnie* by Beckett (and published in Paris in 1980 by Les Éditions de Minuit). Adaptations started in July 1980 when it was broad-

cast by BBC Radio 3, with Patrick Magee. Adaptations for performance soon followed: one at the National Theatre at the Cottesloe, September 1980 (Director John Russell Brown, with Stephen Moore), and one by Mabou Mines in New York, 1983 (Director Frederick Neumann and Honora Ferguson).

29. Eileen Fisher, "'Company': A Mabou Mines Production at the Public Theater, New York City," *Journal of Beckett Studies* 10 (1985) 165–68. Quotation p. 165.

30. *Ibid.*, p. 166.

31. *Ibid.*, p. 167.

32. Samuel Beckett, *Company*, p. 64.

33. *Ibid.*, pp. 13–14.

34. *Ibid.*, p. 14.

35. The failure of self-identification structures Beckett's play *Not I*. Its protagonist constitutes a perfect example of the incapacity of going through the looking-glass of pronominal mimesis. See also Chapter Three.

36. Samuel Beckett, *Company*, p. 27. Emphasis mine.

37. Paul de Man, "Autobiography as De-Facement" in *The Rhetoric of Romanticism* (New York: Columbia University Press, 1984) pp. 67–81. Quotation pp. 70–71.

38. Samuel Beckett, *Company*, p. 15.

39. Linda Ben-Zvi, "Fritz Mauthner for Company," *Journal of Beckett Studies* 9 (1984) 65–88. Quotation p. 66.

40. *Ibid.*, p. 69.

41. Samuel Beckett, *Company*, pp. 7–8.

42. *Ibid.*, p. 70.

43. *Ibid.*, p. 75.

44. We have only to understand the mirror stage *as an identification,* in the full sense that analysis gives to the term: namely, the transformation that takes place in the subject when he assumes an image [. . .] This jubilant assumption of his specular image by the child at the *infans* stage, still sunk in his motor incapacity and nursling dependence, would seem to exhibit in an exemplary situation the symbolic matrix in which the *I* is precipitated in a primordial form, before it is objectified in the dialectic of identification with the other, and before language restores to it, in the universal, its function as subject.

Jacques Lacan, "The Mirror Stage as Formative of the Function of the I as Revealed in Psychoanalytic Experience." Lecture delivered at the 16th International Congress of Psychoanalysis, Zurich, July 17, 1949. Published in *Ecrits: A Selection*, Alan Sheridan, trans. (New York and London: W. W. Norton & Company, 1977) pp. 1–7. Quotation p. 2.

45. Samuel Beckett, "Three Dialogues" in *Disjecta*, pp. 138–45. Quotation p. 138.

46. Samuel Beckett, *Company*, p. 9.

47. Paul de Man, "Autobiography as De-Facement," p. 71.

48. Linda Ben-Zvi, " Fritz Mauthner," p. 74.

49. Jacques Lacan, "Mirror Stage," p. 3.

50. *Ibid.*, p. 2.

51. "The *mirror stage* is a drama whose internal thrust is precipitated from insufficiency to anticipation—and which manufactures for the subject, caught up in the lure of spatial identification, the succession of phantasies that extends from

a fragmented body-image to a form of its totality that I shall call orthopaedic."
Ibid., p. 4. Emphasis mine. The original French reads as follows: "le *stade du
miroir* est un drame dont la poussée interne se précipite de l'insuffisance à
l'anticipation—et qui pour le sujet, pris au leurre de l'identification spatiale,
machine les fantasmes qui se succèdent d'une image morcelée du corps à une
forme que nous appellerons orthopédique de sa totalité." *Écrits* (Paris: Éditions
du Seuil, 1966) p. 97.

5. Visibility, Semiosis, and Representation in *ill seen ill said*

Ways of Saying as Ways of Seeing

As in many of Beckett's previous works, the main theme at the core of his short prose piece *ill seen ill said*[1] is the relationship of a personal subject with a spatial object. As a consequence, Beckett's concern involves space and, specifically, the "modality" of space, which is explored and illustrated as being both a way of seeing and the result of a way of seeing. This twofold aspect of seeing (as a mode and as a result) is in turn shown to be determined by what is said, and eventually by what can actually be said. Quite literally, then, in *ill seen ill said* what is visible is shown as the effect of figurality: the visible is captured and endowed with permanence by linguistic figurations.

My reading of this work aims at elucidating the complexity of the structure of seeing that emerges from the narrative, while offering some observations on Beckett's epistemology of perception. In fact, the close connection of seeing and saying, synthesized as it is in the title of the work, entails far-reaching epistemological issues, regarding not so much how we see what we know, but how we know what we see. The issue of the translatability of the said into the seen, and vice versa, determines the development of this narrative, where subject and object (that is, a seer and a seen) keep changing points of view, and even exchange places as one "predicates" the other. The protagonist, a woman we first encounter in the act of star-gazing, becomes the "seen" for a mysterious "seer-sayer," and the two are, in turn, "seen-said" by an impersonal speaker. In the course of the narrative, the saying takes the place of the seeing, leading us away from the "first sight" of the thematic level and disclosing to us the pervasiveness of language.

The metamorphosis linking the seen and the said constitutes the full cycle of a hermeneutics of experience, understood at first as "said as seen" and progressively transformed into a "seen as said," until the fallacy of each individual statement is deconstructed in the narrative, into the problematics of a recurrent "ill seen ill said." The philosophical implications of this "narrative" can perhaps be synthesized by borrowing one of Jacques Derrida's questions from *Writing and Difference:* "is it by chance that the book is, first and foremost, volume?"[2] Indeed, is it by chance that space and language are implicated?

Beckett's epistemological attention to different ways of seeing develops according to an oscillatory and repeated shift of emphasis, from an object to a subject reciprocally related. His analysis of this relation proceeds in such a thorough way that readers become aware of the fact that ways of saying, together with their temporal dimension, are responsible for the determination of visibility. In other words, the reader learns that what is seen has always already been said. In order to develop this theme, *ill seen ill said* employs a large number of accurate details dealing with physical, mental, metaphorical, or figurative ways of looking and seeing, ways that involve both a perceiver and an object, often very minutely described. However, as we shall see, Beckett's reproduction of reality refuses a traditional illustration, and his critical, suspended mimesis becomes the only means that enables him to develop his critique of seeing as produced by saying. Therefore, I will take into consideration the many facets of the structure of seeing, its wavering exteriority (developed in relation to a skyline and a landscape) and its interiority (developed in relation to a "skullscape"). Not surprisingly, at the end of the novel space will be found coextensive with reality and intimately related to time. Space will be designated as a horizon both physical and mental, unreliable when defined, most significant when impalpable.

The opening of the "novel" can be taken as an example of the descriptive quality of narration, of the critical mimesis that structures the entire work:

> From where she lies she sees Venus rise. On. From where she lies when the skies are clear she sees Venus rise followed by the sun. Then she rails at the source of all life. On. At evening when the skies are clear she savours its star's revenge. At the other window. Rigid upright on her old chair she watches for the radiant one. Her old deal spindlebacked kitchen chair. It emerges from out the last rays and sinking ever brighter is engulfed in its turn. On. She sits on erect and rigid in the deepening gloom.[3]

Here the referential quality of star-gazing is fragmented, but also supported by a narration that minutely takes into consideration respectively: 1) the conditions of seeing external to the observer, either remote from her ("when the skies are clear"), close to her ("in the deepening gloom"), or simply related to her ("the last rays"); 2) the attitudes of the observer ("she rails," "she savours," "she watches for"), which are shown to determine the object which is seen ("Venus" at first, "Venus [. . .] followed by the sun," "the star's revenge," and finally "the radiant one"); 3) the positions of the observer, which are again conditions of seeing but determined by the observer herself ("from where she lies," "At the other window," "On her old chair").

Seeing is denoted as the result of those interacting conditions that define it as a changing fact and as a system of transformation, in spite of the chosen stillness of the observer. In the novel, everything changes, except for the "rigidity" of the protagonist ("rigid upright on her old chair [. . .] she sits on erect and rigid"), a rigidity which is itself problematically lingering on the borders between a mental and a physical state. Yet her determination (both mental and physical) cannot guarantee the appearance of the real world: the very choices that allow the articulation of a vision obstruct the articulation of different visions. As a consequence, seeing is always connoted as an "ill seeing," because reality would remain invisible were it not rigidly determined by a frame, "willed" by a choice. It is always an "ill saying" because those determinations obstruct the visibility of an indivisible real, that is, the un-iconic real that can perhaps be imagined but can never be seen.

Furthermore, in *ill seen ill said* physical traits and mental states are evoked together, to complete a vast catalogue of modes and ways of seeing so accurate as to be almost obsessive, and yet visibility is shown as having no more relation to the physical world than to words. In fact, descriptions become efficacious in portraying things because of recurrent repetitions through which the text becomes self-reflecting, reinforcing the iconic effects of portraiture. Visibility is thus connoted as the outcome of a linguistic process involving discourse rather than the solidity of objects, which enter narration through referents or pseudo-referents. From the very beginning of the novel, the establishment of reference depends on repeated narration and the physicality of the objects is conveyed by the confirmations of anaphorical signs and indexes.[4] It is reasonable to read Beckett's descriptions while keeping in mind the hypothesis that description is just a form of discourse, the choice of a self-reflective code with no direct connection to reality. Yet, this type of narration also discloses the fact that language founds the visibility of phenomena, and that this "foundation" happens in the "real" world, even outside the field of literature, whenever speech acts determine the social visibility of the world.

In order to show the modeling and constructive role of language Beckett's narrative strategy constantly produces a doubtful reference; the erratic syntagmatism of his narration scatters the pieces of the descriptive puzzle, rather than correlating them according to a mimetic expectation. Thus, the systematic complexity of the opening description (its elaborate internal parallelisms) and the stratifications of its allusiveness (producing a polymorphic approach to seeing) can easily be lost if the novel is dismissed on the ground of its unsystematic fragmentariness. But, in fact, only ellipsis and repetition can portray "groundless" objects: even stars and chairs can merge into one another, with the help of pronominal vagueness:

> she watches for the radiant one. Her old deal spindlebacked kitchen chair. It emerges from out the last rays and sinking ever brighter is engulfed in its turn.[5]

No ontological or objectifiable conception of space is posited in this narrative; instead, the borders of objectivity and subjectivity are eroded within a vision of space that always configures it as both mental and physical.[6] The complexity of seeing is literally portrayed as the modeling of the world, and the actual seeing, inextricably linked to saying, is shown to be the only means apt to establish a world, even when the borders and structure of seeing are problematic.

Furthermore, the theme of the "mobile subject before an evanescent object," which according to Ruby Cohn and a number of other critics is "Beckett's major chord,"[7] develops here as a denunciation of the inadequacy of sight (the radical "ill seen"), and of the limits of any discourse about the world (the radical "ill said"). We must note that a special emphasis seems to underscore the inevitability of such illness, once the vision is achieved, if it is achieved. The past participle ("seen," "said") is used to express this cognitive condition, which is connoted as an overt failure (*"ill* seen," *"ill* said"). Even when nothing is taken for granted, not even the empirical materiality of objects, as soon as anything is seen and named (or vice versa), a recurrent, inescapable illness pervades cognition. The possibility of grasping time, and of understanding that "it dissolves when unaided" by saying, because it would be deprived of stabilizing iconic traits, reinforces the theme of the ill seen-ill said:

> See the instant see it again when unaided it dissolved. So to say of itself. With no help from the eye.[8]

The paradox of cognition is epitomized in these short sentences: for anything to be known it has to be "aided" by language. However, as soon as language formulates it, it is "dissolved" as well. Permanence is an effect of language, but language cannot capture the actual duration or presence of things. In recent times both de Man and Derrida have developed this idea. In his *Memoires: for Paul de Man* Derrida notes:

> I shall simply stress one point here: the impossibility of naming without in some way appealing to the order of the law.[9]

The "order of the law," it is implied, is not the state of things but a sort of *Gestalt* through which things are apprehended. The "gap" between being and saying, and the possibly wider gap between being and the written word, are explored by de Man who explains them in this way:

> When he states the law, the poet does not say Being, then, but rather, the impossibility of naming anything but an order that, in its essence, is distinct from immediate Being.[10]

The differentiation between "order" and "immediate Being" constitutes one of the important areas of critical investigation in *ill seen ill said* and develops according to distinct complementarities: subjectivity and identification, self-identification and consciousness, mental eye and physical eye, and even left eye and right eye.[11] Most of the time these complementarities are the expression of a skillful narrative strategy portraying a perceiver perceiving a perceiver, but occasionally we can find overt thematic confirmation of them:

> No longer anywhere to be seen. Nor by the eye of flesh nor by the other.
> [. . .]
> Close it for good this filthy eye of flesh. What forbids?
> Careful.
> [. . .]
> Eyes closed in the dark. To the dark. In their own dark.[12]

Beckett's analysis shows how in ordinary experience we feel that the "seen" precedes the "said," how we naively think that we name something only after having seen it, and how we tend to assume that the verbal process always follows and imitates the perceptive process. This "Cratylian fallacy" can be deconstructed by a phenomenological reduction: an accurate analysis of what is seen reveals that the seen is often the result of what is said, and not its cause. In fact, we recognize what we have already endowed with the distinctness of a name, and we simply do not see what we cannot name.

Furthermore, the categories of "immediacy" and "mediation" are reflected in reverse by the mirror of consciousness, so that the effect appears as the cause, the after appears as the before, and the "thing in itself" seems to precede the vision of it. Beckett's refusal of a conventional narrative mimesis certainly does not lead to a final denouement, but it allows the illustration of these perceptive fallacies. Thus, Beckett's manipulation of saying provides an important knowledge about the habitual, but hidden, "ill seen."

By rejecting the traditional separation of subject and object, and by expressing an idea of "nature" as "a composite of perceiver and perceived,"[13] Beckett opts for a new form of representation, one that can portray the "becoming of things." We could apply to him what he says of the Irish poet Thomas McGreevy: "He neither excludes self-perception from his work nor postulates the object as inaccessible. But he knows how to wait for the thing to happen."[14] Furthermore, Beckett's short piece *Still* (1972) can be taken as the beginning of his "late" experimental trend, because it already implies a conception of the literary text as ongoing communication rather than as a linguistic object. Against the stillness of illustration and description, and against the closure of metalanguage, Beckett represents the presence of language. *Still* indicates the duration of a relationship between text and reader ("still there"), rather than the immobility of the text. In this sense it subverts the closure of narratives, determining reference as a process, transforming the narrative into narration.[15] Also the experimental nature of a "novel" like *ill seen ill said* is linked to a mimesis of "happening things," and is constituted by diachronic images that denounce the fallacy of any "still life."

Art's "Insuperable Indigence" and Beckett's "Fidelity to Failure"

As we have seen, Beckett's critical mimesis provides a cognitive reflection on the "ill seen" of ordinary experience. Now we can say that, by depriving things of logocentric stability, he reveals the intentionality of mental acts and plays it against the determinations of the linguistic system. The interplay of desire and signifiers is shown as determining the creation of what

Rainer Maria Rilke calls "the interpreted world,"[16] the world in which we live, the world both as we conceive it and as it is. Objects are shown to exist as determined by the intentionality of mean*ing* and by the available forms of language, and Beckett devises an unusual narrative strategy to reveal to us our logocentric determination of "nature." Furthermore, his literary mimesis does not aim at reproducing the "thing in itself," but at producing reference as a result of a process of identification. Thus, reference is an achievement that takes into account different diachronic components of the perceptive process. Here is an example of how the intentionality of saying is shown to affect the determination of "the thing." In fact, the will and purpose of the perceiver are given as components of the referent:

> Close up of a dial. Nothing else. White disk divided in minutes. Unless it be seconds. Sixty black dots. No figure. One hand only. Finest of fine black darts. It advances by fits and starts. No tick. Leaps from dot to dot with so lightening a leap that but for its new position it had not stirred. Whole nights may pass as may but a fraction of a second or any intermediate lapse of time soever before it flings itself from one degree to the next. None at any moment overleaping in all fairness be it said. Let it when discovered be pointing east. Having thus covered after its fashion assuming the instrument plumb the first quarter of its latest hour. Unless it be its latest minute. Then doubt certain nights of its ever attaining the last. Ever regaining north.[17]

This example illustrates one of the ways in which narrative mimesis can manifest the discrepancy of "seeing" and "saying." Something, "organized" by language in the course of perception (as a "watch"), is organized further, under the pressures of a different teleology (as a "compass"). Obviously, this produces an interesting allusion as to the proximity of time and space, as to the translatability of one into the other, and of seeing into saying. This literary mimesis displays the power of linguistic conceptualization both in the articulation of vision and of description. Furthermore, it shows that, while the seeing of an eye identifies an object, the seeing of a mind's eye *signifies* a subject through that object. In this sense the eye cannot "tear itself away from the remains of a trace," in spite of a previous dream of "Blackness in its might at last. Where no more to be seen. Perforce to be seen."[18]

The uncertainty of the boundary between subject and object is one of the major themes of this narrative, and it develops by eroding the conceptualization that would keep such boundaries clearly distinct. Description does not denote objects, but alludes to their subjective implications and to the possibility of connotative residua in any repetition of naming. For example,

Beckett introduces several points of view in his descriptions, views that can eventually be arranged in a hierarchical order, but only after we have read the entire text. In fact, they are expressed or illustrated with no authorial classification of their role, and according to no expected mimetic order. Thus, the protagonist's "seeing" is simultaneously reproduced as interiority and as exteriority, as a literal seeing or as a figurative one, and, specifically, together with a viewer's view of her. The unexpected, unsignaled changes of point of view suggest relativization, not only because they constitute a limitation of intentionality and map out a conflict of wills about the inter-pretation of the world, but also because the manifestation of these different points of view is never inscribed into the final, absolute will of a narrative affirmation. Rather, the will of the text appears as a desire to show the happening of contrasting wills, as a conflict irresolved to the point of drowning the will of the text in the allusion to other world determinations and descriptions.

At the level of discourse, stylistic variations reveal the presence of a "desire in language," of a will that, on one hand, has to face the compelling imperatives of a linguistic system (independent of a conscious subject), and on the other appears precisely as the result of a series of choices. Thus the definition and the investigation of the radical illness of seeing and saying comes to deal with the signifier, without which, according to Lacan and also according to Beckett, there would be no subject.[19] Yet a special attention for the signifier, within the context of an investigation of the "ill seen ill said," cannot result in a purely metalinguistic endeavor. It has to open onto the problematic territory of the power of rhetoric, investigating it in relation to the *potentia rerum,* the power of things. The Ciceronian belief in the stability of things, and the subsequent view of words "follow-ing them" (*"Res tenent, verba sequentur"*), is subverted to the extent that the issue of expressive adequacy can no longer be grounded in a simple analogi-cal presupposition. Beckett's readers are asked to confront the problem of phenomenalism from a modern perspective, with the awareness of the fact that a lot is yet to be known about our interpretations, and consequently about our (interpreted) world. This task requires the capacity of bearing a "confusion" that works as an antidote to the generally accepted "ill seen ill said." The "confusion" advocated by Beckett is in fact the opposite of a metaphysical, logocentric way of thinking:

No matter. No matter now. Such the confusion between real and—how say its contrary? No matter. That old tandem. Such now the confusion between them once so twain. And such the farrago from eye to mind. For it to make what sad sense of it may. No matter now. Such equal liars both. Real and— how ill say its contrary? The counter-poison.[20]

The epistemological implications of this passage are very important. First of all they contest "the old tandem" of binary oppositions, rigid distinctions that polarize "eye" and "mind," the physical and the mental world, into an untenable dualism ("such now the confusion between them [. . .] such the farrago from eye to mind"). Furthermore, the passage deconstructs these oppositions, by showing the power of language in the articulation of (pseudo-)opposites, and by producing a resistance to the accomplishment of the binary pair ("between the real and—*how say* its contrary?"). In fact, thanks to this suspension, we come to see that the "unreal" is not the opposite of the real; it is only a "partial object," a ready-made, complementary product of conceptualization that actually closes movement within the real, and betrays it, with a closed, frozen image. The serious attempt to "say its contrary" reveals that the "real" is an all encompassing, pervasive procession of *différance,* a limitless movement "from eye to mind," including every kind of reality. The real has no "real" contrary, therefore the only way of speaking about such "contrary" is conceptually "ill said." The theme of the inescapability of the real also appears in the play *A Piece of Monologue* (1980), where the main character, assuming positions that are similar to the ones of the protagonist of *ill seen ill said*,

Stands there staring beyond at that black veil lips quivering to half-heard words. Treating of other matters. Trying to treat of other matters. Till half hears there are no other matters. Never were other matters. Never two matters. Never but the one matter.[21]

Again, it is an indigent type of discourse that in Beckett expresses basic "truths." In this case, the revelation of the pervasiveness and inescapability of the world, given as a "half-heard" discourse, comes to match the denunciation of the "ill said" expression: "the contrary of the real." Once more, impotence and negation constitute Beckett's "counter-poison" to the dogmas of logocentrism; once more a reduction opens our eyes onto something unseen. In this case we see the effects of the play of *différance* against the closure of an "ill said" common sense.

Beckett has always defended an "art unresentful of its insuperable indigence,"[22] but at the same time he has also denounced the fallacy of absolute negation and refused the seduction of dogmatic nihilism. His description of Abraham van Velde as an artist who "cannot paint, since he is obliged to paint,"[23] and "who was among the first "to desist from [. . .] estheticized automatism"[24] certainly reflects his idea of an exploring artist. Coherently with it, right in the midst of his critique of the "ill said," Beckett prompts a preference for incomplete expression, and modes that keep discourse open. The disclosure of a closed "ill said" cannot rest in its being a denunciation. Thus, of his "fidelity to failure" Beckett makes

> a new occasion, a new term of relation, and of the act which, unable to act, obliged to act, he makes an expressive act, even if only of itself, of its impossibility, of its obligation.[25]

A "fidelity to failure" is Beckett's strategy in the pursuit of a knowledge that finds in art its expression. Obviously, it has to be an art that chooses no external finality, being totally absorbed in the exploration of its obligation, of its destiny. The artist's "no desire to express, together with the obligation to express"[26] can explain why he does not deny the existence of perceiver and perceived, even though he does not formulate their relation in terms of an ontological distinction, and thus does not keep them separated in his "confused" narrative.

As I have said, Beckett's "novel" starts from the relation of perceiver and perceived ("she sees Venus rise"), but the exploration of seeing soon multiplies and mingles the traces of perceiver(s) and perceived(s). Their involvement with one another is repeatedly expressed, their "farrago" is given as a datum of reality, and yet, in order to be given, it has to engender the unintelligibility of the story that reproduces it. The ill-said order of the universe appears through the difficult saying of narration, a lucid, critical "half-saying" that transforms the scope of mimesis from traditional imitation to critical investigation. As a result of this process, nature can be portrayed in *ill seen ill said,* but according to Beckett's definition, as an experience, not as a *datum.*[27] He had expressed a similar interest in the existential aspects of representation when he praised Thomas McGreevy's poems because "it is the act and not the object of perception that matters"[28] in them, and the "act of perception" obviously demands the active relation of perceiver and perceived.

Along this line of thought Beckett admired McGreevy's ability to "wait for the thing to happen," eventually leaving the perceiver to wonder why he or she had not seen it before. This effect of surprise is the antidote to the dogma of the inaccessibility of things, which *can* appear, after all; that is, after the conscious vision or the habitual visibility of things is modified. A radical openness is demanded as the only way to let this "happening" be inscribed into the "ill said" and modify it. An openness is invoked, respectful of time as revealed by change:

> Scrapped all the ill seen ill said. The eye has changed. And its drivelling scribe. Absence has changed them. Not enough. Time to go again. Where still more to change. Whence back too soon. Changed but not enough. Strangers but not enough. To all the ill seen ill said. Then back again.[29]

Reciprocal Reflections: Words and Visibility

We normally think of visibility as a primary, intrinsic quality of objects, that are seen simply because they are objects. However, things are seen as repetition, as a result of the use of language. They are seen when a word exists to name them, and consequently they are seen as an effect of how they are named. This fact is expressed quite simply in the Genesis story of Adam where we learn that "the Lord God formed every beast of the field and every bird of the air, and brought them to the man to see what he would call them; and whatever the man called every living creature, that was its name."[30] Naming is not a descriptive, passive technique, and the Eden story is a reminder of the fact that the name is a determination of the thing, a determination which characterizes the human relation to an otherwise inaccessible "living creature." The statement "whatever the man called [. . .] that was its name" is not purely tautological, but should be read as intrinsically performative.

Today, although we know of the arbitrary nature of the link between things and words, we still tend to ignore the fact that words imply a determination. Similarly, although we believe that there is no simple analogy between syntactic structures and connections among phenomena, we use syntax as if it were directly expressive, or faithfully representative, of the happening of those phenomena. It is thanks to major scientific and epistemological revolutions that we are forced to remember that syntax works precisely because it is a model, not the "objective correlative" of the connections of what happens. Thus, when something previously unseen appears, it is because a previously unexplored expressive possibility of the linguistic system begins to work and produces its results. The effect of suddenness that often accompanies this seeing is a mere surprise, rather than the result of the "objective" speed of its happening or the sign of a real beginning.

The history of science and of epistemology is full of instances of the fact that a new concept or a new icon can create the visibility of the unseen.

Once we see visibility as a semiotic effect, we can no longer believe that seeing is originated only by "things-in themselves." On the contrary, we have to take into consideration the effect, and question the degree of linguistic determination. So, on one hand, saying is not directly descriptive (it is not a mere registration of the form of the "thing in itself," which does not exist) and, on the other hand, seeing is not altogether passive or "formless." Saying and seeing determine one another in turn, "ill" from the inevitable, yet unseen contamination, "ill" from a constant, mostly unrecognized mingling. Semiotic and grammatological theories have helped us to investigate this "contamination." According to Charles Sanders Peirce, an object can be defined by a sign, but "every sign that is understood gives rise to another sign in the mind of the interpreter. This second sign is the interpretant of the first,"[31] so the determination of an object is always linked to an interpretant. Furthermore, according to Jacques Derrida, "the signified always already functions as a signifier."[32] Thus, we can say that one "illness" of seeing ensues from a belief in the dependence of the interpretant on the object, or from a belief in the "secondarity" of signifiers. This could explain why in *ill seen ill said* nature is expressed with total disregard for the metaphysical notion of the "adequacy of expression." This "composite of perceiver and perceived" is expressed by transforming referents, which "enter the game" so that the lines of communication remain open. Instead of invoking *le mot juste* Beckett underscores the "Beneficient Fecundity of the Imperfect,"[33] which sets us free from the ideal "notion of an unqualified present—the mere 'I am'."[34] The fecundity of ever imperfect signifiers derives from the temporal quality of their difference, from their unlimited semiosis. *Différance* is the antidote to a crystallized, atemporal "ill said" that engenders or perpetuates the "ill seen." The difference between the seen and the said, between designation and expression, between referents at different moments of notation, or between referents of different sign systems, can be perceived only within the horizon of what *is* said or expressed, of what must be said or expressed in order to be susceptible of transformation.

We must also remember, however, that when a discrepancy between the seen and the said is perceived, as well as when duration manifests itself as a component of the referent and of the segnic function, disquieting effects of unfamiliarity are produced. This seems the warning implied by these Beckettian words:

The already ill seen bedimmed and ill seen again again annulled.[35]

Kant describes such surprising effects as the "dynamical sublime," not without revealing to us the vertigo produced by an "indeterminate concept of reason,"[36] a vertigo which might generate the unreliable, groundless belief in the actual existence of an infinite signified, as a remedy to the contingent limitations of language. Yet, as we have seen, the revoking of the referral of signifiers produces an "ill seen" that cannot account for the discrepancies of visibility that often characterize perception. Beckett, on the contrary, exploits the power of the literary system in relation to the semiotics of the natural world, so as to reveal the primary role of the signifier and the importance of time in the structuring of our cognitive systems. He produces and shows discrepancies between interpretants and objects defined by them, between designation and visibility, between the seen and the said. Even though the linguistic system does not coincide with presence (with non-linguistic experience), in *ill seen ill said* he shows us that time provides the ground for the actual transformation of signifiers, and for the suspension-translation of certain cognitive systems into different ones. Were it not for time, no transformation could occur, but on the ground of duration signs of a system can suspend their designative value and express a different signified, which can be used within the same system or assumed by a different one, as a signifier. All the critics that have worked on *ill seen ill said* have underscored the referential difficulty of the text. In fact, I think that reference is hard to establish because narration expresses duration as a component of the referent, and time as the ineliminable element of any categorization. Repeated temporal indications pervade the novel, and they are structured in such a complex way that the passing of time is far more than just a theme of the story. The system of temporality is here based on the most sophisticated semiotic systems, combining denotation and expression, which, interacting with one another, transform diegesis into mimesis, narration into enactment.

Deconstructing Literary Representations: Back to Reference

A critical approach to language characterizes all of Beckett's works, and in *ill seen ill said* a sort of semiotic passion develops his elucidation of seeing. As I have noted, modes, ways, and times of seeing are explored and redefined, always implying and proving that none of them could achieve permanence without language. The "novel" develops all those aspects of the theme of the "ill seen ill said" in extreme depth, multiplying points of view that focus on seeing, and multiplying ways of saying, so that new ways of seeing can be represented or expressed in the narrative. Thus, the literary work becomes a gnoseological and critical discourse, questioning and exploring the basic aspects of experience that are normally taken for granted, but that should reveal their intrinsically problematic nature. Beckett expresses this need for investigation with a paradox against the power of blind acceptance of "facts" or answers:

If there may not be more questions let there at least be no more answers.[37]

His rhetorically winded pseudo-syllogism implies the clear awareness of the fact that the advancement of knowledge is not provided by answers, but by endless questions. The play of negations comes to denounce the fact that intellectual laziness produces answers that in fact blind us to the strength of endless questions, and close the pursuit of knowledge. Beckett's ethical resentment may well be related to the denunciation of modern literary tautologies, artifacts that build questions to fit their own answers, works of art that could even be metalinguistic, but are essentially un-communicative. An art that is "unresentful of its insuperable indigence and too proud for the farce of giving and receiving"[38] is in fact the opposite of a self-reflective artifact, a work that sustains itself by being autarchically self-sustained, by being a closed system of answers to pseudo-questions. Against systems of predication that have lost their relevance in relation to "reality" (to the play of signifying differences), and against the unity of a discourse that would distort the actual lack of coherence of phenomena, Beckett produces a work that provides no answers, and multiplies the questions. Even descriptive passages are pervaded by the awareness that there cannot be "no more questions." See, for example, the problematic presentation of

The cabin. Its situation. Careful. On. At the inexistent centre of a formless place. Rather more circular than otherwise finally. Flat to be sure. To cross it in a straight line takes her from five to ten minutes. Depending on her speed and radius taken. Here she who loves to–here she who now can only stray never strays. Stones increasingly abound. Ever scanter even the rankest weed. Meagre pastures hem it round on which it slowly gains. With none to gainsay. To have gainsaid. As if doomed to spread.[39]

The multiplicity of opinions expressed about "the cabin" does not eliminate the referential quality of the place, even though reference is animated by many questions, often focused also on the means of description, focused on discourse, when discourse is open onto the problem of reality and is concerned with the state of things as a result of specific formulations.

In Beckett's recent prose works, discourse is self-reflected in order to question its relation to the "real and—how ill say its contrary?" This means that self-reflection is not functional to express the gratifications of mere literary wit. The metanarrative quality of Beckett's discourse is not just a contemporary practice of self-reflective devaluation of traditional narrative conventions, for whatever literary purpose. Unlike many postmodernist writers (such as Barthelme, Sukenick, Barth), Beckett probes into the question of literary reference, and he does so with no intention to create a metanarrative answering-device, merely reflecting the literary text onto itself. Rather, he leaves the issue of reference radically open, so that it displays its problematic nature. An open question, which may seem meta-narrative but whose scope is clearly oriented towards reference, can be found at the end of the description of "the cabin":

> And from it as from an evil core that the what is the wrong word the evil spread.[40]

The metalinguistic question embedded in the text mirrors linguistic choices, but critically, that is, only in order to foreground the pervasiveness of language in relation to reality. Reflection becomes reflexivity, because the production of narrative images is never an end in itself, never a complacent reflection. Thus, even though Beckett certainly does not naively assume that "referentiality is the basic mechanism of the literary mimesis,"[41] yet he is deeply concerned with the presentation of reality, and uses literary re-presentations to focus on the issue of referents. He is concerned with the issue of signs referring to objects, whether mental or physical, rather than focusing on signs referring only to signs.

At this point, it may be useful to remember the fact that the term "mimesis" covers a wide semantic area, and that it acquires a different meaning depending on its relation to "semiosis" or to "diegesis." In relation to this twofold context, Robert Scholes defines mimesis as follows:

> Holding its traditional sense of imitation or representation, this term is now used in two more specific senses. Opposed to diegesis, it means enactment of what is represented as opposed to imagination of the events based on a verbal text. [. . .] In another context mimesis is opposed to semiosis. Here, mimesis is the attempt to take language as literally representational.[42]

Beckett's works clearly show a profound interest in mimesis, in relation both to diegesis (as enactment versus narration) and to semiosis (as degrees of literality). In fact, his works for the theater are intrinsically mimetic, enacting "acts without words" but also testing the limits of mimesis by representing "acts of narration." His prose works, on the other hand, test the boundaries of mimesis by manipulating narration, transforming description into performative indications (see for example the repeated "On," "Careful," "Gently," "Quick," etc. in *ill seen ill said*). Because of their experimental and iconoclastic perspective, Beckett's works clearly show that he shares Riffaterre's view, according to which realism is a convention, not a universal category, and thus

> if we try to arrive at the simplest and most universally valid definition of the representation of reality in literature, we may dispense with grammatical features such as verisimilitude or with genres such as realism, since these are not universal categories.[43]

However, Beckett's primary concern, especially since *The Unnamable* (1956), seems to be more radical than the denunciation of devices that make literature a pseudo-universal artifact. The "intertextual mimesis" that Riffaterre describes can be found particularly in Beckett's early stories, such as "Dream of Fair to Middling Women" (1932), *Murphy* (1938), and "First Love" (1945), where intratextual mimesis is exploited to produce distancing effects, effects of unfamiliarity (see Chapter One, on "Typologies of Meaning"). However, his most recent works do not just follow the usual procedure whereby "it is in and through intertextual mimesis that literature challenges representation."[44] Given that "the mimetic text is not composed of words referring to things but of words referring to systems of signs that are ready-made textual units,"[45] Beckett challenges mimesis with his brilliant unwording. His "poetics of the unword," as described in his essays and realized through his works, indicates an attempt to "subtract" further, from "words referring to systems of signs," thus tending towards the production of "words referring to things." In other words, he deconstructs literariness against the background of reality, and his texts strive towards the production of a retrieved reference, of words referring to "things."

A fragment from *ill seen ill said*, which radically challenges the possibility of maintaining objective distinctions about physical and mental realities seems to illustrate the typically Beckettian erosion of literary referents. Here Beckett is not theoretically invoking the abolition of a difference between referents and literary referents. Unlike some critics, who maintain that the distinction "literary/non-literary" is untenable because of the centrality of language, he does not argue, but *enacts* his un-wording, thus showing that subtraction can be done. He starts from a literary text, but nothing prevents the reader from imagining the "ending" in a speech act. Here is an example of how the erosion within a literary artifact can open onto the "reality" of reference:

> Already all confusion. Things and imaginings. As of always. Confusion amounting to nothing. Despite precautions. If only she could be pure figment. Unalloyed. This old so dying woman. So dead. In the madhouse of the skull and nowhere else. Where no more precautions possible. Cooped up there with the rest. Hovel and stones. The lot. And the eye. How simple all then. If only all could be pure figment. Neither be nor been nor by any shift to be. *Gently gently. On. Careful.*[46]

Thematically, the passage indicates that it is not meaningful (nor would it be successful) to equate reality with a purely willed mental state. The project of a freedom ensuing from "no more precautions to be taken" is bound to end in the awareness of "no precautions possible," and in the image of a "coop," a mock-prison of the perceiver as perceived. It is a prison of the woman, in this case, but only as a "she" thought by her, or, to paraphrase one of Beckett's paradoxes, the image of "her skull doing its best without her."[47] We must notice that the very movement that should subsume the physical world articulates the impossibility of its success, not only because success is given as "wishful thinking" ("*If only* she could be pure figment. Unalloyed [. . .] *If only* all could be pure figment."), but because the "grammar" of phenomena cannot be suspended, according to the wish of "neither be nor been nor by any shift to be." The impossibility of suspension reveals the fact that the content of the project is a mere abstraction, betraying what exists, and confining it to the realm of a mere possibility, ironically expanding: "if only *she* [. . .] if only *all* could be pure figment."

Furthermore, the "skull and nowhere else" as the space of the abstraction that includes the perceiver (if only as perceived) remains a residuum, the condition and the sight of an impossible inclusion.

It is also important to notice that the passage begins by suggesting the abolition of a distinction between "things and imaginings," but that the argument is developed through a rhetorical paradox. By recalling a "confusion amounting to nothing," it renders unanswerable the referentiality of that "nothing." Is the confusion creating "nothingness," or does it "amount to nothing" (to no confusion)? The very structure of the question destroys its informational power, since it establishes de facto the conditions of an impossible answer.[48] The paradox of an unanswerable question proves the fact that meaning is not determined in direct relation to things, but that narration develops by contradicting a closure of discourse, and opens right onto the present of its enunciation ("Gently gently. On. Careful."). It is also clear, then, that language cannot *ultimately* make a "pure figment" of its referents. Language is open onto the real, open to the different semiotic systems of the natural world, even against itself and the absolute power of its inner differences.

Furthermore, even intertextual mimesis can produce referents, referents of literature, rather than multiplying literary signs. Thus we could say that the passage shows that even though language can be used apart from reality (formulating unanswerable questions, letting rhetoric and grammar fight for the power of meaning), if language persists, it will become a referent of itself, the truth of a lie. That is to say, that the literary lie is bound to turn into the truth of the literary simulation. On a narrative level the impossible closure of literature is also illustrated and enacted by including in the message its enunciation, by transforming the narrative into the performance of a communication, sharing the present of reading.

In this sense Beckett is remote from Saussure's conception of the purely paradigmatic nature of meaning. Rather than believing that it is generated solely by relations among words, Beckett stresses the role of temporality in the play of signifiers ("On."). He is interested in the conditions of the working of the linguistic system, and always aware of the diachrony of linguistic syntagmatism. In this sense he seems much closer to the conceptions of language of phenomenology and semiotics.[49] The evidence of the impossibility of "all" being a "pure figment," thanks to the sense of a temporal economy of signifiers, endows his representations even with the doubt of the inevitability of a certain level of mimesis. For one thing, diegesis is often transformed into mimesis, enacting the act of narration it represents; for another, the inescapability of mimesis in relation to semiosis derives from the evidence that even if figurality cannot be eliminated from a literary narration, the *life* of signs cannot be eliminated by their figurality. In other words, Beckett's literary mimesis posits the problem of the relationship between semiosis and mimesis, literality and figurality, even when the borders of mimesis and diegesis seem dissolved into each other because narration has become enactment, the enactment of itself. Thus, I believe that Beckett radically transforms literary diegesis, and transforms it into an instrument for the investigation of the structure and scope of semiosis.

Repetition and the "Scene of Betrayals"

As we have seen, the power of language in relation to reality is at stake in *ill seen ill said,* and is investigated through literary diegesis, even if it is certainly conceived as extending outside it. In this sense, the "final" scene of Beckett's epistemic quest is beyond narratives, and regards language and reality. The critical denouement at the end of *ill seen ill said* focuses on the problem of semiosis, in the light of the *fact* that

> The eye will return to the scene of its betrayals.[50]

The power of intertextual mimesis, but even more the power of an intratextual mimesis, is exploited in Beckett as the power of a return, of a differential repetition which shows that ultimately the "ill-seen" and "ill-said" portrayed in literature regard the problem of the relationship of signs and reality. Riffaterre's suggestions only explore the field of literary mimesis (that is, of mimesis in relation to diegesis), and in this sense his concern about "intertextual representation" is most suggestive when the boundaries of the literary artifact remain unquestioned. This is why his contribution is most usefully applicable to the study of Beckett's early works, because Beckett probes into a different set of problems in his later ones. Here, the "return to the scene of betrayals," which in a sense is a systematic, pro-grammed form of intratextual reference, can be seen as the scene of un-limited semiosis. In fact, we see that Beckett's critical mimesis is never bound by the specificity of any specific textual image. On the contrary, the differential repetition of nearly identical portions of discourse erodes the literariness of pseudo-representations, with an un-wording that articulates questions of presence beyond literary boundaries. His declaration that "the eye will return to the scene of its betrayals," together with his prompting of progressive reductions in the expressive system, underscores the specific *actuality* of the process of saying, through a mode of literary representation that makes the linguistic system visible, so that it can be questioned in relation to the natural world. Consider "Fragment 50" as another example of a textual "opening" onto reality:

But see she suddenly no longer there. Where suddenly fled. Quick then the chair before she reappears. At length. Every angle. With what one word convey its change? Careful. Less. Ah the sweet word. Less. It is less. The same but less. Whencesoever the glare. True that the light. See now how words too. A few drops mishaphazard. Then strangury. To say the least. Less. It will end by being no more. By never having been. Divine prospect. True that the light.[51]

In Beckett the un-iconic vision of a return modifies the vision of whatever scene was, at any one time, under one's eyes. Besides, when that vision takes place, the literary scene is brought to the verge of showing its actual enunciation. Not surprisingly, Beckett can indicate the "ill said" of diegesis as the result of an "ill seen" occurring when the language of perception accumulates "on itself," and the language of narrative accumulates images that do not relate directly to reality. The problem of perceptive diegesis (of the stories we tell ourselves while perceiving reality) is caused by an "ill" vision, one that accumulates images but does not see the role of repetition in the articulation of vision. See how this process is described in the following passage:

The eye will return to the scene of its betrayals. [. . .] Ever heaping for want of better on itself. Which if it persists will gain the skies. The moon. Venus.[52]

As much as seeing tries to capture reality, some literary texts try to achieve a successful reference, to "gain the skies. The moon. Venus." Unfortunately, they normally proceed only by heaping images of the seen, that is, by multiplying pseudo-references and self-references ("heaping for want of better"). Significantly, *ill seen ill said* keeps representing scenes of the eye's betrayal, and yet, unlike most narratives, it finally opens and includes the enunciation of those scenes.

This narrative moves beyond reproduction, onto the presence of actual communication: it opens to mirror the present of reading. The great many repetitions such as "on," "careful," "gently," convoke the reader to the awareness of the ongoing production of meaning, to the presence of literary signs that are actually (working as) referents. The "on," for example, is an imperative addressed to the reader, as well as a sign of the on-going condition of the process of meaning. It is a temporal referent, narrating a time change and self-reflecting its occurrence in the present. It prompts the recognition of the conventional consistency of pseudo-referents, but it is also an index of literary figurality ("on" is different from all the other iconic determinations of temporality and reality). "On" actually states something about the life of signs, and makes the reader aware of a semiotic system that exceeds the language of literary narration.

Time and *Différance*: "Both. All three."

It is through the play of deferred identification and continuation that reference can be retrieved in *ill seen ill said*. An example of the radical ambiguity of an open difference can be found in the referential complexity of "Fragment 25":

> Stares as if shocked still by some ancient horror. Or by its continuance. Or by another. That leaves the face stone cold. Silence at the eye of the scream. Which say? Ill say. Both. All three. Question answered.[53]

In this passage the means of denoting "mouth" suspends reference within the foldings of the composite expression "eye of the scream." Besides producing suggestive effects (of a "hole" that "sends forth a scream"), an audio-visual concurrence reveals the deep links between seeing and saying, and gives way to questions regarding linguistic options ("Which say?"). The pervasiveness of the linguistic system is such that non-linguistic reality can be organized into a model only through it, which makes the "say" "both," ill and not-ill. Saying is thus "all three": ill, not-ill, and both. The principle of non-contradiction (a = a) is challenged by time, both here and in the previous sentence, which had a similar rhetorical structure: "shocked still by some ancient horror. Or by its continuance. Or by another." The logic of binary opposition, entailing exclusion, is thus deconstructed through a syntagmatic progression that erodes the borders of reference. In this sense we could apply to the narrative strategy of *ill seen ill said* what Barbara Johnson says of the strategy of deconstruction:

> Instead of a simple "either/or" structure, deconstruction attempts to elaborate a discourse that says *neither* "either/or," *nor* "both/and" nor even "neither/nor," while at the same time not totally abandoning these logics either. The very word *deconstruction* is meant to undermine the either/or logic of the opposition "construction/deconstruction."[54]

In *ill seen ill said*, Beckett does not surrender to dogmatic scepticism, and literally prompts the reader to be "careful," not to be too resolute. Even though the invitation can assume ironic overtones, it always retains a pedagogical value in relation to the gnoseological quest expressed by the "novel." It calls for awareness, and takes into account the inescapability of duration, which is indicated by the often following, equally recurrent indication, "On." Thus, what is seen and what is said are placed within a temporal continuity that is indicated, even though it cannot be properly illustrated. In fact, duration must be recognized as the condition of any knowledge, and as the milieu in which discourse itself takes place. It is easy to recall the opening of the "story," when the seeing and the saying of the protagonist ("she sees [. . .] she rails") are inscribed within an inescapable temporal advancement signaled by the recurrent "on" in the narration. Duration can only be alluded to, and cannot be expressed with the traits of a specific reference, lest it be betrayed by conceptual abstraction. This impossibility of naming, made explicit by a rhetoric of present temporality, points to the unseen in a way that casts a shade of "illness" on the integrity of saying.

> What is it defends her? Even from her own. Averts the intent gaze. Incriminates the dearly won. Forbids divining her. What but life ending. Hers. The other's. But so otherwise. She needs nothing. Nothing utterable. Whereas the other. How need in the end? But how? How need in the end?[55]

The impossibility of properly naming one's own life derives from the double paradox of one's own life as *appropriated duration* ("What but life ending. Hers. The other's. But so otherwise"). That woman's life is what "defends her," but it is also an "ending," a terminable duration at the end of which it is impossible even to need ("How need in the end? But how?"), and to miss a personal duration (the "Nothing utterable").

In *ill seen ill said,* the dissolution of the borders of referentiality, through the un-iconic image of duration provides a starting point for a questioning of rhetoric in relation to the borders of perceiver and perceived. In the light of an insufficient rhetoric of duration, the "seen" appears as a probable "ill seen," because of its cogent repression of the temporality required for the articulation of perceptions. Similarly the "said" appears as "ill said" because it provides and records atemporal information. On the contrary, the narrative strategy of *ill seen ill said* shows the irreversible nature of temporal advancement, which devoids illustrated actions of any objective value, and denies the possibility of defining actions according to the "objective" criteria of traditional mimesis.

Semiotic Differences: Visibility and Representation

I have argued that the gap between designation (of the object) and expression (of the signified) is an essential feature exploited by the global narrative strategy of *ill seen ill said*. In a similar way, it is almost as if the text is conceived primarily so as to remind a reader of the difference between thought and speech,

> because to speak is to know that thought *must* become alien to itself in order to be pronounced and appear.[56]

Thus, one of the most important themes developed in *ill seen ill said* regards the difference between visibility and representation, and the means through which this difference can be expressed in fiction. In his essay on the "Theater of Cruelty," Derrida emphasized the novelty of Artaud's conception, a project anticipating that

> The stage, certainly, *will no longer represent*, since it will not operate as an addition, as the sensory illustration of a text already written [. . .] The stage will no longer operate as the repetition of a *present*, will no longer *re*-present a present that would exist elsewhere and prior to it.[57]

The opposition between the illustration of a discourse and its theatrical production helps to elucidate Beckett's experiments in the theater, but also in *ill seen ill said*. In fact, the coordinates of visibility in narration depend on description, in the sense that description may or may not want to indicate its means of notation and its degrees of imitation of the "real world." It is obvious that narration cannot recapture the present of what is narrated, but it *can* strive to indicate this impossibility, rather than repress it in the folds of mimetic conventions. The idea of "*re*-presentation as the auto-presentation of pure visibility,"[58] an idea that Beckett must have encountered through his knowledge of Artaud, offers no concrete suggestions in relation to his diegesis, but points to the use of structural repetition so as to express presence and transform diegetic pseudo-referents into mimetic referents of literature.

A further problem ensues from the attempt to represent visibility, not only because of the complex nature of sight (not purely "optical," but phenomenological), but also because it does not involve the mere diegetic/mimetic alternative and demands a temporal, complex interplay of mimesis and semiosis. In order to illustrate visibility in a literary representation, language has to work as literally representational, as figurative and as meta-representational; that is, it has to question the "representativeness" of its elements, in relation to duration. It has to reproduce the "clarity" of the thing, together with the semiotic systems that have determined that clarity. The attempt to include visibility in the reproduction of the "thing," implies a critique of imitation as literality of mimesis, through a metalinguistic relativization. This point is essential to the understanding of Beckett's recent works, because his use of metanarrative devices does not erase the mimetic quality of his works, but strives to include temporality in represen-tation, by means of a tension of literality and figurality that enacts the play of meaning. Unlike postmodernist writers, he is not primarily interested in the production of metafiction: after all, most metanarratives challenge only the language of literary narration. Beckett's critical mimesis regards the representation of the unrepresented, not only the representation of repre-sentations.

The reproduction of visibility in Beckett's recent works is achieved by means of a suspension of designation, and shows the role of language in the structuring of reality. Suspension hampers an immediate grasp of reference, but can show the fact that saying is responsible for visibility. In fact, a suspended designation makes reference difficult to assess, but reproduces, at least in part, the process through which visibility is achieved. Beckett is fighting against the primacy of signifieds, ill seen abstractions, susceptible of naturalistic imitation because void of duration. As Nicholas Zurbrugg remarked in his reading of the novel: "Neither the narrator nor the reader discovers the nature of [. . .] 'scenes,' for [. . .] in *Ill Seen Ill Said,* details remain infuriatingly elusive."[59]

This elusiveness indicates that here the mimetic process does not repress its own duration. Mimesis becomes a textual movement that reproduces "the thing" as temporally determined. The frustrated desire to find a precise reference derives from the need to maintain an indisputable, authoritative center of representation, something like an omniscient perceiver with an encyclopedic access to an infinite deposit of signifieds. On the contrary, the whole narrative is structured as an observation of observing, through an observer of an observer of an observer (the woman, the narrator, and the implied narrator of both). No predominant point of view can found the linear coherence of the text. Thus in *ill seen ill said* a "true-to-life" narrative coherence requires a constant process of interpretation, a reconstruction of reference, because the "novel" refuses the laws of imitation of abstract images of things. This narrative strives instead to represent the process through which things acquire visibility. Specifically, visibility is shown to be what remains when the seen is unworded from the said.

Visibility is representable when signs involve *supplementarity,* that is, when they are caught in "a movement of play, permitted by the lack or absence of a center."[60] In other words, the "ill said" engenders visibility if it remains open to the successive, diachronic movement of signs. This means that it is then *seen* as "ill said," because a discrepancy between referent and object, between designation and expression, opens the message beyond its pseudo-referentiality. When duration is made explicit, language can appear as a *generative* structure of visibility, as an open, diachronic system of designation. Thus narrative description can be seen as the result of a result: in fact, the progressive development of description starts from the results of the process of naming, a process which has already designated the object.

Yet representation in literature, which must perforce be syntagmatic because it is based on language, can also indicate the linear syntagmatism of language, thanks to an erratic "plot," and through disconcerting and un-familiar narrative sequences. Description itself seems made to include the self reflective question: "what description?, of what?" The progressive linearity of description doubles linguistic syntagmatism, and, as much as the conventions of description are shown, literary representation can also show how the identification of things is the result of a convention, the result of a series of successive determinations that have little, if anything, to do with "what" is "actually there." Beckett's critical mimesis foregrounds how the interpretant determines the object, while the object cannot deter-mine the interpretant. The process of visibility is indeed complex; as Beck-ett suggests:

> The mind betrays the treacherous eyes and the treacherous word their treach-eries. Haze sole certitude.[61]

"Haze Sole Certitude": The Irreducible Ambiguity of Literary Signs

An interesting example of the double impossibility of eliminating referen-tiality and of identifying reference is given in many of the obscure passages of *ill seen ill said*. In fact, these irreducibly puzzling passages resist both a purely metanarrative interpretation and a figurative reading. Significant is the example of "the twelve," a narrative element which remains unclarified throughout the whole work. I will quote from "Fragment 3," where "they" appear for the first time:

> Innumerable white scabs all shapes and sizes. Of striking effect in the light of the moon. In the way of animals ovines only. After long hesitation. They are white and make do with little. Whence suddenly come no knowing nor whither as suddenly gone. Unshepherded they stray as they list. Flowers? Careful. Alone the odd crocus still at lambing time. And man? Shut of at last? Alas no. For will she not be surprised one day to find him gone? Surprised no she is beyond surprise. How many? A figure come what may. Twelve. Wherewith to furnish the horizon's narrow round. She raises her eyes and sees one. Turns away and sees another. So on. Always afar. Still or receding. She never once saw one come toward her. Or she forgets. She forgets. Are they always the same? Do they see her? Enough.[62]

The exegetical effort to interpret elements of this passage is bound to failure if it is oriented towards a specific determination of referents. In fact, not only the "Twelve" (interpreted by some critics as Apostles, the "unshepherded sheep"), but many other elements defy clarification. For example, the referential ambiguity of "they stray as they list" is irreducible, loaded with allusions that indicate (as in the French text) the pleasure of straying, but also a "leaning position." Even a blatant contradiction is suggested as a trait of the description ("still or receding"), and then, when mathematical precision should be exploited as evidence of the objectivity of the scene, we are told that the famous "twelve" are just a random mathematical indication ("A figure come what may. Twelve").

Given the disconcerting impossibility of achieving a precise, successful reference, we are led to the appreciation of the code of the narrative, a code of differences oscillating around an undefined semantic nucleus. This radical uncertainty designates a narrative strategy that constantly and relentlessly shifts from the seen to the said, suspending pseudo-referential discourse and also going beyond a self-reflective one. The second time in which the mysterious "twelve" are mentioned, in "Fragment 9," they have become "*The* twelve," no longer a random figure, but a personification:

> It is evening. Yet again. On the snow her long shadow keeps her company. The others are there. All about. The twelve. Afar. Still or receding.[63]

This personification is more than a rhetorical device: it is the way in which visibility can be represented in the narrative, as the outcome of a process of formalized perception. The expression "The twelve" is here the appropriated synthesis of a long perceptive process that in "Fragment 3" had linked: 1) shapes and attributes ("white scabs [. . .] in the way of animals); 2) "after long hesitation"; 3) for a perceiver, who had thus found something "wherewith to furnish the horizon's narrow round." In retrospect, that narrative concatenation mirrors the generative quality of a thought linking seen and said, whereas in "Fragment 9," the synthetic expression "The twelve" represses the process of such identification. The acquired "objectivity" of "the twelve" is confirmed by all the subsequent passages, where, paradoxically, their determination remains unachievable:

> Weary of the inanimate the eye in her absence falls back on the twelve. Out of her sight as she of theirs.[64]

The full cycle of visibility is thus portrayed: the "seen as said" becomes the "Seen no matter how and said as seen."[65] Yet this continuous oscillation of differences, this constant transformation, also reveals the abstraction at the core of the logocentric fallacy. Significantly, the project of a "real" end, articulated in the narrative as the refusal of "another word," leads to the perception of a discrepancy between absolute verbal negation and "real" void:

> No more sky or earth. Finished high and low. Nothing but black and white. Everywhere no matter where. But black. Void. Nothing else. Contemplate that. Not another word. Home at last. Gently gently.[66]

In fact, the absolute negation "No more sky or earth. [. . .] Not another word" breaks down, under the pressure of a doubt, from the evidence of irreducible, ineradicable, haunting "traces." The end of narration underlines the necessity and yet the impossibility of eliminating "traces," as well as pointing to the impossibility of not having been, and of not having interpreted:

> And what if the eye could not? No more tear itself away from the remains of trace. Of what was never. Quick say it suddenly can and farewell say say farewell. If only to the face. Of her tenacious trace.

> Decision no sooner reached or rather long after than what is the wrong word? For the last time at last for to end yet again what the wrong word? Than revoked. [. . .] Farewell to farewell.[67]

The final passages of *ill seen ill said* emphasize the temporal dimension of the endless metamorphosis of concepts ("Decision no sooner taken [. . .]

than revoked."), and shows temporality as an irrevocable movement, independent from the power of a personal will ("revoked" *is* "the wrong word"). It is not in our power to decide and revoke, implicated as we are in the struggle of our will ("for to end") with (our) duration ("yet again").

The instability of our determinations, together with the erosion intrinsic to our successive interpretations of the world, is reflected in the critical mimesis of this narration. Here the recurrence of a series of *"memento mori"* does not imply the metaphysical distinction of time and eternity, nor a radical dichotomy of life and death. The *memento*s are, each time, one of the many *caveat*s (one of the many "careful"s) that throughout the narrative remind us of the power of misleading, because atemporal, logocentric fallacies. We could apply to Beckett's narrative strategy the description he provided of Abraham van Velde's painting:

> a job that insinuates more than it affirms, which is not positive but for the transient and accessory evidence of the great positive, time that decays.[68]

The only "great positive" is identifiable with the irreversible passing of time also in *ill seen ill said,* where duration runs counter to all the ideological positives conceived by culture, and all the axiological positives successively produced by narration itself. The advancement of death struggles in all the positives of culture, and yet it is regularly repressed in all the images that culture produces, in all its conceptual "stills" of life. The passing of time, unrecorded as it is in the things seen-said at any one point, in the things "fixed" by language, is nonetheless the essential "thing" to be seen. That is why conceptualization must be suspected, as it constitutes an extreme denial of the natural extension of things, the spatio-temporal nature of perceiver-perceived. See another example of how this Beckettian text tries to represent reality, through a process that no binary logic could ever synthetize:

> Reexamined rid of light the mouth changes. Unexplainably. Lips as before. Same closure. Same hint of extruding pulp. At the corners same imperceptible laxness. In a word the smile still there if smile is what it is. Neither more nor less . . Less! And yet no longer the same. True that the light distorts. Particularly sunsets. That mockery. [. . .] There the explanation at last. This same smile established with eyes open is with eyes closed no longer the same. Though between the two inspections the mouth unchanged. Utterly. Good. But in what way no longer the same? What there now that was not there? What there no more that was? Enough. Away.[69]

The passage illustrates how the very definition of "sameness" should take into account the passing of time. In spite of its seductions, even nominalism is rejected ("the smile still there if smile is what it is"), and only duration can explain what remains otherwise unexplainable ("the mouth changes. Unexplainably."). We could say that, implied in this description, Beckett re-proposes the Greek paradox of Theseus' ship, even though he provides a different answer to its question. The Greek philosophers aimed at demonstrating that the ship returning to the harbor was still "the same," in spite of the fact that during the voyage all of its parts had been successively replaced. On the contrary, Beckett emphasizes change, disregarding functional continuity: "the same smile [. . .] no longer the same." We must notice the shift in semantic focus, from physical traits to the temporality of change, from "smile" to "What there now that was not there? What there no more that was?" This type of description foregrounds the fact that change is not necessarily visible ("between the two inspections the mouth unchanged"), even when objective factors of change are taken into account ("True that the light distorts."). Only the "sunset," the natural correlative of an "end-*ing*," "mocks" our abstractions and calls forth the acknowledgment of duration. Thus, time can be seen through changes, even if the representation of single stages of reality perpetuates a synchronic "ill seen," expressed by an abstract "ill said." Time never appears in any one iconic "still" of reality, and so it cannot be adequately represented, except un-iconically, through succession. This mode of vision had also been described by Beckett in his essay on the van Velde brothers, when he was meditating on the problems of representational art:

> right at the core, the same dilemma of plastic arts: how can one represent change? [. . .] Succession cannot be represented except through the stages that follow one another, by imposing onto them such a quick flow that they end up merging into one another, I would tend to say that they almost end up finding stability in the very image of succession.[70]

The Temporality of Hypotyposis: The Double Extension of Space

The desire to represent change, and things as determined by their duration, implies a foregrounding of the temporal dimension of representation as well. This means that the perfect temporality of traditional narratives has to be subverted, or at least questioned from within the narrative itself. Thus

Beckett radically transforms the traditional rhetoric of space, metamorphosing hypotyposis and ecphrasis into a series of suspended references.[71] In the course of centuries rhetoricians have praised those figures of speech, because they can vividly capture the visual quality of things, and put them "before our eyes," be it in the literal sense of Cicero's *ponite ante oculos* or in the modern, allusive sense of Corneille's *figure-toi*.

By combining hypotyposis and ecphrasis, Beckett is now telling us that the extension of space is not only objective and psychological but also temporal. In fact, hypotyposis, however colorful, is not a vivid portraiture of the world as it is, because the objects it puts "before our eyes" are the result of a temporal determination as well as of a subjective metaphorization. When space is represented, it is according to a willed evidence, which can be different, but always with no inherent objectivity. Just like the protagonist of *ill seen ill said*, we have to acknowledge the temporal dimension through which space and images of space are structured and appropriated. We should not forget that the "place" where the protagonist lives is "divided by her use of it alone"[72] and that "she could be seen crossing the threshold both ways."[73] The introduction of temporality into these descriptions of space dissolves all those apparent contradictions, even if it certainly indicates, at the level of discourse, the presence of an unfamiliar mimesis.

I think that there is a profound reason for the unusual, open vision and impersonal narration that puzzles the reader in *ill seen ill said*. As I have said, in the novel an observer observes an observer, virtually endlessly: the "she" is watched while watching, by "somebody" who could be another protagonist narrator, but who could also be the omniscient narrator (so impersonal it could coincide with language itself, disembodied and yet narrating). Even the readers can be convoked by Beckett's imperative ecphrasis: "But quick seize her where she is best to be seized. In the pastures far from shelter."[74] The mimetic narration that puzzles us in *ill seen ill said* is functional to the foregrounding of the actuality of time, while the abstraction of the language of narration totally subverts the emotive subjectivity of description. In order to show time, Beckett has to subtract from the "ill said" every personal implication, including the narrator's. Suspension is not to be confounded with anybody's hesitation. Therefore, Beckett subtracts from narration every illusion of self-expression; his descriptions cannot possibly seem personal accounts, so that the linear syntagmatism of language can emerge as a temporal process, a process that animates description and naming. Time pervades formulations about reality in such a way that the solidity of concepts can be shown as resulting only from a hidden synthesis that abstracts from the temporal flow.

I believe that a naturalistic reader, one too worried about the specific determinations of reference, would miss the innovative strength of the "novel," which is concerned with language and reality, not directly with the specificity of things and beings.[75] *Ill seen ill said* is an amazingly successful experiment of language working impersonally: it shows, perhaps only like *Finnegans Wake* (though by subtractions rather than allusions), how strong is the power of language, and how constructive of our world and of our "nature."[76] It is important to see the referential quality of Beckett's language, because it is only through a suspended reference that we can see language at work. We must remember that it is only in relation to reality that the all-encompassing power of language can be foregrounded. The language of *ill seen ill said,* though impersonal, is referential in the deep sense of its actual connection to reality. I would suggest that we can see it working precisely because it *is* impersonal. The impossibility of achieving a solution to unclear, particular determinations of pseudo-references should by no means affect the perception of the work, which is a masterful sequence of "impersonal and disembodied figures of speech"[77] expressing the effects of time.

If we see a progression in Beckett's gnoseological quest focused on language, and link *The Unnamable* (1956) to *How it is* (1964), we can find in *ill seen ill said* a further step in the exploration of that ambivalent linguistic struggle thanks to which we exist as subjects, but in which we also are subject to the power of the signifier. This text can be read as the illustration of the real power of language, and the referential quality of its words should be seen as the unseen index of *our* implications with disembodied figures. In this "novel" we see language proceed like life, resisting the void it sometimes seeks, while we learn that the face value of our statements is just "ill seen ill said."

Notes

1. Samuel Beckett, *ill seen ill said* (London: John Calder, 1982). All references are to this edition. The original appeared in French as *Mal vu mal dit* (Paris: Les Editions de Minuit, 1981) and was then translated into English by the author. A critical discussion of the translation in relation to the original would reveal an interesting number of semantic and syntactic discrepancies. However, a com-

parative approach exceeds the scope of this chapter, which develops as a reading of the English text, with special emphasis on visibility and representation.

2. Jacques Derrida, "Force and Signification" in *Writing and Difference,* translated with an Introduction and Additional Notes by Alan Bass (London, Melbourne and Henley: Routledge & Kegan Paul, 1981) p. 25.

3. Samuel Beckett, *ill seen ill said,* p. 7.

4. In Charles Sanders Peirce's semiotic theory, a sign can be classified in relation to itself, to the object, or to the interpretant. An index is a sign referring to an object when there is a phenomenal or existential connection between the sign and what it signifies. See *Collected Papers* (Cambridge, Mass.: Harvard University Press, 1966), in particular Vol. 4. Wendy Steiner's *Exact Resemblance to Exact Resemblance: The Literary Portraiture of Gertrude Stein* (New Haven, Conn.: Yale University Press, 1978) describes indexes as "necessary components of reality statements, that is, one cannot identify an object in reality without an index [. . .] the indexical sign is existentially related to its referent. [. . .] Many indexes, such as pronouns, constantly change their referents from context to context." p. 6.

5. Samuel Beckett, *ill seen ill said,* p. 7.

6. I would note that Enoch Brater's suggestions, defining the place inhabited by the protagonist(s) of *ill seen ill said* as a Druidic archeological site, enrich my psycho-physical interpretation of this irreducibly ambivalent space with allusions from symbolism and myth. See Brater's "Cromlechs and Voyelles" in *As no other dare fail: for Samuel Beckett on his Eightieth Birthday,* by his friends and admirers (London: John Calder, 1986) pp. 43–49.

7. Ruby Cohn, "Editor's Foreword" in Samuel Beckett's *Disjecta: Miscellaneous Writings and a Dramatic Fragment* (London: John Calder, 1983) p. 9.

8. Samuel Beckett, *ill seen ill said,* p. 53.

9. Jacques Derrida, *Memoires: for Paul de Man,* Cecile Lindsay, Jonathan Culler and Eduardo Cadava, trans. (New York: Columbia University Press, 1986) p. 8.

10. Paul de Man, *Blindness and Insight: Essays in the Rhetoric of Contemporary Criticism* (New York: Oxford University Press, 1971), p. 261. Quoted by Derrida in *Memoires,* pp. 7–8.

11. A suggestive analysis of the role of eyes in *ill seen ill said* is developed by Aldo Tagliaferri in "Il sacro di Beckett," *Alfabeta* 107, Anno 10 (April 1988) 32–33.

12. Samuel Beckett, *ill seen ill said,* pp. 17, 30, 50.

13. Samuel Beckett, "Three Dialogues" in *Disjecta,* pp. 138–45. Originally published in *transition* (December 1949).

14. *Ibid.,* p. 74.

15. I dealt with the problems of the boundaries of a text, and with mimesis as process, in a reading of *Still:* "Il significante che ha luogo: *Still* di Samuel Beckett" in *La Performance del testo.* Atti del VII Congresso Nazionale dell'Associazione Italiana di Anglistica (Siena: Libreria Ticci—succ. Giubbi & C., 1984) pp. 407–18.

16. Rainer Maria Rilke, *Duino Elegies* (London: The Hogarth Press, 1968). In the "First Elegy" Rilke speaks of "the interpreted world" ("der gedeuteten Welt") in which "we don't feel very securely at home" ("wir nicht sehr verlässlich zu Haus sind in") pp. 24–25.

17. Samuel Beckett, *ill seen ill said*, pp. 45–46.

18. *Ibid.*, pp. 59, 58. The unavoidable necessity of seeing is well conveyed in the original by the French pun "avoir à voir."

19. For a discussion of the role of "The Supremacy of the Signifier" in the construction of the subject, and for a definition of the "imaginary," the "symbolic" and the "real," see Jacques Lacan, *Ecrits: A Selection,* Alan Sheridan, trans. (New York: W. W. Norton & Company, 1977). In particular, see "The mirror stage as formative of the function of the I," "The function and field of speech and language in psychoanalysis," "The agency of the letter in the unconscious or reason since Freud,"and "The subversion of the subject and the dialectic of desire in the Freudian unconscious."

    Also, because of its original focus on the recurrence of certain signifiers in the development of Beckett's "associative monologues," see Marjorie Perloff's reading of *ill seen ill said,* "Between Verse and Prose: Beckett and the New Poetry," *Critical Inquiry* 9, 2 (December 1982) 415–33. Reprinted in *On Beckett: Essays and Criticism,* S. E. Gontarski, ed. (New York: Grove Press, 1986) pp. 191–205.

20. Samuel Beckett, *ill seen ill said*, p. 40.

21. Samuel Beckett, "A Piece of Monologue" in *Collected Shorter Plays* (London: Faber and Faber, 1984) p. 269.

22. Samuel Beckett, "Three Dialogues," p. 141.

23. *Ibid.*, p. 142.

24. *Ibid.*, p. 145.

25. *Ibid.*

26. *Ibid.*, p. 139.

27. "By nature I mean [. . .] like the naivest realist, a composite of perceiver and perceived, not a datum, an experience." *Ibid.*, p. 138.

28. Samuel Beckett, "Recent Irish Poetry," *The Bookman* (August 1934), signed with the pseudonym Andrew Belis. Reprinted in *Disjecta*, pp. 70–76. Quotation p. 74. See also Ruby Cohn in *Disjecta,* p. 174.

29. Samuel Beckett, *ill seen ill said*, p. 51.

30. Genesis 2:19.

31. This definition of "interpretant" is in Robert Scholes's "Glossary" in *Semiotics and Interpretation,* (New Haven, Conn.: Yale University Press, 1982) p. 145.

32. Too many philosophical implications pervade this statement to be discussed here in detail. But a quotation from Jacques Derrida's "The End of the Book and the Beginning of Writing" can help make some of those implications more explicit. He writes:

    language itself is menaced in its very life, helpless, adrift in the threat of limitlessness, brought back to its own finitude at the very moment when it ceases to be self-assured, contained and *guaranteed* by the infinite signified which seemed to exceed it. [. . .] the concept of writing—no longer indicating a particular, derivative, auxiliary form of language in general [. . .] is beginning to go beyond the extension of language. In all senses of the word, writing thus comprehends language. Not that the word "writing" has ceased to designate the signifier of the signifier, but it appears, strange as it may seem, that "signifier of the signifier" no longer defines accidental doubling and fallen secondarity. "Signifier of the signifier" describes on the contrary the movement of language: in its origin, to be sure, but one can already suspect that an origin whose structure can be expressed as "signifer of the signifier" conceals and erases itself in its own production. There the signified always already functions as a signifier. The secondarity that it seemed possible to ascribe to writing alone affects all signifieds in general, affects them always already, the moment they *enter the game*.

Of Grammatology, Gayatri Chakravorty Spivak, trans. (Baltimore: Johns Hopkins University Press, 1976) pp. 6–7. See also Derrida's "Force and Signification" in *Writing and Difference* , p. 25:

But is it by chance that [. . .] the meaning of meaning (in the general sense of meaning and not in the sense of signalization) is infinite implication, the indefinite referral of signifier to signifier? And that its force is a certain pure and infinite equivocality which gives signified meaning no respite, no rest, but engages it in its own *economy* so that it always signifies again and differs?

This idea seems very close to Umberto Eco's conception of "unlimited semiosis"; see *A Theory of Semiotics* (Bloomington: Indiana University Press, 1976).

33. Samuel Beckett, "Dream of Fair to Middling Women" in *Disjecta*, p. 43.
34. *Ibid.*, p. 48.
35. Samuel Beckett, *ill seen ill said*, p. 48.
36. The beautiful in nature is a question of the form of the object, and this consists in limitation, whereas the sublime is to be found in an object even devoid of form, so far as it immediately involves, or else by its presence provokes, a representation of limitlessness, yet with a superadded thought of its totality. Accordingly, [. . .] the sublime [can be regarded] as a presentation of an indeterminate concept of reason [. . .] For the sublime, in the strict sense of the word, cannot be contained in any sensuous form, but rather concerns ideas of reason, which, although no adequate presentation of them is possible, may be excited and called into the mind by that very inadequacy itself which does admit of sensuous presentation.

Immanuel Kant, "Analytic of the Sublime" in *Critique of Judgment*, J. C. Meredith, trans. (New York: Oxford University Press, 1973) pp. 90–94.

37. Samuel Beckett, *ill seen ill said*, p. 43.
38. Samuel Beckett, "Three Dialogues," p. 141.
39. Samuel Beckett, *ill seen ill said*, p. 8.
40. *Ibid.*, p. 9.
41. Michael Riffaterre, "Intertextual Representation: On Mimesis as Interpretive Discourse," *Critical Inquiry* 1,1 (September 1984) 141–62. Quotation p. 141.
42. Robert Scholes, "Glossary," p. 145.
43. Michael Riffaterre, "Intertextual Representation," p. 141.
44. *Ibid.*, p. 159.
45. *Ibid.*
46. Samuel Beckett, *ill seen ill said*, p. 20. Emphasis mine.
47. Samuel Beckett ends his prose piece "From an Abandoned Work" (1957) with these words: "my body doing its best without me." In *Collected Shorter Prose 1945–1980* (London: John Calder, 1984) p. 137.

48. For a discussion of the problems regarding the decidability of meaning see Paul de Man's "Semiology and Rhetoric" in *Allegories of Reading: Figural Language in Rousseau, Nietzsche, Rilke and Proust* (New Haven, Conn.: Yale University Press, 1979) pp. 3–19. He describes "referential aberrations" by relating grammar and rhetoric: "grammar allows us to ask the question, but the sentence by means of which we ask it may deny the very possibility of asking [. . .] Rhetoric radically suspends logic, and opens up vertiginous possibilities of referential aberration "(p. 10)

49. Ferdinand de Saussure emphasized the fact that meaning derives exclusively from the relation of signs to other signs. He stressed the arbitrariness of the conventional relation between the constituents of the sign, between the signifier and the signified. See his *Course in General Linguistics,* Charles Bally and Albert Sechehaye, eds., in collaboration with Albert Reidlinger, trans. Wade Baskin (New York: McGraw-Hill, 1966). On the other hand, Charles Sanders Peirce defines different categories of signs according to different relationships that exist between signifiers and referents: they could be existential in indexes, analogical in icons, and conventional, but only in symbols. See his *Collected Writings,* and also Justus Buchler, *Philosophical Writings of Peirce* (New York: Dover, 1955), in particular Chapter 7.

50. Samuel Beckett, *ill seen ill said*, p. 27.

51. *Ibid.,* p. 52.

52. *Ibid.,* p. 27.

53. *Ibid.,* pp. 28–29.

54. Barbara Johnson, "Nothing Fails Like Success" in *A World of Difference* (Baltimore and London: Johns Hopkins University Press, 1987) p. 12.

55. Samuel Beckett, *ill seen ill said*, p. 16.

56. Jacques Derrida, *Writing and Difference*, p. 303.

57. Jacques Derrida, "The Theater of Cruelty and the Closure of Representation" in *ibid.,* p. 237.

58. *Ibid.,* p. 238.

59. Nicholas Zurbrugg, "*Ill Seen Ill Said* and the Sense of an Ending" in *Beckett's Later Fiction and Drama,* James Acheson and Kateryna Arthur, eds. (Houndmills and London: The Macmillan Press, 1987) p. 150.

60. Jacques Derrida, "Structure, Sign and Play in the Discourse of the Human Sciences" in *Writing and Difference*, p. 289.

61. Samuel Beckett, *ill seen ill said*, p. 48.

62. *Ibid.,* p. 10.

63. *Ibid.,* p. 15.

64. *Ibid.,* p. 22.

65. *Ibid.,* p. 31.

66. *Ibid.*

67. *Ibid.,* pp. 58–59.

68. Beckett's original reads as follows: "un métier qui insinue plus qu'il n'affirme, qui ne soit positif qu'avec l'évidence fugace et accessoire du grand positif, du seul positif, du temps qui charrie." in "La peinture des van Velde ou le Monde et le Pantalon," *Disjecta,* p. 130. Translation mine.

69. Samuel Beckett, *ill seen ill said*, pp. 49–50.
70. Beckett's original reads as follows: "au coeur du dilemme, celui même des arts plastiques: Comment représenter le changement? [. . .] on ne représente la succession qu'au moyen des états qui se succèdent, qu'en imposant à ceux-ci un glissement si rapide qu'ils finissent par se fondre, je dirais presque par se stabiliser, dans l'image de la succession même." in "La peinture des van Velde," pp. 118–32. Quotation pp. 129–30. Translation mine.
71. The Oxford English Dictionary defines *hypotyposis* as "Vivid description of a scene, event, or situation, bringing it, as it were, before the eyes of the hearer or reader." It is interesting to note that, historically, the semantic area covered by the term includes both "lively description" (1732) and "effective metaphor" (1583, 1638, 1897). *Ecphrasis* is defined according to Kersey's quotation (1715) as: "a plain declaration or interpretation of a thing." Both are figures of *evidentia*, that is, they develop illustration (*illustratio*) and description (*descriptio*), which, on the ground of their showing, can become evidence (*demonstratio*). We could say that ecphrasis is closer to evidence, in the sense that what is seen is believed, whereas hypotyposis is closer to illustration, and charged with suggestiveness.
72. Samuel Beckett, *ill seen ill said*, pp. 21–22.
73. *Ibid.*, p. 13.
74. *Ibid.*, p. 15.
75. The debate on issues like the health of the protagonist is part of several readings of *ill seen ill said*. Nicholas Zurbrugg in *"Ill Seen Ill Said* and the Sense of an Ending" emphasizes his belief in the death of the woman, contrasting it with David Read's ("Beckett's Search for the Unseeable and Unmakeable: *Company* and *Ill Seen Ill Said*," *Modern Fiction Studies* 29 [Spring 1983] 111–25) and with Marjorie Perloff's readings. On this issue, Tagliaferri in "Il sacro di Beckett" implicitly takes the side of the latter critics. So would I, were it not that I believe that the "alive/dead" dilemma is the sign of a naturalistic attitude which betrays the radical openness of Beckett's reference, an openness he lucidly keeps, in order to deconstruct conceptual dichotomies and to foreground the importance of duration.
76. An extended discussion of influences between Beckett and Joyce can be found in Barbara Gluck's *Beckett and Joyce: Friendship and Fiction* (Lewisburg, Pa.: Bucknell University Press, 1979) and in Aldo Tagliaferri's *Beckett e l'iperdeterminazione letteraria* (Milano: Feltrinelli, 1979); in English translation see his "Beckett and Joyce" in *Samuel Beckett: Modern Critical Views*, Harold Bloom, ed. (New York: Chelsea House Publishers, 1985) pp. 247–61. Here I would like to quote from David Hayman's "Joyce→/Beckett/Joyce," *Journal of Beckett Studies* 7 (Spring 1982) 101–07, as many of his points closely relate to my reading of *ill seen ill said*. Hayman emphasizes flux as "an essential component of our experience" (p. 102) in both Beckett and Joyce, and asserts that "Joyce was building a world; Beckett was dismantling one, proving the verbal nature of the known" (p. 103). Furthermore, by pointing out that "Statement in Joyce is always ready to give way to anti-statement, although no true synthesis is elicited and the dynamic of the word persists," while in Beckett we witness "words generating words which are later erased," Hayman is implicitly indicat-

ing the specificity of Beckett's unwording, against the background of Joyce's "negative echoes" (p. 104).

77. I am indebted to Nicholas Zurbrugg for recording a conversation with Beckett, in which Beckett himself "described *What Where* as a 'puppet play,' and discussed his preoccupation with impersonal and disembodied figures and speech." See Zurbrugg, "*Ill Seen Ill Said* and the Sense of an Ending," p. 158. I see the same type of preoccupation at work in *ill seen ill said* and in *Worstward Ho.*

6. *Worstward Ho:*
The Persistence of Missaying
Against the Limits of Representation

The Duel-Dialogue of Language

Worstward Ho (1983),[1] Beckett's latest major prose work, can be seen as a synthesis (but not the closure) of his lucid "literature of the unword,"[2] because subtraction and representation are radically implicated in it, and because the narrative itself is structured as a series of subtractions. If we adopt phenomenological terminology, we could say that representation is precisely what is being shown and investigated in this prose piece, through progressive, different, and drastic reductions of representational components.

I think it is possible to talk about a synthesis also in view of the compressed intensity of this "novel," which presupposes not only a previous struggle with language (as both a direct engagement and a critique), but also the structuring of a poetics. As a matter of fact, the typically Beckettian poetics of subtraction derives from a constant linguistic awareness and a sharp linguistic undertaking, which are the visible elements of a life-long process through which Beckett has consistently and boldly probed into various phenomenological and epistemological issues.

Furthermore, *Worstward Ho* synthesizes Beckett's previous and most typical themes: those centered on subjectivity (identification and self-identification), temporality, and the aesthetic reproduction of reality. While operating analytical reductions in each of these thematic directions, he achieves a powerful apotheosis of subtraction as an epistemological instrument, as a procedure for the critical investigation of representation and of the "essence" of language itself.

It is well known that all of Beckett's works are characterized by the presence of phenomenological concerns, and that all of them reveal a keen awareness of the logocentric orientation that characterizes Western thought, especially in the second half of the twentieth century. In the 1970s, the dynamics of Beckett's critical epistemology transforms his original conception of language as alienation into a reevaluation of speech, through the analysis of a series of subtle and important differences whereby the linguistic system is played off against communication, the message against its enunciation, and reference against representation.

I think that *Worstward Ho* constitutes a meditation on the role and structure of the signifier, or, to put it more simply, an investigation of the extent and structure of representation. In order to do so, here as in *Company* (1980) and in *ill seen ill said* (1981), the narrative movement deconstructs designation, and structural repetition corrodes semantic similarity. What remains, then, is the working of the texts, and what is made visible is the event of (its) communication. I believe that these are the "themes" of *Worstward Ho,* a strange narrative in which impersonal language is the protagonist of a duel-dialogue with unavoidable representation.

In his review article of *Company,* John Pilling has described the work as a "palimpsest,"[3] a definition which seems very apt to define not only *Company* (1980), but all the works of the so-called "Second Trilogy" (e.g., also *ill seen ill said* and *Worstward Ho*). In fact, the extreme compression, the reductions to the "most mere minimum. Mere-most minimum,"[4] and the stark lexical poverty of these narratives cannot totally conceal the actual working of subtraction in relation to a great wealth of information that resists reduction, nor can the text hide the strength of the conceptual and critical powers required by the functional specificity of its unwording.

Furthermore, the original complexity of this narrative can easily be related to previous literary artifacts, to works eroded and corroded by their very use and assumption in the novelty of a Beckettian text. Not surprisingly, critics have traced the literary "roots" of *Worstward Ho* as far back as John Webster and Thomas Dekker's *Westward Hoe* (1607), and suggestions have been made to approach the narrative as an interesting, anti-sentimental parody of Charles Kingsley's *Westward Ho!* (1855).[5] However, it is not the aim of my present investigation to pursue the rich suggestions of philological comparisons.

What I intend to do is continue my analysis of the hermeneutical and epistemological implications of the Beckettian canon, underlining the fact that Beckett's early theorization of a "literature of the unword" culminates in a new way of conceiving representation, beyond a "hermeneutics of suspicion"[6] and even beyond his own expressive mistrust (ethical, psychological, and epistemological) of the 1960s and early 1970s.

If the early Beckett saw language only as a source of alienation, as a "veil that must be torn apart in order to get at the things (or the Nothingness) behind it,"[7] in the 1970s he came to realize that the inescapability of the veil constitutes a positive "ground," or at least an indisputable starting point from which a new conception of language and experience can be sketched out. I am not implying that Beckett is opening a discussion on ontology, but I am saying that, without probing into the issue of ultimate reality or primordial being, he is demonstrating the inevitable role of language in the construction of the world in which we live, and upon which we act.

Unwording Evidence and the Epiphanies of Un-Saying

The lucid development of Beckett's "poetics of the unword" and the subsequent awareness of the ineliminability of language in representation can easily be traced as far back as his conception of *Proust* (1931), when he regretted the use of memory as "an instrument of reference" rather than as "an instrument of discovery." Significantly, he observed that "The man with a good memory does not remember anything *because he does not forget anything.*"[8] The necessity of forgetting in order to discover is comparable to the necessity of unwording in order to see how remote we are from reality when we perceive the world through language. So the advisability of breaking down the "uniform memory of intelligence" resides in the discoveries that can be made when a discordance, rather than "a concordance to the Old Testament of the individual" can be achieved.[9]

Over the years, Beckett has defined with greater precision his idea of disruption against semantic uniformity and accumulation, and has repeatedly manifested his decision to work with impotence and ignorance. In this light, it is easy to understand why he kept proclaiming his distance from Joyce, even while he was continually fascinated by the aesthetic problems inherent to Joyce's works. In an interview with Israel Shenker, which appeared in the *New York Times* on May 5, 1956, Beckett declared:

> the more Joyce knew, the more he could. He is tending towards omniscience and omnipotence as an artist. I'm working with impotence, ignorance.[10]

In other words, if Joyce's purpose was that of transforming the word into reality, if his was a myth of transubstantiation of the verb into reality, Beckett's attempt was that of analyzing and eventually acknowledging the reality of the word itself.

These two attitudes entail writing procedures whose tensions (towards some sort of linguistic or epistemic absolute) are similar, but whose orientations are radically different. Beckett himself expressed this idea in his letter to Axel Kaun, dated July 7, 1937. Here, as he was outlining his literary program to his German friend, he wrote:

> With such a program in my opinion, the later work of Joyce has nothing whatever to do [. . .] unless perhaps Ascension to Heaven and Descent to Hell are somehow one and the same.[11]

In this letter Beckett is describing his "poetics of impotence" against the background of Joyce's "poetics of omnipotence," though it is clear that both writers do use language transgressively, and myths irreverently. Furthermore, Beckett's critique of Joyce's "apotheosis of the word" leads him to affirm that

> As we cannot eliminate language all at once, we should at least leave nothing undone that might contribute to its falling into disrepute.[12]

Finally, well beyond parody and "Nominalist irony," the result of Beckett's program of linguistic struggle against language will culminate, as we have seen, in the formulation of the expression "literature of the unword," that is, in a plan to produce a type of verbal art that faces the problem of the visibility of reality by deconstructing the unity of saying. Such a deconstructive program comes to coincide with the following definition of art:

> Art has always been this—pure interrogation, rhetorical question less the rhetoric.[13]

Beckett is saying that a "pure interrogation" can only be structured as a subtraction (of rhetoric from the rhetorical question), and it is clear that subtraction should not be conceived as a metaphysical closure or a result, but rather as a process. Similarly, the prefix in the expression "*un*word" implies the *dynamics* of subtraction, the *movement* of a want which transforms the staticity and stability of words. In fact, the production of a gap or a lack, in a meaning that was previously compact, points to a rhetorical relation between concept and figure, and makes it problematic. In other words, the appearance of a gap in meaning points to a play of truth in tropological movements.

As I will show, repetition is the most common form of Beckett's unwording, because it is above all a way of eroding the useless, if consoling, certainties of tautologies. Repetition in the works of the "Second Trilogy" normally signals a hiatus between the subject and the predicate of the same sentence, and points to the impossibility of an absolute retraction of what has been said (even when it is apparently just "repeated").

At this point, we cannot fail to note that the main polarity implied in Beckett's comparison of himself with Joyce regards the issue of power, an issue which acquires great relevance within an onto-logocentric perspective, and more specifically, in relation to the determination of linguistic visibility. Beckett's preference for "impotence" and "ignorance" can be explained within the framework of broad epistemic issues regarding the relationship between language and reality and the ethical issues connected to them, and regarding the "correctness" of representation. In fact, if language is a powerful falsification (inasmuch as it hides the conflict of concept and figure within the sign), then the weaker language is, the better it shows such a repression; the less powerful language is, the closer it gets to reality.

This linguistic attitude can explain why repetition in Beckett, far from clarifying things, confounds reference systematically, thus showing the reality of semantic instability and the excess of linguistic notations. More specifically, visibility is shown to be the result of the power of linguistic repression, and the subtraction of unwording is invoked to give a chance of expression to whatever is repressed (always an impossible denotatum, anyway). In this sense, the "rhetorical question less the rhetoric" cannot lead to any certainty, nor to the content of a specific revelation, and not even to the positive knowledge that some theorists link with "the anti-foundationalist paradox."[14]

In fact, Beckett's "working with ignorance" suspends the magnetism of certainties, together with the firmness of dogmas and the seduction of analogies. Ultimately, his "working with impotence" is an attempt to make mimetic language less powerful in relation to phenomenalism and to show that it is possible to reduce the meaning-to-say from the said.

Words have the power to mean things, but their mimetic power is so strong that they work mostly as the perfect substitutes for things, while hiding the conventionality that presides over this unquestioned substitution. Words *are* very powerful, especially if we do not ask any epistemological questions about the nature of their power, or about the type of knowledge they convey. However, when words cannot hide their figurality, and when their analogical and mimetic power is questioned, the performative power of such figurality dramatizes ideas rather than representing concepts. This is precisely what happens in an epistemic novel like *Worstward Ho:* logocentric dramatization replaces conventional narrative mimesis.

Logocentric dramatization, this sophisticated reminding of a difference (normally repressed) between the designation of life and the impossible expression of life, seems to point to a concern shared by many modern philosophers, a concern that Emmanuel Lévinas defines as the problem of "the attachment of thought to being."[15]

In other words, Beckett's subtractions seem to ask such passionate questions as "does thought transform matter into being?" and "how far reaching could the consequences be?". Beckett's answers normally point to language as the site of an unjustifiable abstraction, thus connoting it as simultaneously "inane" (a favorite adjective of his) and "excessive."

While many readers may understand and agree with Beckett's refusal of "symbols where none [are] intended," some may go even further and see that the way in which Lévinas describes philosophizing comes very close to Beckett's literary dramatizing, since they both point to a way of representing which develops by subtracting the representative quality (which is conventional, anyway), to what is represented. Lévinas says:

> I have spoken somewhere of the philosophical *saying* as a saying which is in the necessity of always unsaying itself. I have even made this unsaying a proper mode of philosophizing. I do not deny that philosophy is a knowledge, insofar as it names even what is not nameable, and thematizes what is not thematizable. But in this giving to what breaks with the categories of discourse the form of the *said,* perhaps it impresses onto the said the traces of this rupture.[16]

A "saying which is in the necessity of always unsaying itself," but is certainly not led by the charms of positive negation and naive nihilism, characterizes all of Beckett's recent works. It would be difficult to conceive of a legitimate hermeneutical reading of the works produced in the 1970s unless one is willing to grasp the laws of a *movement* articulating meaning in them. In fact, an indivisible movement can be grasped, going from thematization to "revelation" through the denial of thematization; a semantic movement goes from designation to expression, through the denial of any one, specific designation that is posited in the text.

In the tradition of visionary Irish literature from Yeats to Joyce, I suggest we define these Beckettian "epiphanies" as "visions of the immediate," because they do not go, nor do they mean to go, beyond the precise instant of evidence. Beckett's epiphanies are always linked to a Kierkegaardian theatrical knowledge of the immediate, the immediate that is mostly, in fact, unseen.[17]

As we have seen, all of Beckett's works and the passion of his subtractions grow from the strongly felt challenges of logocentrism, and they question the problematic extent of logocentrism, pointing primarily to an epistemological concern, which is congruent with an ethical one. Beckett's unwording and Lévinas's unsaying are broader than an aesthetic interest primarily focused on the use of language in literary representations: Beckett's aesthetic transgressions are, in the words of Lévinas, "a form of the said" that "breaks with the categories of discourse," and the "traces of this rupture" cannot leave literature as it was before, precisely in the sense that literature comes as close to present communication as it could ever be, because it shares the same epistemic concerns and structure of self-reflexive (not only self-reflected) communication.

In fact, in the late Beckett, literature is not questioned from within the conceptual and structural alternatives provided by genre and conventions, but from the exteriority of an epistemic concern that finds in literature the best source of a negative knowledge regarding the relation between words and phenomena. This is why the referential function of language is never abandoned in the late Beckettian texts in favor of an aesthetic (postmodernist?) self-reflection. In turn, that is why a profound, comprehensive reading can only be achieved by going beyond the formal structure of the text (though certainly, through its elements). Reading itself needs to become a radical exercise in unwording, and I hope that the following paragraphs will prove it, as the unfolding of my analysis will bring us closer and closer to the specific, unworded textuality of this prose piece.

The Human Adventure: From the "Somehow" to the "Nohow"

From its very beginning *Worstward Ho* states the irreducible boundaries of representation, and the whole narrative can be seen as an exploration of such boundaries, and in general of the onto-logocentric inescapability of our being in the world. The very first paragraph of the narrative summarizes the hermeneutical cycle into which human beings are caught, subject to a *Geworfenheit* (a state of "Thrownness," i.e., a "being thrown" into the world), somewhat reminiscent of the one described by Heidegger at the beginning of *Being and Time*.[18] In fact, Beckett's narrative opens as follows:

> On. Say on. Be said on. Somehow on. Till nohow on. Said nohow on.[19]

It is plain to see that here the context of human experience is represented by that "on," independent of human will, which provides the background to any understanding or imagining, of every perception and thought. This also means that the human condition of being-in-the-world is shown to coincide with an unavoidable perceptive-interpretive way of being (indicated by "*Say* on."). Being is described as one with understanding, and specifically as one with linguistic perception, however impersonal it may be ("On. *Say* on. *Be said* on.").

Besides, the opening of the novel illustrates human life through the paradigmatic instances of a "*some*how on" leading to a "*no*how on," even if the latter is immediately presented as a condition which can only be imagined but not experienced ("*Said* nohow on.") This means that the limits (*a quo* and *ad quem*) of human life are given within the unquestioned ontology of a duration in which humans perceive their being, through the diversity of their experiences. As a consequence, we can say that the starting point of the narrative, while insisting on the generics of an impersonal being, seems to imply some Kierkegaardian attitudes, whereby

> one who neglects to take into account the relationship between his abstract thought and his own existence as an individual [. . .] is in process of ceasing to be a human being.[20]

The "on" of existence and the many "somehows" of thought and experience construct the presumable protagonist of *Worstward Ho* as an existential interpreter who refuses to divorce abstract thought from existence. Existential attitudes will greatly modify Beckett's critique of the linguistic system, a critique implied by his earlier works, when he seemed to believe in a hermeneutics of strong suspicion. Even though in his later works Beckett still tends to divorce language from personal determinations, he moves progressively away from an absolute linguistic mistrust, and even from the certainties (objective fallacies) they can provide.

Significantly, what is represented in the opening paragraph of *Worstward Ho* is the existential movement (an irrefutable "on") starting with the many "somehows" of existence and leading to the anticipated, imaginable "nohow" of death, the only moment in which the absence of movement occurs, decreeing the end of representation. As we have seen, Beckett admits and underlines the impossibility of saying a referential "nohow," and illustrates the limits of a "nohow" said, connoting it as false, precisely because it hides the existential movement that sustains the very possibility of saying it. A "nohow" conceals in its denotative negation the assertiveness from which the said always derives.

In this light it is possible to see the entire novel as an extreme attempt to deprive language of its false movement and of its progressive abstraction from life. In fact, Beckett manages to show that even the abstractions and self-reference of a text are rooted in reality, being directly dependent on it, and related to it through the enunciation. A text like *Worstward Ho* reminds us of the fact that existence cannot really be suspended by the thought that suspends it, and that the enunciation cannot be revoked by a message that denies it. This is probably the only final (in the sense of "residual") meaning of the end of a text without closure such as *Worstward Ho:* "From out what little left" of the "skull," there is, "into it still the hole." The narrative reminds us that there is always something missing in the "said," and that this unwordable lacking can be seen, a posteriori, as the ground and origin of what is said.

Furthermore, even placed "At bounds of boundless void," the thought of a "nohow" (a dynamic version of the thought of "death") indicates the irreducible intentionality of thinking, still there, at the extreme end of thinking subtractions:

Nohow less. Nohow worse. Nohow naught. Nohow on. Said nohow on.[21]

Similarly, it is very interesting to see how it is precisely through linguistic impersonality that Beckett leaves open the possibility of inferring a subject (which, of course, cannot be denoted). The specificity of linguistic occurrences is shown to express the presence of a being, even while this being is unspecified and remains undefinable. In other words, impersonal and yet communicative language can point to a certain degree of linguistic falsification (pseudo-reference), and also to a "subject" who is always incapable of fully manifesting him- or herself. Yet, this impersonal subject is not totally absorbed or obliterated by the laws of the linguistic system, nor by the indisputable supremacy of the signifier. We must bear in mind the fact that every utterance signifies a subject, even if it denies the denotation of one.

As for the "somehow" of experience, we can say that it can only be acquired as an a posteriori knowledge, a knowledge which, however, always speaks in the present, and to a present being, to a consciousness that can re-present itself as a subjectivity resisting the mental suspension of existence while thinking about it. In fact, as Kierkegaard had anticipated, the "subjective how" *can* be communicated, but only dynamically, as an attempt, an endeavor, a struggle:

> The subjective "how" is transformed into a striving, a striving which receives indeed its impulse and a repeated renewal from the decisive passion of the infinite, but is nevertheless a striving.[22]

Although Beckett is far from the religious connotations and psychological *Einstellung* of the Kierkegaardian definition of the subjective "how," and he never talks about a "passion of the infinite" nor assumes a "self" as a personal subject, it is easy to see that *Worstward Ho* is a text of venture and orientation, rather than the story or the *topos* of a voyage.

Here, the archetypal motif of the journey is transformed into a textual meandering around and through representation, and the subjective "how" is represented by the pervasive use of the so-called "conative function" of language, which replaces the more common (and closing) "referential function" of narratives.[23]

It might be worth recalling the fact that intrinsic to Roman Jakobson's definition of the conative function is an emphasis on the orientation toward the addressee, which is indeed typical of the whole prose piece, where this addressee is not identifiable in stable referential terms (and never will be). Yet, paradoxically, an undefinable speaker and an undefinable addressee highlight the intrinsic subjective striving of any message, even in spite of all its denotative closures.

Consequently, the orientation of the message, its "being open to," is shown to be more pervasive and important than the denotative message itself, and the "subjective how" of communication replaces both the subjective and the objective "what" of information. In other words, even the most drastic unwording cannot eliminate the residual presence of speaking (a "subjective how") and of an addressee who survive the most pervasive and boldest narrative reductions that invest characterization, themes, and authorial authority.

If we adopt Kierkegaard's words, we could say that this is a way in which "the abstract thinker pays his debt to existence, by existing in spite of all abstractions,"[24] at least inasmuch as destination is not determined once and for all. In fact, the question of destination is established, but remains unresolved and undefinable throughout the novel. A narrative that shows one of its *implicit* bases (e.g., its cogent presupposition of an addressee) produces a destination which resists becoming a destiny, even within the boundaries of a story-told, and even against the intrinsic teleology of a novel. The early Beckett probably shared Roland Barthes's idea according to which

> the Novel is a Death; it transforms life into destiny, a memory into a useful act, duration into an oriented and meaningful time.[25]

However, Beckett went on producing novels, and it is reasonable to think that Beckett is still producing prose works (which I would call "epistemic novels"), precisely because he has found a way of maintaining (and showing) an essential relationship to existence through narration. This, of course, involves a series of markedly aesthetic problems, but what I intend to underline now is the fact that Beckett reminds us that there is always a true movement of literature, rooted in the meaningful time of narration, and sustained by incessant representations which are arbitrary in their specificity (and in relation to a context), and yet are unavoidable if narration and experience are to occur.

In this way, the intentionality of representation, that is, the fact that representation is always a "representation of" something, is brought forth in Beckett's latest works. Paradoxically, this intentionality emerges because of a constant, lucid unwording of specific descriptions and pseudo-referents which, when reduced to the minimum, show the ineliminability of the object of representation. Thus we can say that the earlier Beckettian concern with the correctness of description is replaced by a discovery and an analysis of the ineliminability of representation, a concern which will lead Beckett to describe the narrative process as a

> From now say for be missaid.[26]

In the light of the entire narrative and of its communicative strategy I believe that the expression "say for be missaid" does not refer to literary narratives only, but relates to the most elementary perceptions as well. The full epistemological value of such an expression demands the prohibition of breaking it down with conceptual abstractions. In fact, the "say" represents the present of communication, which becomes visible only as a posthumous "said," thus having become somewhat "missaid" in the process.

The inclusion of the conceptual "missaid" within the present of "say" expresses the fullness of the expressive (perceptive and hermeneutical) cycle: "*Be* missaid." It is interesting to notice that Beckett is thus underscoring the temporal condition of representation, due to the fact that

> It is impossible to conceive existence without movement, and movement cannot be conceived *sub specie aeterni*.[27]

Representation (that is, the way in which "we conceive existence") is shown to be related to a "subjective how" which functions diachronically, and the efficacy of representation is no longer related to some analogical quality of signs and denotata, but to the subjective duration of the intentionality of thought. Obviously, by "intentionality" I mean here the necessary content of thought produced by thinking, rather than a specific will to mean.

This interpretation can easily explain why representation can best be seen when an unwording of specific representational instances takes place, and its legitimacy is shown to reside in its double nature of evoking and obliterating repetition posited by consciousness. In this sense we can understand the Beckettian description of words as "wanting in inanity" (p. 20), that is, too powerful to obliterate reality completely, but also too weak to evoke it. *Worstward Ho* proves that existence can best be represented as change, and through movement, given that the representative quality of narration derives from the consciousness that founds it (or finds it), as a significative, diachronically structured content.

It is important to notice that the very title of this work evokes a movement related to the flux of consciousness. *Worstward Ho* denotes a dynamic orientation, psychologically charged with an evaluative dimension. Besides, it reveals the subtractive passion of all of Beckett's epistemic reductions, because "worst," as we shall see, expresses a methodological ideal related to quantity (of information), rather than an ethical evaluation related to goodness.

"Somehow on": Human Knowledge and the Limits of Representation

As we have seen, the quest for the meaning of being in *Worstward Ho* is not separable from being itself, and this inseparability derives from a specific narrative denotation of being as coextensive with an interpretive way of being, which is sustained in the narrative with the requirements of an existentialist methodology of epistemic investigation. Without indulging in a number of philosophical questions regarding the primordiality and the definition of being, questions which have kept Western philosophers busy for hundreds of years, Beckett represents our finding ourselves in the world, involved in and related to an existential-hermeneutical horizon which is not chosen, but is irrefutably implied by perception.

Obviously, Beckett's representation of this situational beginning dismisses as unanswerable all the questions regarding the truth or verifiability of statements such as "On. Say on." since they are given in the form of an imperative or performative, that is, as linguistic expressions which are not liable to a truth test. Closer to a speech act than to a description, this narrative systematically avoids the form of an arguable statement. In fact, though the sentence "On. Say on." could convey a degree of doubt (the "on" being given as the result of a convention, and "*Say* on" merely meaning "granted on," and expressing a pure hypothesis), the issue of continuity (and being) remains a non-debatable issue. This is perhaps a high form of Beckettian irony related to his conception of human life as an "existential contract" which cannot be revoked even when its value is severely doubted.

From these imperative sentences we can infer that, according to Beckett, the understanding of the foundation of what is given as ontology is impossible, since language, the only instrument apt to analyze it, cannot represent being in a doubtful form. Therefore, a sound epistemological conclusion leads Beckett to a renewed declaration of linguistic mistrust, a declaration which, however, does not express a pure negation or a generalized suspicion, but which is directed precisely on the philosophical problem of the logocentric determination of being. When Beckett writes:

Say for be said. Missaid. From now say for be missaid,[28]

the "missaid" has definitely replaced the positing of silence as an absolute. Furthermore, in the light of the continuation of narration, the worthiness of this "missaying" begins to appear, and its value is explained. In fact, the inescapability of failure constitutes a sort of "ground," and in that sense a hermeneutical improvement, if compared to a purely abstract linguistic negation. This attitude can explain the explicit invitation to failure proposed by Beckett:

All of old. Nothing else ever. Ever tried. Ever failed. No matter. Try again. Fail again. Fail better.[29]

This is much more than a stoic statement prompting endurance, and more than an ironic statement pointing to a repeated failure; it is an epistemological conclusion, deriving from the fact of taking into account the inescapability of existence ("All of old. Nothing else ever"), and from emphasizing the evolutionary state of knowledge rather than its absoluteness ("Try *again*. Fail *again*. Fail better."). Although it shows an awareness of its cogent limits ("Ever tried. Ever failed."), this passage also implies a recognition of the value of ongoing approximations ("Try again. Fail again. Fail *better*"). The immutability of reality ("All of old?"), which is in fact an ever-changing phenomenon, can be related to the negative transience of knowledge, but also to the positive value of know*ing*, a knowledge always in need to establish itself "again" and "again," in accordance with the passing of time, in order to avoid dogmatic anachronism. It is perhaps worth recalling that a very similar preoccupation is expressed in *A Piece of Monologue*, where again the exteriority of language in relation to phenomena is charged with negative ethical connotations, in view of the linguistic staticity unknown to the living world.[30]

We can easily notice that, rather than surrendering before what he perceived as a mere linguistic failure, Beckett has gone all the way into the exploration of this alienation, and the usual Beckettian radicalization, through a *via negativa,* has transformed the unavoidable limit of linguistic suspicion into the acquisition of a revocatory knowledge. In other words, by providing positive evidence about the limits of human understanding Beckett shows us that even a negative truth can prove enlightening and liberating.

At the beginning of *Worstward Ho* Beckett very clearly defines the boundaries of human knowledge:

Know minimum. Know nothing no. Too much to hope.[31]

The usual Beckettian refusal of absolute negation ("nothing no") is specifically thematized here as inevitably "limited knowledge," and the investigation of limits is then carried out with the very instruments that produce such knowledge. The knowable *limen,* in the sense of both an opening threshold and a restriction, in fact becomes the object of narration. Thus, representation is investigated in its active and passive aspects, both as perception and recollection, as specific will and general, cogent intentionality of thought.

Furthermore, the reader is brought to see that subtraction can provide the best evidence for linguistic ineliminability; that is, subtraction can show the minimal, ineliminable knowledge (the "know minimum") which is eluded by positive assertions, but which always constitutes representation. So the text develops as a radical "un-saying" of the general "mis-saying," the "unwording" being both a process and a procedure which deserve further discussion, and which will in fact be one of the objects of my subsequent analysis.

Now, I would like to underline the fact that in *Worstward Ho* the worlds of perception are no longer kept separate from the worlds of the mind, so that Beckett, far from his earlier marked dualism, which opposed concrete (physical) and abstract (mental) realities, can show us the pervasive, shaping role of language, a creative role which works in the representation of both things that are present or absent. See for example the mingling of perception and conceptualization (of "seeing" and "saying," as Beckett usually puts it in his "late" works) in this passage:

> First the body. No. First the place. No first both. Now either. Now the other. Sick of the either try the other. Sick of it back sick of the either. So on. Somehow on.[32]

It is very important to notice here the double field of reference evoked by a double series of referents related either to the physical world ("body," "place"), or to the mental world ("both," "either," "the other"). This apparently rigid polarization is in fact contained within a vaster psycho-linguistic constructionist perspective, which reveals the fallacy of precise boundaries between perception and conceptualization. A referent such as "the either" reveals that the product of conceptualization can easily become a referent of the physical world, as much as reference can easily become self-reference in a text.

It seems to me that what Beckett is interested in showing in the 1970s and the 1980s concerns the inescapability of linguistic representation and the extent of the intentionality of thought, rather than trying to justify meaning in relation to signs (by ridiculing the repression of the discrepancy between signs and things) as he did in his early works. This reveals that very significant changes have occurred in Beckett's linguistic preoccupations, even if the novelty of his attitudes towards language derives from the metamorphosis of his old questions. In fact, rather than denouncing a Cratylian fallacy, Beckett wants to investigate the intrinsic intentionality of thought and the actual effects of communicative language. In his recent works he is showing us that speaking, like thinking, is always a "speaking of" (a "thinking of"), independent of the presumed mimetic quality of signs, and that speaking always signifies a subject, even without denoting it.

Here, the sign still reveals its impossible justification in relation to phenomena, but it also shows its impossible disappearance and its impossible total transparence. Signs, always charged with the ambiguity of a notation, happen, and their happening cannot be revoked, even when their meaning is revoked. In this sense they are ineliminable diachronic traces, moving endlessly, disappearing but not ending. It is an accurate unwording that can prove that the sign is always a "sign of," that it always implies representation. The event-quality of representation is manifested by repetition, which produces in the reader the awareness of the fact that this narrative always points to a "saying" which exceeds the "said." Let us examine, for example, a passage in which the conditions of knowledge and sign production are clearly stated, and evolve in the course of narration:

> Unknow better now. Know only no out of. No knowing how know only no out of. Into only. Hence another. Another place where none. Whither once whence no return. No. No place but the one. None but the one where none. Whence never once in. Somehow in. Beyondless.[33]

The theme of the ultimate unverifiability of knowledge, already present in *Company*,[34] is reasserted here: "no knowing how know," but following the declaration of the impossibility of an absolute absence of knowledge: "Know nothing no. Too much to hope." (p. 9).

Also the unquestioned present of the context in *Company* ("*A voice comes to one in the dark. Imagine*") finds a parallel in the unchallenged and unverifiable present of perception in *Worstward Ho*: "*Dim light* source unknown." and "Know only no out of" (p. 9). The epistemological adventure of these narratives begins within these unverifiable, and yet undeniable, present situations. In *Worstward Ho* the *spatial* metaphor "no out of" ("No knowing how know only *no out of*. Into only.", p. 11) reiterates the unverifiable and undeniable *temporal* designation of the "on" which had opened the narrative ("On. Say on. Be said on").

Furthermore, far from being a mere tautological reduplication, the specification "Into only." structures an alternative ("no out of"/"into only") which opens before our eyes a whole fictional world ("Hence another.

Another place where none"). In other words, here we can see perception transformed and sustained by conceptualization.

It is important to notice that the gripping power of this description is no less powerful because of the fact that the designation of space resists iconic representation ("no place but the one where none"), which proves that the intentionality of representation is independent of the specific semiotic nature of signs (icons, indices, or symbols) articulating representation itself.

Besides, the fact that Beckett shows us that what seems to be an irreducible denotation ("into"/"out of") is in fact a fertile spatial metaphor, may lead the reader to notice the ineliminable spatialization of language itself, which, though mostly unseen, still allows conceptual elaboration.

In a passage like this we can also easily see the creative role of the signifier, particularly because of the progressive discrepancy between narrative signs and narrative referents. See for example a sentence like "No place *but the one,*" immediately followed by "None *but the one* where none." Far from producing a semantic contradiction and a subsequent erasure, the movement of codification points to a multiplication of meaning, because of the establishment of a relation of contextual elements with co-textual ones. We can see that space is denoted both in relation to the reality of the world ("No place but *the one*"), and in relation to the text itself ("None *but the one where none*"). In other words, the text speaks of fictional spaces both as pseudo-referents (of real space) and as elements of the co-text (of the textual space). Thus we are made aware of the narrative enunciation thanks to an apparent semantic contradiction.

Without going further into the problem of semiosis and symbolization, I can say that *Worstward Ho* formulates more clearly than any of Beckett's previous works his idea of the strength of linguistic creation, moving beyond his early radical rejection of language as mere alienation or pure falsification. The fact that the "said" and the "saying" are played off one against the other, as in the example above, points to a relevant epistemic reciprocity and to a significant *différance*. In this light, representation must be implied as an event, rather than as an analogy, and language as a communicative act, rather than as a system. In fact, in *Worstward Ho* Beckett often substitutes diegetical equivalents with mimetic repetitions, so that his new conception of language reveals both an uncompromising rejection of metaphysics and an equally strong interest in an *on*going reality, perceived and perceivable as *différance*.

Here Beckett does not start from meaning in order to justify or explain the sign, but rather, he shows how the signifier always defers the signified and thus creates meaning. In the following example we can see very clearly that the reoccurrence of the signifier regulates the specificity of meaning within each re-presentation:

> It stands. What? Yes. Say it stands. Had to up in the end and stand. Say bones. No bones but say bones. Say ground. No ground but say ground. So as to say pain. No mind and pain? Say yes that the bones may pain till no choice but stand. Somehow up and stand. Or better worse remain.[35]

Certainly the semantic transformations of "stand," however surprising, are not enough to account for the complexity of this discourse, whose concern is the expression of difference, either as: 1) semantic variation ("stand," progressively transformed into "bear" and "remain"); 2) as referential variation ("Say bones. No bones but say bones. No ground but say ground."); and 3) even as thematic variation (the sentence "Say yes that the bones may pain till no choice but stand" is the product of a pure narrative combination, not the textual registration of a referential inference. It points to co-textual coherence, rather than to logical referential unity).

The separation of language from presence could not be stated more forcefully, nor could the evidence of the effective, actual structuring role of language be better outlined. The semantic development of the text dramatizes the interrelated process of perception and conceptualization, reflected in the dialectics of text and co-text. The difference between designation and expression is enacted by this text, which skillfully avoids the establishment of a firm pseudo-reference, but which also points to the co-text as the horizon of textual self-reference and coherence. Thus, the ordinary need for a unity determined in relation to reference alone, is continuously broken because of the visibility of cotextuality which is somewhat dependent on, but extraneous to, reference. In other words, a narrative syncretism (combining heterogeneous representational elements) replaces the merely logical development of specific pseudo-referents. In this sense we can say that here syntax enacts a true movement between narrative levels, rather than being subservient to a simple combination of conceptualized elements of the same referential level. In this complex semantic palimpsest, thematization includes textual self-reference (but does not wholly coincide with it).

Shown together, literary pseudoreference and textual self-reference represent representation. In other words, the text shows its true being as "other" than "the other" (reality), together with its being an actual representation of pseudo-referents. Because of the acquired visibility of their interdependence in a narrative text, pseudo-reference and self-reference enact and show the ineliminable re-presentational quality of narration. Let us consider another example, of a description developed at both the textual and co-textual levels:

> Nothing to show a child and yet a child. A man and yet a man. Old and yet old. Nothing but ooze how nothing and yet. One bowed back yet an old man's. The other yet a child's. A small child's.[36]

The problem of visibility pervades the passage, in a series of reiterated contrasts (*"nothing to show* a child/*and yet* a child; a man/*and yet* a man; old/*and yet* old."*). They indicate that visibility has little to do with iconic perception, but a lot to do with the working signifiers. In this sense representation can be defined as a "Nothing but ooze," a diachronic way of signifying, rather than a specific, static content. In other words, representation is a "how nothing and yet," and the sign (visible as an a posteriori resistance, as "and yet") is the double agent of persistence ("how") and obliteration ("nothing"). Furthermore, we must notice that the accomplishment of meaning here requires the intervention of co-textuality as a semantic component of it. In fact, single sentences such as "A man and yet a man," "Old and yet old," and "The other yet a child's" would have no referential meaning were it not for the anaphoric links which relate them to other sentences in the text. Specifically, in the first two cases, a man and his age attribute constitute the problematic object of showing ("nothing to show [. . .] and yet"); in the second case, the pattern of narrative repetitions confers a complete meaning to an otherwise impossible denotation (at first we hear about an old man's "bowed back," so that we can understand that "The other yet a child's. A small child's" refers to a child's back).

This elaborate syntax of visualization mirrors the necessary role of language in the construction of reality, and the complexity of the irreducible relation between perception and conceptualization, between being and understanding.

If we bear in mind the lucidity of these narrative strategies (which skillfully combine repetition, negation, semantic suspension and referential ambiguity), we have to admit that it is far too reductive, at this stage of Beckettian production, to maintain that Beckett's narrative incongruence is just a way of denouncing literature as demystification and of showing the work as a mere artifact. After all, there are different ways of producing incongruence, which, however, entail different meanings. It seems to me that the combination of pseudo-reference and self-reference in these "late" works investigates the role of fictions in relation to the development of human knowledge, rather than connoting them as mere artifacts.

We must remember that the tension of the text producing the denunciation of an artifact cannot be bound or contained by the self-reflective and purely abstract quality of the artifact itself. The denunciation of literature here is effective precisely because of the relation of literature to reality. Thus, far from becoming secondary, the issue of reference is sharpened by the linguistic complexity of this literary text, where the coexistence of a thematization of experience (pseudo-reference) with textual self-reflection constitutes an endless opening of ordinary mimesis. This means that the wavering boundary between textuality and referentiality is actually represented in the text, because the text succeeds in showing its enunciations, through endless repetitions.

As we have seen, particularly in Chapter Two, it is true that some of the comic strategies of Beckett's very early works produce denunciations of the novel as mythology, or use Literature as a target, but his later works do not exploit incongruence in a teleology of clarification, nor for the unveiling of a truth.[37] Beckett's humor in the "Second Trilogy" is not cathartic but disturbing, because it is conceptually irreducible and based on the constantly deferring openness of meaning. All we can say is that this late humor is always endowed with an epistemic nature: its openness underscores the impossibility of conceptual closure, and the diachronic positing of both meaningfulness and meaninglessness.

Let us consider an example from *Worstward Ho* where the semantic exploitation of the expression "words for what" produces comic effects in relation to penultimate and unchangeable realities:

> All seen and nohow on. What words for what then? None for what then. No words for what when words gone. For what when nohow on. Somehow nohow on.[38]

As we can see, an ironical denial of the possibility of self-expression and of a perlocutionary teleology is produced here ("What words for what then?"), but without denying the value of some sort of linguistic ontology, the value of a present communication. In fact, in this passage words are said to be purposeless when they are "gone," that is, when they have named the "seeing" and transformed it into a "seen."

The use and value of words are discussed here in relation to time, showing that words of the past ("then," "when words gone") or words of an impossible time ("when nohow on") have no purpose. Their impossibility to express derives from the fact that a semantic determination transforms a present will-to-mean into a posthumous meaning. The analysis of temporal indications can lead us to see that it is the repression of the present of the enunciation in the determination of reference which falsifies it, producing the dramatic divorce of words from presence. The expression "Somehow nohow on" does not indicate a logical contradiction, but points to an undeniable presence of communication ("Somehow [. . .] on"), paradoxically revealed by the impossibility of purposeful expression ("nohow on"). From a passage like this we learn that perlocutionary utterances do not live outside time ("No words for what [. . .] when nohow on."), and they are for "Nothing save what they say" (p. 29) in the present of saying. Their value is precisely in the communicative quality they possess; it is in the proximity of presence that characterizes them.

It is no wonder that at this point of narration Beckett can be more precise about the limits of human knowledge. His investigation reveals that it is the impossible inclusion of the meaning of saying into the meaning of the said which constitutes an insurmountable linguistic alienation:

> Enough still not to know. Not to know what they say. *Not to know what it is the words it says say.* Says? Secretes. Say better worse secretes. *What it is the words it secretes say.* What the so-said void. The so-said dim. The so-said shades. The so-said seat and germ of all. Enough to know no knowing. *No knowing what it is the words it secretes say.* No saying. *No saying what it all is they somehow say.*[39]

The limits of knowledge are manifested by the impossible inclusion of the meaning of words and the meaning of the actuality of speech in a totality of meaning. Words keep splitting between *what* they mean and their mean*ing:* "no saying what *it all* is they somehow say." Indications such as "it says," "it secretes" embedded into the description of "what it is the words say" emphasize the importance of the enunciation, and can explain why the notion of reference is given as a "so-said," as an inevitable expressive compromise, justified only by its own occurrence, and by no intrinsic similarity with the denotatum. After all, a determination through disappearance is what characterizes literary pseudo-reference, a reference produced by what Derrida calls "the responsibility of *angustia,*" that is, the choice of "the necessarily restricted passageway of speech against which all possible meanings push each other."[40] A work like *Worstward Ho* constantly oscillates between repeating and unsaying itself. It is as if Beckett is explicitly appropriating Derrida's words: "Speaking frightens me because, by never saying enough, I also say too much." His writing keeps putting before our eyes "the moment at which we must *decide* whether we will engrave what we hear. And whether engraving preserves or betrays speech."[41] The total equivocality of an answer to this dilemma sustains the unattainable catharsis we long for and never experience in this *Worstward Ho* journey.

From Ecphrasis to Representation: Subjectivity Without a Self

Beckett's "unwording" and his pervasive use of repetition point to a lucid and constant refusal of abstraction, in the sense that every description is deconstructed while it is formulated, and the dialectics of text and co-text show meaning as a process, and narration as the process of meaning.

The implication of a *movement* of meaning as the actual and cogent meaning of the text obviously transforms the nature of description and narrative, and subverts the canonical distinction between text and extratextual reality, showing the conventionality of such boundaries. Beckett does not attempt to describe life, nor to illustrate it; rather, he brings the impossibility of pure description before our eyes, showing how blurred the distinction between "said" and "saying" can be, and also how even diegesis can be both an imitation of reality and an event.

It is interesting to note that these problems, concerning the limits between diegesis and mimesis, and between literature and ordinary utterances, had been faced by Beckett many years earlier, and have been discussed in his critical essays. As a matter of fact, these works can be read in retrospect as a sort of theoretical anticipation of the semantic effects produced by his subsequent fictions and plays.

For example, if we take the famous essay on the paintings of the van Velde brothers (ca. 1945), we can find a precise, pervasive orientation which even then emphasized the temporal (diachronic and dynamic) dimension of the work of art. Beckett wrote:

> The work considered as pure creation, and whose function stops with its genesis, is destined to nothingness.

And again:

> There are some Braque [paintings] which seem plastic meditations on the means put into the work. Hence, a peculiar impression of hypothesis which originates in them. What is definite is always for tomorrow. It seems that this observation is relevant for the greater, and not the smaller part, of what we call modern living painting.[42]

The intrinsic openness of a modern work, including its metasemiotic components ("meditations on the means") and its self-reflection ("plastic meditations" in a painting), is unmistakably part of Beckett's conception of "modern, *living*" art, and we can easily infer that a true dynamics of reading is invoked as the necessary answer to an open encoding. In fact, the artistic text is seen as cogently metamorphic: "What is definite is always for tomorrow."

It seems important to note that Beckett emphasizes the metanarrative quality of the text because of its expressive effects (of uncertainty and novelty, against the *déja vu* of a closed work), and not because self-reflection would develop and point to innovative devices. In other words, according to Beckett, a reflection on the medium is important because it creates a "peculiar impression of hypothesis" in the message, not just because it circumscribes it, pointing to the means that create an artifact. Metanarrative devices are seen as functional to the creation of a possibly stronger relation to reality, rather than as sanctioning the definitive closure of the text. In this sense Beckett should not be considered a postmodernist writer, at least in relation to the definition of postmodernist art which foregrounds an aesthetic of ironic *bricolage*.

Beckettian critical attitudes should be borne in mind when reading his works; it is sad to see that a fairly common way of ignoring their referentiality occurs precisely when metalinguistic and metaliterary readings are invoked, not without an excessive structuralist ingenuity (which ignores the impossibility of conceptual closure, a typical trait of Beckett's later works).

His remarks on painting well reflect his endeavor as a writer, and the specificity of his metaphors describing the means (in the sense of components, and meaning in a broad sense) of the van Veldes' paintings, can aptly be applied to the description of the means of his own writing:

> What can we say of these surfaces which slide, of these shapes which vibrate, of these bodies almost cut out of fog, of this balance that a nothing can

disrupt, which breaks and reforms as we look? How can we speak of colours that breathe, that pant? [. . .] Here everything moves, swims, escapes, comes back, is undone and done again. Everything ends endlessly. [. . .] This is what literature is.[43]

As we can see, Beckett himself operates the translation from the strictly iconic field of painting to the verbal field of literature, and not only in this description, but also in his works. His lexical units "slide" and "vibrate," never acquiring the referential stability that can place them out of a designative "fog." Syntactic movement endlessly animates what has always already ended, that is, the literary referents, which are, strictly speaking, only pseudo-referents. Yet, though always void of referential presence, his texts always breathe the life of literature; that is, they are endowed with the truth of the literary lie.

If we keep these observations in mind, it is easy to see why Beckett progressively transformed his narratives into dramatizations: a word is never a "thing" in them, but never remains just a word, either. What happens is that we are shown that it becomes a thing *qua* word in the world of communication. Significantly in the van Velde essay he wrote ironically:

every time we want words to perform a real trespassing, every time we want them to express something different from words, they line up in such a way that they annihilate themselves. This is undoubtedly what makes life so charming.[44]

This statement proves that Beckett is conceptually far removed from a Cratylian fallacy which simplistically identifies words and things, but he is also far from formalistic oversimplifications, as he prefers the "charm of life" to the fictitious charm of the autonomous, self-contained existence of words on a page. He declares that words annihilate themselves when we want them to express "something different from words" (when we want them to coincide with things), but he also points out the fact that things do not disappear when we want them to coincide with words. In this sense, the impossibility of "a real trespassing" invests both the conventionality of signs and the ontology of things.

Against the false movement of traditional diegesis and textual closure Beckett points to the "charm of life," to a real movement which, of course, can only be perceived through, and as, change. So, here again, the issue of language and presence is put before our eyes, through the ironic complexity of an ambiguous statement: life is so charming because no notation can ever annihilate the world.

This awareness obviously modifies the way in which we can talk about life, because we have acquired the disquieting knowledge of a lack of symmetry between words and things. Linguistic alienation derives from the fact that words talk about life as if they had the power to convoke it and revoke it, but this is only a logocentric fallacy.

Having seen that life cannot be abolished by words, Beckett's work develops as an investigation of what happens to life when words are progressively reduced, perhaps even abolished. He will discover that there is no human life when words are unconceived, and ironically enough, he will have to reintroduce in his epistemic work (particularly in *Worstward Ho*) the idea of a necessary representational subjectivity ensuing from language, even after his radical critique of the subject (in *Company,* for example).

This process, leading to the vision of the ineliminability of representation from human experience, is structured as a series of progressive, daring, and unexpected reductions of representational components. These subtractions will also entail the evidence of the implication of subjectivity in the structuring of any significant content of representation, a content determinable only in relation to some sort of consciousness. In other words, the movement of the signifier signifies a subject precisely when the signifier forecloses him or her as real. Beckett's "imaginative transactions" point to what is inescapably human in representation, as well as showing the impossibility of adequately representing a real subject.

In line with his early theorization of a "literature of the unword," the rhetorical modality found by Beckett to represent existence in his later works is a form of subtractive "ecphrasis," that is, a sort of progressively reductive description (negative and diachronic) which will show representation itself.

According to a classical explanation, ecphrasis is a figure of *evidentia,* that is, a plain indication, and specifically "a plain declaration or interpretation of a thing" (Kersey's definition, 1715).[45] Beckett exploits the simplicity of this representational solution, and combines it further with a rhetorical strategy which runs counter to all figures of accumulation. He operates reductions on both the iconic and un-iconic components of plain indications, till the movement of subtraction shows representation itself.

To this effect, he employs a wide variety of signs, characterized by different representational relations. Symbols, indices, and descriptive icons in this narrative are all subservient to a reductive logic which creates an original hermeneutics of experience, a hermeneutics which is interested in a minimum of unavoidable (thus irrefutable) knowledge, rather than in maximum information.

Reductions on repeated portions of semantic content make it clear that representation is an informative content, but also that it is the inevitable mark of human thought, variously described as the primordial *arché,* the irreducible intentionality of thought, the Lacanian signifier. Beckett formulates the same idea in the performative, non-arguable, existentially rooted form of a "known minimum" (p. 9). Reduction indicates that the means of cognition are inextricably involved with the cognitive content they indicate, and that all forms of knowledge involve representation (even as representation of the unknown).

It is no wonder that the only narrative rule explicitly stated and repeated in the text forbids addition:

> Pending worse still. *Add a–. Add? Never.*
> [. . .]
> From merely bad. *Add–. Add? Never.*
> [. . .]
> *Add others. Add? Never.*[46]

Accordingly, the aesthetic ideal formulated in the text coincides with an "unlessenable least" configuring an irreducible residual knowledge, a sort of Husserlian result of a transcendental-phenomenological reduction, a "best worse":

> With leastening words say least best worse. For want of worser worst. Unlessenable least. Best worse.[47]

It is obvious that, in order to reach the "unlessenable least," the extent of the "unwording" has to become superlative, so that the failure of images and definite denotations can reveal the presence of the signifier as the symbolical matrix which, through the endless deferral of the signified, constitutes our interpreted world.

Yet, the extreme subtraction which makes visible the ineliminability of representation, also reveals both the figurality and the diachrony of discursive figures. This means that, although no denotation can constitute an object definitely, the figural detachment from the object also reveals a definite quality inherent to figurality: its temporal determination, which is to say that words cannot be totally revoked, even when their meaning is superseded. In fact, the specificity of (imperfect) designation occurs through a perfect temporal specificity of figures. In other words, the processing of words, their irreversible temporal sequence, shows that expressive inanity is one with an effective, definite, ontological figurality, one with a sort of excess of presence of the same circumscribed image, an excess within the same circumscribing but existing, present word.

> What words for what then? How almost they still ring. As somehow from some soft of mind they ooze. From it in it ooze. How all but uninane. To last unlessenable least how loath to leasten.[48]

This way of writing shows how powerful (how "uninane") words are, because they have an unlessenable duration ("to last unlessenable least"). Here, the problem of presence in language is foregrounded against all conceptualization, against all abstractions, vis-à-vis of duration. We are led to see that it is precisely an ontological order inherent to discourse (and not the order of the rhetorical laws of discourse) which makes language communicative, even if the presence of the subject is forever banned from words by the law of the signifier. Thus, ineliminable figurality is the ambiguous scandal of speaking phenomena, because figurative language in action (the only one in which also the subject is made somewhat visible precisely by appearing as that which is banned from language) is an ontologically structured aporia.

Furthermore, repetitions of quasi-identical textual segments can represent the diachronic structure of significant contents, and show that even what seems an immediate perception always involves a temporal doubling, an interpretive handling of information.

It is interesting to note that the development of this idiosyncratic Beckettian technique, combining subtraction and repetition, goes back to the early 1960s, when Hugh Kenner remarked that in *How it is:*

> a few dozen expressions permuted with deliberate redundancy accumulate meaning even as they are emptied of it[49]

Though the narrative strategy is basically still the same in *Worstward Ho,* a significant change has occurred in the late works, because the protagonist of the narrative has disappeared into syntactic impersonality. In other words, the disfiguring of meaning is not carried out by a specific subject who says that he "says it as he hears it" (as in *How it is*), but occurs through a pure textual and representational movement. Even if a he or a she is not denoted, a subject is signified by representation: textual movement is

impersonal but conative and communicative. Impersonality does not nul-
lify a linguistic function which at least presupposes an addressee, nor does it
abolish syntax, which, together with a lexicon and a semantic system
constitutes the representational system (of both a language and the novel).
So, the disfiguring of meaning can be fulfilled without the determination of
a subject, but it cannot destroy the presence of subjectivity so long as there
is representation. Actually, we could say that the addressee becomes the
agent of the addresser's visibility.

Let us consider an example, taken from the beginning of *Worstward Ho,*
where the reduction of representational components serves to show that it
is not possible to extinguish representation, nor the subjectivity implied by
it:

> Say a body. Where none. No mind. Where none. That at least. A place.
> Where none. For the body. To be in. Move in. Out of. Back into. No. No out.
> No Back. Only in. Stay in. On in. Still.[50]

As we can see, a reductive movement goes successively from a "body," to
a "mind," a "place," an "in," an "out," to a "No," soon revoked, like all the
other paradigmatic alternatives. Through a series of positings followed by
negation, this movement shows the ineliminable "On in" of existence,
rather than emphasize the specificity of representational occurrences. A
synonym of the more synthetic "Still," this "on in" indicates the ontological
condition which warrants the perception of the different "somehows" of
experience. In turn, the deferring "some*hows*" (indefinite referents, or oscillating meanings, here summarized and epitomized by "stay" at the end of
a paradigmatic sequence) lead back to the irreducible, modal, representational "some*how*" in which life necessarily presents itself.

It is precisely the synonymical repetition of "On in" (followed by "Still")
which reproduces the fullness of a hermeneutical circle regarding human
existence, by both signifying and signaling the "on in" which links the
experiential "somehows" to its cogent "somehow" (thanks to the permanence of the "On in" expressed by "Still"). What this repetition shows is the
fact that "on in" is both the object and the condition of its representation:
both ontology and figurality are thus foregrounded by repetition, through
the actual doubling of synonymic figures.

In that sense, it is interesting to note that the duplication of figures ("On
in. Still.") introduces polydoxy into an apparently compact discourse, not
only because the semantic focus is shifted (from space to time, and then
from transience to persistence), but also because repetition, by literalizing a

double point of view, shows the impossibility of certain inclusions in discourse, inclusions which would be necessary to maintain mimetic adequacy, but which would disrupt the inevitable syntagmatic linearity of discourse.

The text resists monological reduction by portraying the "same" reality from different points of view, besides showing the impossible inclusion of the diachrony of ontology in the discursive portraiture of things. The "On in. Still." is more than the perfect oxymoron of a "moving stillness"; this repetition shows that the *centrality* of language in human experience is not to be confounded with the establishment of *one center* of signification. In other words, although the determination of reality is inevitably logocentric, it should not appear unquestionable. Even if logocentrism is the cogent mark of human understanding, the centrality of linguistic experience is not to be mistaken for a center of specific logocentric determination. In other words, representation is a function of human understanding, as well as a possible content of that understanding. Yet, the two should not be confused, seeing that a content can never constitute a stable center, fixed once and for all.

One of the antidotes to dogmatic logocentrism is the creation of multivocal, "plural" texts. Polyphony and polydoxy appear in Beckett's works either through frequent discursive ruptures, or even through an overt thematization of the limits of unified and univocal denotations. For example, a thematization of polydoxy is explicitly formulated in *Worstward Ho* as an indication of the impossible inclusion of the instrument of thinking into thought:

> the head said seat of all. Germ of all. All? If of all of it too. Where if not there it too? There in the sunken head the sunken head.[51]

A passage like this underlines the Beckettian commitment to reality, precisely through the repetition of tropes. The use of logical operators, that is, of words that join prepositions, is rigorous here: "in the sunken head the sunken head" is the perfect, logical conclusion deriving from a previous narrative assertion that the head is "said seat of all" (p. 18). Such an image provides a narrative thematization of the existential condition in which knowledge is possible, and also foregrounds the ambiguous nature of the image itself. Thematically, a question like "where is the sunken head if not in the sunken head?" brings to our attention the fact that "thought is in the thinking," even if that thinking is extraneous to consciousness, repressed by that very thought. In other words, thinking produces thought which cannot include the thought of thinking. In this sense, it is important to note that repetition underlines the difference between the first and second "sunken head," thus indicating the instrument and the product of thought, respectively.

Yet, far from closing with this clarification, far from accepting a conceptual definition of "head" (as "instrument" and as "product"), the text exploits the synonymity of figures to emphasize the impossibility of an actual inclusion of "head" into "head," of thinking into thought. Thus, against the evidence of an assimilation produced by figures ("There in the sunken head the sunken head."), repetition also points to the foreclosure (impossible representation) of the subject and to its symbolic abolition through a metonymical negation.

Through this narrative we are led to see that the conflicting forces of signification are not just in texts but at the very beginning of our hermeneutics of experience, in the primordial re-presentation of the world in perception. In this sense, perception is the original repetition, which establishes the origin as origin, the "pure phenomenon" as "a thing," yet not without foreclosing "the real," which can surface into knowledge only as the impossible representation.

Furthermore, the fact that the expression "sunken head" oscillates between figurality and literality enhances a critique of the implication of metaphors in the language of science (specifically, here, of psychology, philosophy, and epistemology), and develops a critique of the relation between methodology and object of investigation. Furthermore, the iconic quality of the image, doubled in the repetition of an acoustic image, highlights the semantic gap between "head" and "thought," which confirms the inescapable centrality of language in the definition of experience, in spite of the variousness of linguistic determinations.

It is plain to see that *Worstward Ho* shares the sophisticated linguistic skepticism of Beckett's earlier works, but it is also clear that here expressive mistrust does not close with the denunciation of a linguistic lie. In fact we are led to see that there are collisions within language, and collusions of language with reality, which fiction can foreground and which acquire epistemic stability and relevance thanks to such an accurate formulation.

In the following passage, for example, the task of literature seems to be that of offering an original production of a way of seeing which foregrounds the quality of invisibility of the unseen:

Old dim. When ever what else? Where all always to be seen. Of the nothing to be seen. Dimly seen. Nothing ever unseen. Of the nothing to be seen. Dimly seen. Worsen that?[52]

The epiphanic content of this passage is enlightening in relation to a peculiar form of human ignorance, made visible by the fact that when the unseen becomes visible, we often re-cognize it as something that was always already there, under everybody's eyes, but that was awaiting a perceptive repetition in order to acquire full visibility.

A discursive sequence like: "Nothing ever unseen. Of the nothing to be seen" includes in the paradox of a referential coincidence a great semantic difference, linked to the subjectivity of representation (e.g., to its significant content). The coincidence of the "nothing unseen" with the "nothing to be seen" foregrounds the power of denotation, but without repressing in it the struggle of concept and figure.

Furthermore, in this Beckettian narrative notation is the ambivalent realization of a symbolic missaid which has the unusual power of indicating the expressivity of inexpressivity, that is, the expressivity of what has no desire "to be seen," to express itself through figurality, but which only surfaces through representational figurality as in the pure ontology of "Nothing ever unseen. Of the nothing to be seen."

From *Worstward Ho* we learn that reference should never entail an illusion of objectivity, because even a referent is determined as a significant content, in relation to a subjective representation ("all always *to be seen*"), rather than by reality itself (which does *not have to be seen,* being denoted as the "all [. . .] Of the *nothing to be seen*"). Reality is literally and imperatively a "nothing to be seen," and figuratively and phenomenologically a "nothing ever unseen." The ambivalence of this logocentric determination allows the emergence of subjectivity through a surprise repetition which shows what is not-seen as the "nothing unseen."

Another concern with the subjectivity of representation is thematized by the narrative example of a rigorous attempt to reduce, or even abolish, the subject. Ironically, the example ends in the admission of an unavoidable subjectivity linked to representation:

Whose words? Ask in vain. Or not in vain if say no knowing. No saying. No words for him whose words. Him? One. No words for one whose words. One? It. No words for it whose words. Better worse so.[53]

This passage reveals how dramatically a subject struggles with(in) language, rather than being expressed by it. In particular, it thematizes the unsuccesful attempt to find a subject in his or her words, or to directly relate the subject of the enunciation to the message: "No words **for him** *whose words*," "No words **for one** *whose words*," "No words **for it** *whose words*."

Any subject is disfigured and betrayed by words, and yet some sort of subjectivity is manifested by a resistance which shows that discourse cannot totally dissolve the question of its origin (a resistance expressed by the repetition "whose words"). Incapable of appropriating what seems to be his own language, a language by which "he," or "one," or "it" is uttered, the unrepresentable subject resists as problematic subjectivity, a subjectivity implied by the question deriving from repetition: "who/what speaks in what is spoken?". If, on the one hand, we see that the presence of the subject in language is impossible, on the other hand, subjectivity always surfaces through what is uttered, signaled and renewed in each one of its instances.

As we have seen, through iconic displacement and metonymic reductions, Beckett manages to show that representation cannot be eliminated from human understanding, and that it inheres in linguistic consciousness. In this sense, this idea of representation, pervasive in *Worstward Ho,* seems to coincide with the "obligation to express" described by Beckett in his "Three Dialogues" with Georges Duthuit (1949) when he talked about

> The expression that there is nothing to express, nothing with which to express, nothing from which to express, no power to express, no desire to express, together with the obligation to express.[54]

This "obligation to express" is certainly not a psychological or ethical object (a compulsion or a duty), but should be understood as the intentionality of thought and the representational cogency of perception, be it either about mental or physical realities. In this passage, object, instrument, origin, power and desire of expression (respectively given as "nothing . . . , nothing with which . . . , nothing from which . . . , no power . . . , no desire to express"), are deconstructed and shown as masks of an "obligation to express" which is concealed but irrevocable in all of them.

If Beckett can say that representation is irreducible ("an obligation"), it is precisely because he has tried, unsuccessfully, to eliminate it throughout his entire production, and has discovered that human life is just inconceivable without representation, in spite of the fact that specific images are not direct mimetic equivalents of life. In this sense we can say that his later works develop further his earlier perception of the fact that "the impetus toward meaning destroys the experience of the word."[55] This new idea of representation as the cogent feature of human hermeneutics is added to Beckett's earlier critique of the sign, and produces the awareness of the irreducible representational nature of any "experience of the word."

Better Failures: From the Thought of the End to the Repetitions of Ending

The exploration of the "obligation to express" radically transforms the quality of Beckett's fiction, and involves a new idea of reference as the significant content of representation and as "con-figuration," rather than as the linguistic correlative of any objective reality.

For example, the recurrent concern of Beckett's earlier fiction regarding meditations on the "end" culminates in showing the impossibility of naming such an "end," because his or her own death is, literally, a perpetually impossible referent for the speaker. So, rather than being expressed by a superlative metaphor such as the word "end," the "end" should be expressed only as movement, in accordance with the actual, existential experience of dying. Everything humans can know about the "end" is the "Worstward Ho" of our life-journey, because even an un-iconic "nohow" can only be conceived after the "hows" of experience.

Furthermore, both of these configurations ("Worstward Ho," and "nohow") are shown to be the product of an "obligatory" interpretation of experience, best perceived as a residual, unavoidable representation which, in turn, has emerged from the subtraction of knowledge (always needing to redefine itself, anyway) from knowing.

Wolfgang Iser's analysis of Beckett's early concern with the end has convincingly demonstrated that "In order for knowledge of the end to remain permanent, life must continually be given a new interpretation—and in such a way that the interpretation coincides with life itself."[56]

This is exactly Beckett's intention, but his expressive procedures before the late 1970s were different from those of his later works, because, at first, a thought-of-the-end was still possible for him, to the point that Clov could assert: "The end is terrific." However, because of his fidelity to the existential principle according to which interpretation should coincide with life itself, the transcendental closure implied by a thought of the end has disappeared from Beckett's later works. The early thought (of a perpetually unattained, though longed for, end) was transformed into the perception of the experience of ending, which, as such, became the focus of Beckett's new epistemic concerns. After all, it is only the experience of ending, and not the experience of the end (transcendentally posited as a limit *ad quem*), which can actually be felt (and analyzed) in life, even if the various existential instances of ending create the anticipating thought of the end, which is, however, purely logocentric.

Consequently, in *Worstward Ho,* the end remains, strictly speaking, the only "un-tellable" how, the "nohow" of human life, and the experience of the ending can be expressed only by the mean*ing* of the textual *movement*. Significantly, Dougald McMillan has pointed out that: "*Nohow* [. . .] is a disastrous confirmation of the impossibility of ever reaching an end."[57] In fact, it is a designation in which the struggle of figure and concept is made apparent as irreducible.

In particular, for Beckett, language and linguistic experience represent the scenario of his perception and subsequent representation (here in the sense of the reproduction of an already structured meaning) of the experience of ending. In fact, the gap of figurality and presence in language is an existential aporia whose meaning (of *lack of* experience, of *want of* life) becomes an anticipation of the meaning of "the end," a semantic expectation which makes one's own death intelligible to oneself. In other words, "the end" represents and anticipates itself in the irreducible figurality of language which inevitably forecloses death as real (even when such a foreclosure is also the only way in which it is possible to allude to it). In other words, the conceptualization of "the end" produces the failure to recognize the ending so that the *experience of death* is rejected as something that does not exist.

At this point, it should be very clear why Beckett, in line with his early preference for "ignorance and impotence," is now proposing a program of incessant "failures," which he realizes through repetition. Failures are the existential accomplishment (the existential *perfection*) of impotence and ignorance, and precisely because of their actuality, they can be regarded as correct procedures for the exploration of reality. In other words, "missaying" (revealed by worsening repetitions), shows the "will of meaning" and the representative intentionality which are normally hidden in any denotation. On the one hand "missaying" shows an inevitable power which is repressed in what is "well-said," while on the other hand, repetition shows that no sooner is something said, than it becomes "missaid":

Said is missaid. Whenever said said said missaid.[58]

A poetics of "better failures" reveals that the mimetic ideal of good representation (based on the criterion of adequacy) should be replaced by the awareness of incessant semiosis, and by a preference for texts characterized by a perpetual regeneration of figures. Significantly, the object of the narrative epiphany in *Worstward Ho* is the movement of the symbolic function which exceeds every semantic determination, and which undermines the very possibility of textual closure.

Furthermore, given that the only possible knowledge of "the real" (always foreclosed by language) is produced by actual indications that language cannot express it, the development and refinement of such indications (i.e., the exploration of such impotence), becomes the only way to pursue legitimate epistemic purposes. This project is well summarized in Beckett's own words:

> Back try worsen [. . .] Till words for worser still. Worse words for worser still.[59]

Failures can reveal a quality of impotence which inheres in linguistic expression, as well as address a quality of ignorance which is an essential feature of human hermeneutics. In this sense, repeated, actual failures are the only means for providing actual knowledge, that is, negative knowledge. Thus for Beckett the experience of ignorance, as Barbara Johnson has described it, becomes an epistemic and ethical imperative:

> *Ignorance,* far more than knowledge, is what can never be taken for granted. If I perceive my ignorance as a gap in knowledge instead of an *imperative that changes the very nature of what I think I know,* then I do not truly experience my ignorance. The surprise of otherness is that moment when a new form of ignorance is suddenly activated as an imperative.[60]

Actually, what Beckett seems to propose in *Wordsworth Ho* exceeds even the advisability of ignorance as imperative, by connoting it also as a necessity, since ignorance is posited as the only condition of the human epistemic endeavor. No hermeneutics of experience is conceivable beyond ignorance, and it is only the repetition of failures (i.e., a practice of the "ignorance imperative") which can constitute human knowledge as a series of "better failures," that is, as a perpetual ignorance which can nevertheless show its perpetual need to be defined over and over again.

Beckett tells us that our understanding is nothing but the diachronic ignorance of ignorance, which can however be activated as an imperative, and without the illusion of ever reaching the truth of "the real" or the stability of determinations. It is no wonder that the opening of *Worstward Ho* combines the sense of duration, as a condition of knowledge, with the sense of failure, as a mode of knowledge, and turns this awareness into an epistemic program:

> On. Say on. [. . .] From now say for be missaid. [. . .] Try again. Fail again. Fail better.[61]

From such a statement, and from many others similar to it which we encounter throughout the narration, we can infer that description can be correctly conceived only as a series of successive recantations, since nothing is ever denotable as something fixed and incontrovertible. Not even negative absolutes can acquire semantic stability, and in this sense it is clear that the later Beckett is far removed both from a Manichaean system of significations and from naive nihilism.

For example, the experience of the void, which is central to the iconography of *Worstward Ho*, is shown, just like the experience of the end, as the impossible denotation of a pure "void," on the one hand, because anything that surfaces in language obeys the rules of figurality (so it is not referentially "pure"), and on the other hand, because the noun "void" is inevitably endowed with an inherent meaning of existence, which originates from logocentrism, but obviously collides against the semantic determination of "void."

So Beckett tells us that we can name the "void," but that we should use denotation only to the extent to which we are aware of its limits and are ready to analyze them, because we have come to experience them as ignorance. We can use the word "void" so long as we know that it produces a semantic failure (a "say for be missaid"), and try to improve it (making it a "better failure"), by exploring the evidence of ignorance it entails. In this way "the void" is not expressed as a concept, nor as a semantic negative absolute; we learn that only repetition can evoke it correctly, because it has the power to deconstruct what lexis and syntax posit. A significant illustration of this form of deconstructive description can be found in the following example:

> The void. Unchanging. Say now unchanging. Void where not the one. The twain. So far where not the one and twain. So far.
>
> The void. How try say? How try fail? No try no fail. Say only—[62]

Through this definition, the "unchanging void" is proven to be changing precisely by the attempt to say how it is not changing. Temporal determination and spatial specification produce the curious image of a "void so far," that is, they produce the contradictory image of a void subject to change. Thus, the hermeneutical circle evoking it has to start all over again, reflecting on the linguistic means which have determined such a semantic contradiction. Hence, description is followed by a metanarrative indication which reveals the risk of descriptive failure, but which also asserts the value of failure by connoting it as an actualization of the expressive attempt, which can always be improved further, by acting upon it through subtraction ("No try no fail. Say *only*—").

Through the combination of repetition and semantic reduction, the void can be represented as a sort of unnamable "nohow" because, by revoking all the iconic components of description, the connotations of being are progressively subtracted from it ("Say only—"). The unattainable pure void, that is, the "grot in that void" (p. 16), is made visible through the anticipations of a linguistic paradigm which is then, however, progressively reduced, and whose epistemic legitimacy is thus shown to lie in the actualization of a communicative performance (the "*Say* only—"), rather than in the specificity of its lexical units. In other words, none of the given images is an adequate image of the void, but the fact of actually failing is the only way that an unrepresentable void can be suggested, by making visible both the attempt and the impossibility of actually expressing it.

This also means that the knowledge of the limits of logocentric positing produces a more refined experience of ignorance, which obviously cannot be fixed once and for all, and which can appropriately be called "the surprise of otherness," because of the irreducible nature of this "other" which resists linguistic assimilation.

At times, the "other" is actually a referent expressed as an unnamable excess beyond the pseudo-referents of literary representation. In fact, by changing the visibility of a pseudo-referent through narration, Beckett shows that its referential quality can be questioned, both because of the intrinsic figurality of any referent, and because of its pre-established meaning upon its inclusion as a pseudo-referent into narrative.

Yet, through subtractive repetitions, it is also possible to point to a referential "other," that is, to an undenotable referent, alluded to by the failure of pseudo-referents: "With worsening words. Worsening stare. For the *nothing* to be *seen.* [. . .] As now *by way of somehow on*" (p. 27).

We could say that in Beckett's later works the referent comes to coincide precisely with anything that cannot enter language explicitly, and yet can be perceived because it resists incorporation into it. In this sense repetition is a typical Beckettian "referent;" that is, it is a perfect textual element with an impossible textual denotation. Repetition becomes a powerful instrument of failure which can indicate the inescapability of linguistic representation, as well as an ever-recurrent want of better words. The ambivalence of repetitive improvement derives from the combination of expressive failure with the actual perfection of a communicative attempt:

> Preying since last worse said on foresaid remains. But what not on them preying? What seen? What said? What of all seen and said not on them preying? [. . .] They then the words. Back to them now for want of better on and better fail.[63]

Furthermore, Beckett's thematization of certain realities whose correct phenomenological denotation requires the use of repetition (such as "the end" or "the void") produces the evidence of the diachronic structure of perception and the urge to express this diachrony as a component of denotation.

Beckett is obviously interested in showing us the temporality of the symbolic movement, since seeing and saying are dialectically and inextricably linked within the duration in which the visibility of things is produced. As the following example suggests, a reciprocal, temporal dialectic of seeing and saying determines the "whatness" of things: "What when words gone? None for what then." (p. 28). When words are gone, there is no way of expressing a quality of being, the "what-quality" of realities determined as "things." Thus words can be used, but only so long as we are aware of the logocentric power which engenders this articulation of meaning.

The evidence of denotative limits (including the semantic instability of referents) also foreshadows, as I have already suggested, the inescapability of representation, an ineliminable necessity in a human hermeneutics of experience.

The following example effectively illustrates the ineliminable role and value of the human symbolic function (beyond any referential determination), for even a drastic reduction in the phenomenological components of perception ("*Know* no more. *See* no more. *Say* no more.") cannot prove successful in eliminating the key elements of a worstward ho phenomenology of experience:

The void. Before the staring eyes. Stare where they may. Far and wide. High and low. That narrow field. Know no more. See no more. Say no more. That alone. That little much of void alone.

On back to unsay void can go. Void cannot go. [. . .] Then all go.[64]

Following a phenomenological reduction of "the void," the invitation to "unsay" derives from the fact that the "void" remains "That little much of void alone," that is, the ineliminable residuum of a deconstructed but irrevocable representation. "Unsaying" produces the condition in which it is possible to see "remains of mind," that is, the "Worsening words whose unknown. Whence unknown." (p. 29).

In this context, a sentence like "As worst they may fail ever worse to say" means that the unutterable "other" which determines the condition of failure can be alluded to only so long as previous representations are not fully revoked, even when perception has ceased. In fact, the event-quality of representation is revealed by signs whose obvious semantic failure underscores the irreversible quality of their diachronic determination. Significantly, "the void" of the given example becomes "*That* little much of *void alone*," which is to say that subtraction has produced another Beckettian iconography of ruins, residual traces, linguistic leavings, and world-precipitates.

The temporal dimension of representation is also emphasized in an epistemic Beckettian program which intends to move "From bad to worsen" (p. 23), a program which wants to dissolve the entity posited by certain predicators ("From bad") with successive transformations, in accordance with the decreasing duration of existence ("to worsen"). It is certainly not a chance event that the main thematic structure involving characters indeed regards the diminution of life experienced by all the protagonists, regardless of their age.

On a structural level, repetition rather than denotation fosters the expression of the temporality of things, a duration which is normally repressed in the canonic figures of *evidentia*. Both extension and succession are shown here as essential components of objects, and Beckett's aesthetic reproductions should be praised for not repressing either of them. He has certainly achieved, and probably surpassed here, the aesthetic results which he had praised in the paintings of the van Velde brothers. In fact, Beckett's lucid de-contextualization of referents is similar to Abraham van Velde's manifest idealization in the illustration of space, while his subtractive repetitions are similar to Gerardus van Velde's representation of reality as irreducible change.[65] In Beckett, it is repetition which inscribes mortality into the illustrated thing, manifesting the cogent *différance* of language and meaning as a want of presence. Thus, life itself, unlike concepts, can be connoted as the penultimate approximation, a "ruin" which, however, cannot be totally dissolved or revoked, in spite of its constant lessening.

It is interesting to see how the morphosyntactic variations of "least" dramatize the conflict between duration and denotation, in the following example:

> With leastening words say least best worse. For want of worser worst. Unlessenable least. Best worse.[66]

The imperative invitation to "say least" radically transforms the concept of an "unlessenable least" and makes it the open object of innumerable, successive destinations. This "least" can endlessly express the "want of," rather than fix and name a need once and for all. Thus, through the indication of a necessary enunciation, Beckett can allude to what would otherwise remain inchoate and which can, on the contrary, become a verbalized anticipation of the knowledge of an "Unlessenable least" (a definition derived from the experience of absence and blown up into conceptually superlative proportions).

Represented by subtraction, which deprives any posited superlative of consistency (through the indication of a "want of wors*er* *worst*"), any Beckettian object of experience remains irreducibly "other," forever unassimilated, resisting assimilation into concepts. In this sense, it can be said that rather than welcoming the charms of nihilist negations, Beckett seems to have accepted an irreducible phenomenological hermeneutics of experience. At this point, the value of saying is fully acknowledged, because only the "saying" is shown as being capable of defining the horizon of human knowledge, even if successive denotations can never ultimately stand, challenged as they are by ever-changing phenomena. The following example can be used to summarize the epistemic adventure of *Worstward Ho* that I have been describing:

> Less. Less seen. Less seeing. Less seen and seeing when with words than when not. When somehow than when nohow. Stare by words dimmed. Shades dimmed. Void dimmed. Dim dimmed. All there as when no words. As when nohow. Only all dimmed. Till blank again. No words again. Then all undimmed. Stare undimmed. That words had dimmed.[67]

Here we find a typically Beckettian reproduction of a full hermeneutical cycle regarding the objects of *evidentia* and the structure of visibility. It is an existential cycle comprising perception and verbalization as the ineliminable dialectical components of human experience. We move from a "seen and seeing *when with words*" to a "*no words again*" and then back to a problematic something or other "that words had dimmed." No other passage summarizes so well the triumph of "saying" together with the inevitable failure of "the said," showing the ineliminable linguistic structure of perceived reality (the "somehow with words") and even explaining the possibility of a linguistic anticipation of death (as the "nohow," "when not [with words]").

From a passage like this, we can easily infer that the value of saying can only be assessed through the rejection of concepts and a critique of denotation ("All there as when no words"). However, it is possible to assess such a value precisely because the "try say" has occurred, and the "said" has appeared as a "From now said alone." (p. 37), that is, as the dynamic result of subtraction.

In this sense, *Worstward Ho* is very different from previous Beckettian works because of its overt acknowledgement of the value of saying, a value which had never been expressed so clearly before and which finds a positive affirmation here, in relation to failure. Actually, the premises of this argument are to be found at the beginning of the narrative, in the "From now say for be missaid" (p. 7), a statement which at that time of narration may have summarized Beckett's earlier linguistic suspicion, but which by the end of the novel should also be seen as the condition through which the positivity of linguistic failure can be discovered. In fact, although it is only perceived as negative knowledge, and is only expressed through failure, the value of saying is disclosed in the novel as the existential expression of the ignorance-imperative, a need placed by Beckett at the same, deep level as the human "obligation to express."

Following the present analysis, it should not be at all surprising to see why this narrative is haunted by repetition, functional as it can be to the development of a reductive strategy which eventually manages to put an irreducible, existentially rooted, residual knowledge into focus. There would be no evidence of the ignorance-imperative without the subtractive doubling of certain elements throughout the novel. Subtractive repetitions allow a condition to be represented in which knowledge could coincide with knowing, and in which thought could overlap with thinking. Expressible only in the "on" of duration (which, by the end of narration, becomes part of representation, thanks to repetition), and expressed by the various "how(s)" of representation, this knowledge also configures its cogent "somehow" (i.e., the intentionality of thought) as the inevitable modality of thinking.

Repetition, far from fixing a cognitive content, becomes the means to illustrate our diachronic intelligence of phenomena, and even the only means of denoting our understanding of the inexplicable. In this sense, any doubling can also be shown to be expressing a force of signification which can disrupt the semantic compactness of denotations, by putting a strategy of discourse against the meaning engendered by that discourse. Repetition shows that it is only the lack of an assimilation of meanings to words that permits the movement of signification, even if the impossibility of this inclusion could un-do the logic on which meaning has been built.

In fact, in *Worstward Ho* we can see that it is only through a struggle of signification (i.e., through a semantic πόλεμος) that the conditions in which visibility can define itself are established. Visibility is thus connoted just as a surviving figure of *evidentia,* a victorious notation which surfaces after the repression of the inevitable conflicts of signification. Furthermore, we must remember that the visibility of specific "things" is necessarily bound to variation, also because of the fact that it is rooted in time, a time shown by the "on back" which Beckett employs in his critical deconstruction of a traditional, more cohesive, narrative "then."

Finally, repetition is shown to abolish the distinction between narratives and speech acts, producing much more than a transgression of canonical genres. It shows that the idea of mimetic adequacy can only have a basis in endless semiosis, and specifically, in a diachronic genesis of "wanting" meanings. Repetition demonstrates the fact that linguistic signs of a second order system (the narrative) function because they re-present signs of a first order system (ordinary language). In other words, the repetition of literary signs in literature doubles the figurality of the signs of the first order system, but obviously without reproducing their (referential) value.

In this sense we can say that this is the crucial and disquieting epiphany of *Worstward Ho:* the literalization of figurality in the doubling of fictional discourse, undoing the very distinction between figure and phenomenon. As a matter of fact, this is perhaps the most dramatic and "beyondless" revelation of a radically open "self-reflective artifact."

Notes

1. Samuel Beckett, *Worstward Ho* (London: John Calder, 1983). All references are to this edition. In the case of short quotations the page number will be given directly in the text.
2. Samuel Beckett, "German Letter to Axel Kaun" in *Disjecta,* pp. 51–54. English translation pp. 170–73. Quotation p. 173.
3. John Pilling, "Review Article: *Company* by Samuel Beckett," *Journal of Beckett Studies* 7 (Spring 1982) 127–31. Quotation p. 130.
4. Samuel Beckett, *Worstward Ho,* p. 9.
5. See Brian Finney, "*Still* to *Worstward Ho:* Beckett's Prose Fiction Since *The Lost Ones*" in *Beckett's Later Fiction and Drama,* James Acheson and Kateryna Arthur, eds. (Houndmills and London: The Macmillan Press, 1987) pp. 65–79; and Enoch Brater, "Voyelles, Cromlechs and the Special (W)rites of *Worstward Ho*" in *ibid.,* pp. 160–74.
6. For a synthetic definition of this expression, by now current within the contemporary hermeneutical debate, see Hans-Georg Gadamer, "The Hermeneutics of Suspicion" in *Hermeneutics: Questions and Prospects,* Gary Shapiro and Alan Sica, eds. (Amherst: University of Massachusetts Press, 1984) pp. 54–65.
7. Samuel Beckett, "German Letter," p. 171.
8. Samuel Beckett, *Proust* (New York: Grove Press, 1957) p. 17. Emphasis mine.
9. *Ibid.,* p. 19.
10. Israel Shenker, "An Interview with Beckett," *New York Times,* May 5, 1956, Section II, 1,3. Reprinted in Graver and Federman, pp. 146–49. Quotation p. 148. See also Chapter One, pp. 60–62.
11. Samuel Beckett, "German Letter," p. 172.
12. *Ibid.,* The expression "apotheosis of the word" is also here.
13. Samuel Beckett, "Intercessions by Denis Devlin" in *Disjecta,* p. 91.
14. For example, Linda Hutcheon quotes Stanley Fish's formulation of what she calls his "anti-foundationalist paradox" as follows: "Ye shall know that truth is not what it seems, and *that* truth shall set you free." in "Beginning to Theorize Postmodernism," *Textual Practice* 1,1 (Spring 1987) p. 18. Formulated as it is, however, this paradox posits a closure to the mobility of tropes, and presupposes the possibility of positive knowledge. In this sense I do not believe it can ultimately be applied to Beckett's works.
15. Among the many works of Emmanuel Lévinas that deal with this problem see *De l'évasion* (Paris: Fata Morgana, 1982), Chapter VIII in particular.
16. Emmanuel Lévinas, "The Glory of Testimony" in *Ethics and Infinity* (Pittsburgh: Duquesne University Press, 1985) pp. 107–08.
17. These aspects of the immediate as a "Kierkegaardian theatrical knowledge" in Beckett's works have been discussed at length in Chapter Three, "Beckett's Theater Since the 1970s"; see note 3. For a direct reference see Søren Kierkegaard, "Repetition," in *Repetition* with *Fear and Trembling,* Howard V. Hong and Edna H. Hong, eds. and trans., *Kierkegaard's Writings* VI (Princeton, N.J.: Princeton University Press, 1983).

18. A thorough analysis of the similarities of thought between Heidegger and Beckett can be found in Lance St. John Butler, *Samuel Beckett and the Meaning of Being: A Study in Ontological Parable* (London: Macmillan Press, 1984). See in particular Chapter 2, "Heidegger's *Being and Time* and Beckett," pp. 7–74. Several critics have discussed Beckett's works in relation to Heidegger's; I will now mention Ruby Cohn, "Philosophical Fragments in the Works of Samuel Beckett" in *Samuel Beckett: A Collection of Critical Essays,* Martin Esslin, ed. (Englewood Cliffs, N.J.: Prentice-Hall Inc., 1965) pp. 169–77; Jean Onimus, *Beckett* (Paris: Desclée de Brouwer, 1968); and David H. Hesla, *The Shape of Chaos: An Interpretation of the Art of Samuel Beckett* (Minneapolis: University of Minnesota Press, 1971).

19. Samuel Beckett, *Worstward Ho,* p. 7.

20. Søren Kierkegaard, *Concluding Unscientific Postscript,* Walter Lowrie, trans. (Princeton, N.J.: Princeton University Press, 1941), excerpted as "Concluding Unscientific Postscript" in *Deconstruction in Context: Literature and Philosophy,* Mark C. Taylor, ed. (Chicago and London: University of Chicago Press, 1986) pp. 169–90. Quotation p. 179.

21. Samuel Beckett, *Worstward Ho,* p. 47.

22. Søren Kierkegaard, "Concluding Unscientific Postscript," p. 177.

23. Roman Jakobson, "Linguistics and Poetics" in *Selected Writings,* Vol. III: *The Poetry of Grammar and the Grammar of Poetry,* edited with a preface by Stephen Rudy (The Hague, Paris, New York: Mouton, 1981) pp. 18–51. See in particular the definitions on pp. 22 and 23.

24. Søren Kierkegaard, "Concluding Unscientific Postscript," p. 170.

25. Roland Barthes, *Writing Degree Zero,* Annette Lavers and Colin Smith, trans., Preface by Susan Sontag (New York: Hill and Wang, 1968) p. 39.

26. Samuel Beckett, *Worstward Ho,* p. 7.

27. Søren Kierkegaard, "Concluding Unscientific Postscript," p. 182.

28. Samuel Beckett, *Worstward Ho,* p. 7.

29. *Ibid.*

30. Samuel Beckett, "A Piece of Monologue" in *Collected Shorter Plays* (London and Boston: Faber and Faber) pp. 263–69. As regards the problem of ontology and judgement, see in particular the quotation: "Trying to treat of other matters. Till half hears there are no other matters. Never were other matters. Never two matters. Never but the one matter." p. 269. The play is discussed at length in Chapter Three.

31. Samuel Beckett, *Worstward Ho,* p. 9.

32. *Ibid.,* p. 8.

33. *Ibid.,* p. 11.

34. Samuel Beckett, *Company* (London: John Calder, 1980). See in particular: "Only a small part of what is said can be verified. As for example when he hears, You are on your back in the dark. Then he must acknowledge the truth of what is said. But by far the greater part of what is said cannot be verified." pp. 7–8.

35. Samuel Beckett, *Worstward Ho,* pp. 8–9.

36. *Ibid.,* pp. 44–45.

37. For a discussion of different teleologies of humor in Beckett, see Hugh Kenner,

Flaubert, Joyce and Beckett: The Stoic Comedians (Boston: Beacon Press, 1962); Ruby Cohn, "The Laughter of Sad Sam Beckett" in *Samuel Beckett Now,* Melvin J. Friedman, ed. (Chicago: University of Chicago Press, 1970) pp. 185–98; and Edith Kern, "Black Humor: The Pockets of Lemuel Gulliver and Samuel Beckett" in *Samuel Beckett Now,* pp. 89–102. See also Chapter Two in this volume for an analysis of Beckett's comic strategies.

38. Samuel Beckett, *Worstward Ho,* p. 28.

39. *Ibid.,* pp. 29–30. Emphasis mine.

40. Jacques Derrida, "Force and Signification" in *Writing and Difference,* translated with an Introduction and Additional Notes by Alan Bass (London, Melbourne, and Henley: Routledge & Kegan Paul, 1978) p. 9.

41. *Ibid.*

42. "L'oeuvre considérée comme création pure, et dont la fonction s'arrête avec la genèse, est vouée au néant," and: "Il y a des Braque qui ressemblent à des méditations plastiques sur les moyens mis en oeuvre. D'où cette étrange impression d'hypothèse qui s'en dégage. Le définitif est toujours pour demain. Il semble que cette remarque soit pertinente pour une grande partie, et non la moindre, de ce qu'on appelle la peinture moderne vivante." Samuel Beckett, "La peinture des van Velde ou le Monde et le Pantalon" in *Disjecta,* pp. 118–32. Quotations pp. 119–120, and p. 127.

43. "Que dire de ces plans qui glissent, ces contours qui vibrent, ces corps comme taillés dans la brume, ces équilibres qu'un rien doit rompre, qui se rompent et se reforment à mesure qu'on regarde? Comment parler de ces couleurs qui respirent, qui halètent? [. . .] Ici tout bouge, nage, fuit, revient, se défait, se refait. Tout cesse, sans cesse. [. . .] C'est ça, la littérature." *Ibid.,* p. 128.

44. "chaque fois qu'on veut faire faire aux mots un véritable travail de transbordement, chaque fois qu'on veut leur faire exprimer autre chose que des mots, ils s'alignent de façon à s'annuler mutuellement. C'est, sans doute, ce qui donne à la vie tout son charme." *Ibid.,* p. 125.

45. See *The Oxford English Dictionary* and Chapter Five, n. 71.

46. Samuel Beckett, *Worstward Ho,* pp. 21, 23, 25.

47. *Ibid.,* p. 32.

48. *Ibid.,* p. 33.

49. Hugh Kenner, *Spectrum* (Spring 1961) 3–20. Quoted in Graver and Federman, p. 242.

50. Samuel Beckett, *Worstward Ho,* p. 7.

51. *Ibid.,* pp. 18–19.

52. *Ibid.,* p. 24.

53. *Ibid.,* p. 19.

54. Samuel Beckett, "Three Dialogues" in *Disjecta,* pp. 138–45.

55. Wolfgang Iser, "When is the End not the End?" in *The Implied Reader* (Baltimore and London: Johns Hopkins University Press, 1974) p. 269.

56. *Ibid.,* p. 259.

57. Dougald McMillan, "Worstward Ho" in *On Beckett: Essays and Criticism,* S. E. Gontarski, ed. (New York: Grove Press, 1986) p. 209.

58. Samuel Beckett, *Worstward Ho,* p. 7.

59. *Ibid.*, p. 41.

60. Barbara Johnson, "Nothing Fails Like Success" in *A World of Difference* (Baltimore and London: Johns Hopkins University Press, 1987) p. 16. Emphasis mine.

61. Samuel Beckett, *Worstward Ho,* p. 7.

62. *Ibid.*, p. 17.

63. *Ibid.*, pp. 30–31.

64. *Ibid.*, p. 18.

65. This is how Beckett describes the van Veldes' endeavor in "La peinture des van Velde ou le Monde et le Pantalon" (p. 128):

   Mettons la chose plus grossièrement. Achevons d'être ridicule./ A. van Velde peint l'étendue./ G. van Velde peint la succession./ Puisque, avant de pouvoir voir l'étendue, à plus forte raison avant de pouvoir la représenter, il faut l'immobiliser, celui-là se détourne de l'étendue naturelle [. . .] Celui-ci, au-contraire, est entièrement tourné vers le dehors [. . .] C'est la représentation de ce fleuve où, selon le modeste calcul d'Héraclite, personne ne descend deux fois.

66. Samuel Beckett, *Worstward Ho,* p. 32.

67. *Ibid.*, p. 39.

Index